Economic Trends
in the MENA Region, 2002

Economic Trends
in the
MENA
Region, 2002

The Economic Research Forum for the Arab Countries, Iran and Turkey

An Economic Research Forum Edition
The American University in Cairo Press
Cairo · New York

This edition published in 2002 by
The American University in Cairo Press
113 Sharia Kasr el Aini, Cairo, Egypt
420 Fifth Avenue, New York 10018
www.aucpress.com

in association with
The Economic Research Forum for the Arab Countries, Iran, and Turkey
7 Boulos Hanna Street, Dokki, 11123 Cairo, Egypt
www.erf.org.eg

Copyright © 2001, 2002 by the Economic Research Forum for the Arab Countries, Iran, and Turkey

All rights reserved. No part of this publication may be reproduced, stored in a retrieval system or transmitted in any form or by any means, electronic, mechanical, photocopying, recording or otherwise, without the prior written permission of the publisher.

Dar el Kutub No. 4142/02
ISBN 977 424 717 5

Printed in Egypt

Table of Contents

Acknowledgments

List of Contributors

Chapter One: Macroeconomic Trends in the Middle East and North Africa — 1

A "Crisis of Growth" — 1

Macroeconomic Performance and Economic Stability — 7

Institutional Reform — 19

Annex — 23

Chapter Two: Financial and Capital Markets, Privatization and FDI — 31

Financial Markets Hit by Turmoil — 31

Governments Work to Sell Their Assets — 36

FDI Grows Worldwide — 40

Measuring Risk in MENA Countries — 43

Annex — 50

Chapter Three: Export Competitiveness: Where the Region Stands — 53

Low but Intensified Product Diversification — 53

Export Competitiveness — 56

Regional Integration: Should Intra-MENA Trade Increase? — 57

Water Resources and Free Trade — 61

Strategies that Raise Competitiveness — 65

Chapter Four: The Challenge of MENA Competitiveness in Industry — 67

Absence of Innovation-intensive Manufacturing Activity — 67

Science and Technology — 68

Trade Liberalization and Innovation — 73

Intellectual Property Rights — 74

Lack of Programs to Enhance Competitiveness — 82

Chapter Five: Labor Markets and Human Resource Development 87

The Challenge to Provide Jobs 87

Unemployment in Select MENA Countries 89

Relaxing Restrictive Labor Regulations 94

Women in the Labor Force 95

Labor Markets and Poverty Reduction 99

Annex 108

Acknowledgments

This report is the fourth in a series published by the Economic Research Forum for the Arab Countries, Iran and Turkey (ERF), under the general direction of Managing Director, Heba Handoussa. The report is based on background papers prepared by an impressive number of ERF Fellows and affiliates, and draws upon the reservoir of knowledge and quality research accumulated over a two-year period, under the auspices of ERF.

ERF is most grateful for the participation of its Research Fellows, Associates, and other distinguished colleagues, and would like to thank them for their invaluable contribution to this publication. It is largely their time and effort extended over two years of hard work which made this publication possible. A special word of thanks is due to H. Abu-Schneif, A. Abu-Shokor, S. Atallah, M. Boughzala, H. Esfahani, A. Jalali-Naini, M. Louis, M. Nabli, S. Ozmucur, U. Panizza, K. Shehadi, E.H. Valsan, E. Yeldan (Chapter One); Y. Allam, R. Al-Mashat, M. Al-Shroogi, T. Hafsi, M. Kandil, M. Louis, J. Speakman (Chapter Two); M. Amerah, C. Astrup, S. Dessus, G. Gaulier, D. Unal-Kesenci, A. Ghoneim, M. Haddad, B. Hamdouch, S. Sayan, K. Sekkat, A. Shinnawy, T. Yousef (Chapter Three); B. Al-Zu'bi, H. Cottonet, N. Mulder, S. Ghali, F. Ghantous, A. Kubrosi, A. Mansour, L. Mazhar, T. Pamukcu, M. Sehal, A. Shinnawy (Chapter Four); A. Abu-Shokor, S. Al-Qudsi, R. Assaad, I. Tunali, M. Boughzala, N. Fergany, M. Khorshid, S. Nagi, S. Radwan, T. Yousef, Z. Tzannatos (Chapter Five).

This volume benefited from data provided by the Arab Fund for Economic and Social Development, the Arab Monetary Fund, the Economist Intelligence Unit, ESCWA, ILO, IMF, UNCTAD, UNIDO, and the World Bank, as well as regular statistical bulletins published by the central banks and national statistical agencies of MENA countries.

ERF indicators, data manipulation and forecast computation were conducted by Maryse Louis, who also managed and coordinated the project, with help from various ERF staff: Particular thanks go to Abda El Mahdi, who pulled together much of Chapter Five, and Azza El-Shinnawy, who was responsible for Chapters Three and Four. Patrick Werr was the principal editor, and Heba Handoussa and Gillian Potter edited the final draft of the report. Iskandar Fadlallah provided artwork.

ERF is also grateful for the continued financial support of its core donors and for the grant received from the MENA Vice Presidency of the World Bank towards the preparation and publication of this report both in hard form and on the ERF website.

List of Contributors

Abda El Mahdi	Economic Research Forum, Cairo, Egypt
Abdel Fattah Abu-Shokor	University of Nablus, West Bank, Palestine
Ahmad Jalali-Naini	Institute of Research in Planning & Development, Iran
Ahmed Farouk Ghoneim	Cairo University, Cairo, Egypt
Antoine Mansour	ESCWA, Beirut, Lebanon
Atef Kubursi	McMaster University, Canada
Azza El-Shinnawy	Economic Research Forum, Cairo, Egypt
Bachir Hamdouch	Institut National de Statistique et d'Economie Appliqué, Rabat, Morocco
Bashir Al-Zu'bi	Jordan University, Amman, Jordan
Claus P. Astrup	The World Bank, Washington, D.C., USA
Deniz Unal-Kesençi	CEPII, Paris, France
E. H. Valsan	American University in Cairo, Egypt
Erinç Yeldan	Bilkent University, Ankara, Turkey
Elias Ghantous	General Union of Chambers of Commerce, Industry and Agriculture for Arab Countries, Beirut, Lebanon
Guillaume Gaulier	CEPII, Paris, France
Hadi Salehi Esfahani	University of Illinois, USA
Heba Abu-Shnief	Economic Research Forum, Cairo, Egypt
Hélène Cottenet	CEDEJ, Cairo, Egypt
Isnan Tunali	Koç University, Istanbul, Turkey
John Speakman	The World Bank, Washington, D.C., USA
Kamal Shehadi	Connexus Consulting, Beirut, Lebanon
Khalid Sekkat	Université Libre de Bruxelles, Brussels, Belgium
Lotfi Mazhar	Federation of Egyptian Industries Project Management Unit, Cairo, Egypt
Magda Kandil	International Monetary Fund, Washington, D.C., USA
Maryse Louis	Economic Research Forum, Cairo, Egypt
Mai Serhal	General Union of Chambers of Commerce, Industry and Agriculture for Arab Countries, Beirut, Lebanon

Mehmet T. Pamukçu	Université Libre de Bruxelles, Brussels, Belgium
Mohamed Saad Amerah	Ministry of Economics and Commerce, Abu Dhabi, UAE
Mohammed Al-Shroogi	Middle East Regional Director, Citibank
Mona Haddad	UN-ESCWA, Beirut, Lebanon
Mongi Boughzala	Université de Tunis, Tunisia
Motaz Khorshid	Cairo University, Cairo, Egypt
Mustapha Nabli	The World Bank, Washington, D.C., USA
Nader Fergany	Almishkat Center for Research & Training, Giza, Egypt
Nanno Mulder	CEPII, Paris, France
Ragui Assaad	Humphrey Institute of Public Affairs, University of Minnesota, USA
Rania Al-Mashat	International Monetary Fund, USA
Saad Nagi	Ohio State University, Ohio, USA
Sami Atallah	Ministry of Finance, Beirut, Lebanon
Samir Radwan	Development &Technical Cooperation Dept., International Labor Organization, Geneva, Switzerland
Sebastien Dessus	The World Bank, Washington, D.C., USA
Serdar Sayan	Bilkent University, Ankara, Turkey
Sofiane Ghali	Université de Tunis, Tunis, Tunisia
Sulayman Al-Qudsi	JECOR, Riyadh, Saudi Arabia
Suleyman Ozmuçur	University of Pennsylvania, USA
Taieb Hafsi	Université de Montreal, Quebec, Canada
Tarik Yousef	Georgetown University, Washington, D.C., USA
Ugo Panizza	American University in Beirut, Lebanon
Yasmin Allam	Economic Research Forum, Cairo, Egypt
Zafiris Tzannatos	The World Bank, Washington, D.C., USA

CHAPTER ONE

MACROECONOMIC TRENDS IN THE MIDDLE EAST AND NORTH AFRICA

A "Crisis of Growth"

The "performance of Middle East and North Africa (MENA) economies in the last two decades has been disappointing. Per capita GDP decreased by an average 1.0 percent per year in the 1980s, a rate worse than that of any other developing region, except Sub-Saharan Africa. Although per capita income stopped contracting in the 1990s, it still grew by a mere 1.0 percent per year. This was especially discouraging considering that growth elsewhere in the world was rapid. High-income countries in the West, especially the United States, made the most gains, while many Asian and Latin American developing economies also made impressive strides. The economies of Russia, Brazil and East Asia, which faltered during the financial crises of 1997-99, have since begun to recover. With the exception of Latin America, which was held back mainly by Brazil, the region's giant, and later by Argentina, MENA continued to grow more slowly in the late 1990s than any other region in the world (Figure 1.1).

The human consequences of low or negative growth have been serious. If the oil-rich countries of the Gulf Cooperation Council[1] (GCC) are not included, the unemployment rate in MENA now averages close to 25 percent—the second highest of any region of the world. In several countries, including Iran, Syria, Libya and Yemen, as many as one-third of the labor force is unemployed. Even among citizens of the GCC, where unemployment has averaged a relatively low 5 percent, joblessness has begun to grow (Figure 1.2).

The biggest impact has mostly been on first-time job-

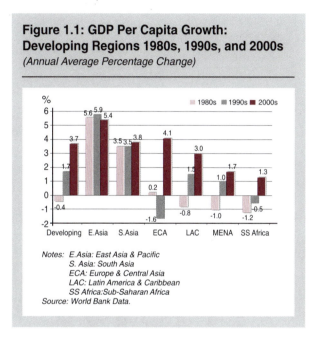

Figure 1.1: GDP Per Capita Growth: Developing Regions 1980s, 1990s, and 2000s
(Annual Average Percentage Change)

Notes: E.Asia: East Asia & Pacific
S. Asia: South Asia
ECA: Europe & Central Asia
LAC: Latin America & Caribbean
SS Africa:Sub-Saharan Africa
Source: World Bank Data.

seekers and the young. Unemployment among those under 25 years in MENA is about twice as high as national averages. To its credit, the region has greatly expanded access to education. Between 1960 and 1990, the average level of education increased by 140 percent, a growth rate not matched by any other region, and illiteracy has fallen precipitously. This investment in human capital has the potential to increase productivity substantially, especially if the high unemployment among the young is reduced. However, high unemployment rates among those young deny the education payoff in the growth of the region. This is can be characterized as a "human capital crisis" in the region (Figure 1.3).

Economic Research Forum

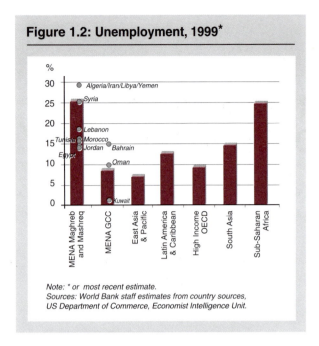

Figure 1.2: Unemployment, 1999*

Note: * or most recent estimate.
Sources: World Bank staff estimates from country sources, US Department of Commerce, Economist Intelligence Unit.

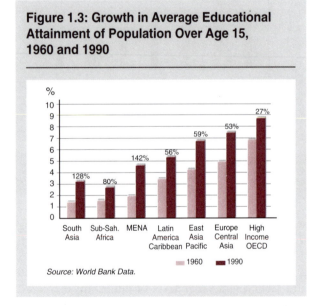

Figure 1.3: Growth in Average Educational Attainment of Population Over Age 15, 1960 and 1990

Source: World Bank Data.

The Diversity of the MENA Region

These broad growth numbers hide a great diversity within the region. Countries such as Egypt, Jordan, Morocco and Tunisia that implemented macroeconomic reforms from an early date, liberalizing trade, reducing budget deficits, tightening monetary policies and privatizing state-owned enterprises, reaped benefits as early as the mid-1980s. The reduction in the budget deficits reduced inflation rates, improved external performance in terms of growth of exports, reduced current account deficits and increased foreign exchange reserves.

The oil exporting states of the GCC generally achieved macroeconomic stability, but have been slow to make structural reforms. Their achievements include: encouragement of greater foreign and private investment in certain areas and the rolling back of some of their cradle-to-grave welfare benefits by increasing fees for social services.

A third group of economies in the region either has not achieved successful stabilization, such as Lebanon and Turkey, or has achieved macro-stability but has not yet significantly moved from socialist, state-dominated management of their economies, such as Algeria, Iran, Yemen and Syria. Lebanon, for example, has run a high budget deficit and borrowed heavily on local markets to finance the reconstruction of its physical and human capital after its civil war.

As a group, the early reformers performed substantially better than either the oil-exporters or the late reformers. Their economies grew by an average 4.5 percent a year (2 percent per capita) in the 1980s, compared with only 0.8 percent among GCC countries (minus 4.2 percent per capita), and 1.6 percent a year among the late reformers (minus 1.6 percent per capita).

By the 1990s, even though the performance of both the Gulf and the late reformers improved significantly, they still lagged behind the early reformers. From 1990 to 1999, GCC economies grew an average 3 percent a year (minus 0.8 percent per capita), late reformers 2 percent (1.2 percent per capita) and early reformers 6.8 percent (1.8 percent per capita).

Growth Prospects Over the Next Decade

Even before the terrorism attack on the US on the 11th of September, the world was entering a slow-down phase where less favorable economic and social conditions were unfolding. The three major economies of the world were facing a downturn. Japan had slipped back into recession, the US' economic growth had dropped to near zero and Europe's economy was slowing sharply.

Growth forecasts figures have been revised downward but at this point, there are as yet no confirmed figures as to how the economies of the world will react to the crisis. However, initial figures of the World Bank show that the growth rate of the US and the OECD countries are expected to be lower by an average of 0.75-1.25 percentage points from the initial forecasted figures for 2002. As for developing countries, growth rate was already forecasted to fall from 5.5 percent in 2000 to 2.9 percent in 2001, mainly due to the global slowdown. However, this figure is now expected to decrease by another 0.5-0.75 percentage points for 2002.

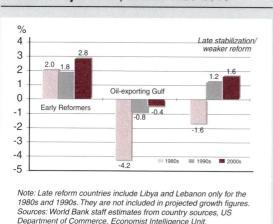

Figure 1.4: GDP Per Capita Growth and Growth Projections, MENA 1980-2010

Note: Late reform countries include Libya and Lebanon only for the 1980s and 1990s. They are not included in projected growth figures.
Sources: World Bank staff estimates from country sources, US Department of Commerce, Economist Intelligence Unit.

The MENA region was forecasted to grow at a rate of 3.8 and 3.6 percent in 2001 and 2002, a decreasing rate from an average of 4.0 percent in 2000. However, these figures are now likely to be even lower. Expectations of decreasing global growth have pushed prices lower, including oil prices which have fallen from $31/b in September, 2001 to $19/b by mid-October, 2001. It is likely that the OPEC will ensure that the price per barrel will not go lower then $22/b. Export prices will decrease but shipping costs will increase. Tourism revenues are being hard hit in the MENA countries due to the perceived fears of using air transportation and the increasing tensions in the region. Increased risk perceptions of the region may also hit FDI flows, which were expected to fall regardless, due to the global slowdown.

As a result of decreasing growth, the number of poor in developing countries will also increase by an estimated 10 million more people than expected for the year 2002. This will be largely a result of the decrease in commodity prices in general, and agricultural prices in particular, and will increase the burden of poverty in rural areas in particular.

There is no doubt that countries of the MENA region will be hard hit by the latest events. However, the depth of the post September shocks on MENA and the speed of recovery will depend on the nature of each market and on how policy makers will respond in order to overcome the crisis.

Long Term Projections for Growth

In the long term, MENA's GDP as a whole will grow by an average of 3.6 percent a year from 2000 to 2010, a rate slightly less than in the Latin America region and significantly less than in the East Asia/Pacific and Southeast Asia regions, according to the December 2000 World Bank forecasts.

Per capita GDP in the MENA region is likely to grow by less than 2 percent a year from 2000 to 2010, according to the World Bank Global Economic Prospects. This compares to 2.3 percent throughout the world, 3 percent in Latin America and 5 percent in East Asia. Only in Sub-Saharan Africa is per capita growth projected to be lower than in MENA.

Growth prospects in the long term for the MENA economies vary, with better performance foreseen for those more advanced in their reforms. Growth among the early reformers is expected to increase to 4.6 percent a year (2.8 percent per capita) up from 3.8 percent the previous decade. That compares with annual growth of 2.6 percent (minus 0.4 percent per capita) among oil economies and about 3.6 percent (1.6 percent per capita) for the late reformers (Figure 1.4).

Despite its expanding labor force, continued macroeconomic stability and past investments in human capital, MENA's growth prospects continue to be hindered by institutional and policy constraints.

Savings and Investment Performance

Saving rates in the MENA region are lower than in other developing regions. In MENA, Saudi Arabia has the highest saving rate (Annex Table A1.2). In general, saving in oil-exporting countries tends to be higher. The high proportion of young and dependant people throughout the region tends to limit the ability of households to shift direct income into savings. Also, a large portion of the population works for the state, whose low salaries leave little surplus for saving (Figure 1.5).

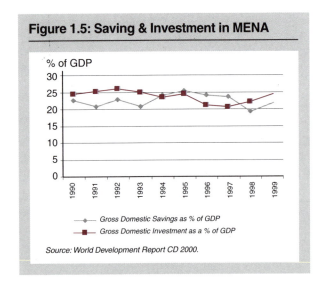

Figure 1.5: Saving & Investment in MENA

Source: World Development Report CD 2000.

Saving rates are determined mainly by interest rates and the sophistication of financial markets. Savings can be increased through policies that liberalize financial markets and deepen financial intermediation by allowing more players into the market and letting them expand the types of financial products they offer. These products include new types of saving instruments in areas such as postal savings and pension funds that are designed to provide easier access to households and other small savers. Governments can increase a country's total savings by increasing their own savings. Several countries, especially in North Africa, have included financial reform in their structural adjustment programs.

In the coming decades, the ratio of the working population relative to retired persons will increase in MENA countries. This may help boost savings, especially if encouraged by the introduction of new savings instruments and improvements in the overall macro environment.

The low rates of saving in MENA countries are matched by similarly low rates of investment (Figure 1.5). Investment in Arab countries increased in 1999 by a mere 1.1 percent from 1998. Algeria, Egypt, Lebanon, Mauritania, Morocco, Saudi Arabia, Tunisia and the UAE accounted for most of this growth, with the highest increase in Egypt. Much of the poor performance can be accounted for by a fall in public sector investment as governments tightened their budgets. Many MENA countries are now encouraging the private sector to take up the slack. This could be achieved by speeding up privatization and by reallocating public investment.

Macroeconomic Stability and Better Management of Volatility

By the early 1990s, most countries had begun macroeconomic stabilization programs that focused on reducing budget deficits. Creditors helped by canceling and rescheduling large parts of government debt, reducing pressure on central banks to financial deficits by creating more money (Figure 1.6). As a result, inflation has fallen to acceptable levels throughout the region. MENA countries show no sign of abandoning this commitment to macroeconomic stability anytime soon (Figure 1.7).

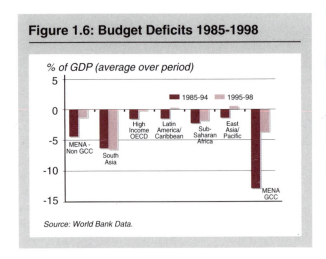

Figure 1.6: Budget Deficits 1985-1998

Source: World Bank Data.

Apart from Algeria, Tunisia and Yemen, and more recently Iran, most MENA countries fix their currency exchange rates as part of their macro-

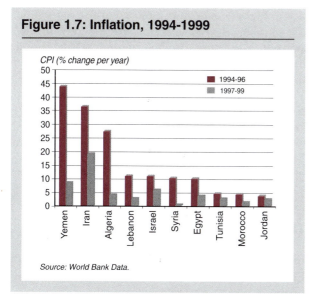

Figure 1.7: Inflation, 1994-1999

Source: World Bank Data.

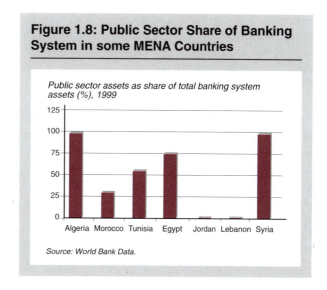

Figure 1.8: Public Sector Share of Banking System in some MENA Countries

Source: World Bank Data.

economic programs. Usually the pegs overvalue local currencies, discouraging exports. This is contrary to the policy of encouraging exports that the East Asian Tigers have pursued for the last three decades. Some MENA countries, notably Egypt, are looking for ways to abandon the pegs to boost economic growth.

Oil remains a regional bellwether. Fluctuations in prices, revenue and related aid flows and worker remittances will continue to affect economies. The hard-won gains in macroeconomic stability of recent years in the face of lower oil prices will need to be preserved even as prices rise. Mechanisms such as higher savings during booms need to be found to deal with future volatility.

The Financial Sector and FDI

With a few exceptions, the unhealthy state of the region's financial institutions continues to constrain growth and private development. The banking sector, crucial for promoting investment and savings, needs further reform, and the sale of state banks needs to be accelerated in Algeria, Egypt, Tunisia, Iran, Syria and elsewhere (Figure 1.8).

Progress has been made in privatization in general, particularly in Egypt, Morocco and Tunisia. However, only about 10 percent of the more than $100 billion in assets that the region's governments have promised to sell has actually changed hands.

GCC states have opened up their economies and are competing to attract foreign business. They offer investment incentives that include tax holidays, long-term leases, greater foreign ownership rights and simplified entry rules. The competition is particularly notable in services. Dubai and Bahrain are both trying to serve as the region's financial hub, Dubai, Bahrain and Qatar are seeking to attract tourists, while Oman has opened port services to private companies. However, despite exceptionally high returns in other developing countries, investors are still staying away from the region. MENA countries must work to make themselves more attractive.

The Role of Trade Liberalization

MENA restricts trade more than almost any other region. Tariffs remain high and non-tariff barriers plentiful, slowing the region's integration into the global economy. However, a number of policy changes across the region should lead to greater openness and, it is hoped, stimulate growth.

The European Union signed trade agreements with Israel and Tunisia in 1995, followed by others with Morocco in 1996 and Jordan in 1997. After several years of negotiation, the EU finally signed a similar agreement with Egypt in May 2001, and one with Lebanon in January 2002. The EU is also seeking agreements with Algeria and Syria. The accords with Tunisia and Morocco dismantle tariffs on European industrial exports over a twelve-year period while postponing discussion of agricultural barriers. The accord with Egypt dismantles tariffs over 16 years. In addition, Jordan recently signed a free trade agreement with the US.

A number of countries have also committed themselves to lowering tariffs, including those on telecommunications and financial services, by joining the World Trade Organization. WTO rules will further open the economies of the GCC, which are already relatively liberal, by discouraging laws stipulating that goods be imported through exclusive commercial agents. Indeed, Bahrain amended its Commercial Agency Law in 1998 to allow foreign companies to import goods and spare parts directly.

Jordan, Morocco, Tunisia, Egypt and other countries have been working to boost exports, while exporters, particularly in Jordan and Morocco, are pressing their governments to devalue their currencies to make their products cheaper abroad. Many countries have programs to modernize local industries and services.

Higher Industrial Productivity

The world's economic environment in the next decade will differ dramatically from that of the 1980s and 1990s. Competition is intensifying and the basis of success changing. MENA economies have made few inroads into the new economy. With only a few exceptions, they have lagged behind in promoting technological development and have failed to invest sufficiently in research and development. There has been little technological innovation in manufacturing.

Developing countries have not yet come to grips with the notion of intellectual property rights. The MENA region's pharmaceutical industry in particular faces a tremendous challenge as countries are increasingly being forced to comply with property rights. Various government support organizations can help ease the transition. But so far many have not lived up to expectations.

Demographics

Population growth in the region should help to increase production. MENA's population grew on average by 2.8 percent a year from 1980 to 1998, one of the highest rates in the world. At the same time, the number of people of working age grew by 2.45 percent while the number of dependent people increased by only 0.25 percent. This represents a net 2.2 percent annual increase in employable people. This fall in the dependency ratio suggests that from now until 2015, MENA economies will enjoy the biggest demographic gift in the region's modern history. In other words, demographic aging of the population has the potential to induce an extra 2.2 percent percentage point rise in MENA's GDP growth, similar to the phenomenon which occurred in East and South East Asia during the 1980s.

This swelling of the working-age population makes it all the more urgent for governments to liberalize their labor markets to pave the way for more jobs. Employment in the MENA region will have to grow by more than 4 percent a year merely to absorb the new workers, let alone provide jobs for the existing unemployed. One major source of new jobs is housing construction, where a huge pent-up demand has been accumulating for years.

As governments liberalize, they must take care not to let those who are vulnerable to poverty fall through the cracks. Most social programs in MENA were put in place during the oil-rich years of the 1980s. However, most governments have set aside very little of their increased revenue from those days as a provision for the day when oil prices fell.

Political Development

Cross-country evidence suggests that economic growth accelerates as political freedom expands, especially in societies that enjoy fewer political rights to begin with. Participatory political systems facilitate the conditions necessary for collecting and processing the reliable information that businesses and governments need to take decisions.[2]

Political development in the MENA region is progressing slowly. Although many countries held pluralistic parliamentary elections in the 1990s, the political processes have fallen well short of the criteria demanded in modern representative democracies. The executive branch of government remains generally uncontested and continues to exercise vast power. The judicial and legislative branches are partially independent, if at all. New political parties need government permission to form, while existing opposition parties have limited access to media. Voters are often coerced to cast their ballots in favor of ruling parties.

Participation of Women

Economic development is also linked to the status of women. Growth is hindered when women have less access than men to health and education. It is likewise impeded when women are denied access to jobs. In the high-growth economies of East Asia, for example, increased female participation in the labor force accounted for an increase in real per capita growth of between 0.6 percent and 1.6 percent a year from 1966 to 1990.

MENA ranks poorly in terms of gender equality. Despite great improvements over the last two decades, the number of adult females who can read and write is, on average, only two-thirds that of men. This compares to 98 percent in Latin America, 76 percent in Sub-Saharan Africa and 86 percent in East Asia. Likewise, only 31 percent of MENA women are employed, compared to 72 percent in East Asia, 41 percent in Latin America, 43 percent in South Asia and 62 percent in Sub-Saharan Africa.

Domestic Structural Economic Reform

While these factors, mentioned above, played and will continue to play an important role in determining growth in the region, it is domestic economic reform that remains the most important factor. The large size of the public sector, which accounts for as much as 40-60 percent of gross domestic output and employment in some MENA countries, has been a drag on the region's growth. This is because government-run institutions tend to be far less productive than their private counterparts. The region's governments have sought to sell many of their businesses, reduce the number of employees or offer incentives to improve performance. However, the effort has been slow and half-hearted.

Private investment represents only 40 to 45 percent of the total in the region, an especially low rate compared to the 75 to 80 percent in Latin America and East Asia. Moreover, much of that private investment has flowed into fixed assets such as housing and real estate and not into the manufacturing and services which have export potential. For private companies to become engines of growth, governments must liberalize trade faster, improve customs and other state functions, better guarantee property rights, reform and speed up their legal systems, improve mechanisms to enforce contracts and develop a more robust financial sector.

But these steps alone will not be enough. The region's private companies have often developed under government patronage, flourishing not so much by being dynamic in a competitive environment, but by selling to protected domestic markets or as state-supported monopolies. The private sector should see itself as independent; governments must allow and encourage competition throughout the economy; and society must support the change.

Macroeconomic Performance and Economic Instability

In industrial countries, fluctuations such as those caused by monetary disturbances and productivity shocks are considered the main factors that cause an economy's business cycle to change. To what degree these fluctuations affect the economy depends on the country's structural and institutional setup. For example, unemployment and falls in output caused by negative shocks normally last longer if employment contracts are long and labor and product prices inflexible.

Studying business cycles[3] in MENA countries does not necessarily imply studying classic cycles or searching for cycles most frequently observed in the industrial countries. In modern usage, cycles mean fluctuations with no particular pattern, or a unique and universal impulse. How long these effects endure and what the short-run impact of the disturbances is on output depends on the structure and institutional setup of the economy.

There are factors specific to developing countries that are usually introduced in empirical analysis in search for sources of fluctuations. In oil-exporting MENA countries, such fluctuations are mainly caused by changes in the demand for oil. When oil demand changes, the effect on the economy tends to be much larger than fluctuations in other MENA countries. When demand for oil collapsed in the early 1980s, for

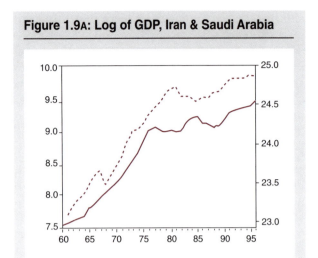

Figure 1.9A: Log of GDP, Iran & Saudi Arabia

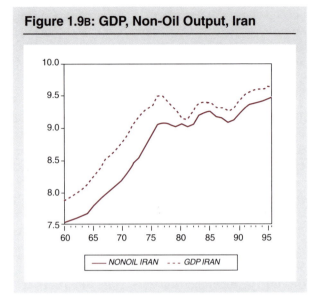

Figure 1.9B: GDP, Non-Oil Output, Iran

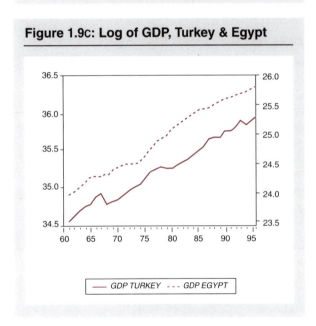

Figure 1.9C: Log of GDP, Turkey & Egypt

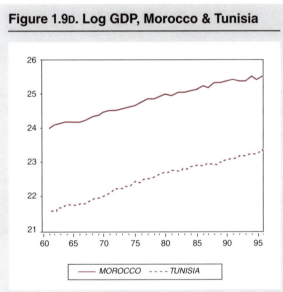

Figure 1.9D. Log GDP, Morocco & Tunisia

example, GDP growth in both Iran and Saudi Arabia slowed significantly during the decade. In Iran, the decline in the price of oil also had a lasting negative impact on the non-oil economy.

Features of Aggregate Fluctuations in Selected MENA Countries

A study of the cyclical fluctuations in a small sample of MENA countries showed that these fluctuations tend to be much larger in oil-exporting countries than in other MENA countries. Output series tend to be smoother in Egypt, Morocco, Tunisia, and Turkey (countries that do not depend much on oil exports) than in Iran and Saudi Arabia (Figures 1.9 A, C and D). The time trend for GDP in Iran and Saudi Arabia reflects a significant growth deceleration in the 1980s. In both countries, once the oil-price-boom ran out of steam, trend growth broke down. Figure 1.9B shows that non-oil GDP in Iran has a similar trend to that of GDP (including oil), which implies that the decline in the real price of oil has had a lasting impact on the behavior of the non-oil economy.

Business cycle studies in industrial countries tend to show that consumption is significantly less volatile than GNP, and investment and foreign trade are significantly more volatile than GNP. For MENA countries we observe similar, though not identical patterns. In the case of Iran, exports are the most volatile component of real aggregate demand. Investment fluctuates more than consumption and non-oil GDP. Further inspection of aggregate data shows that oil exports are more volatile than non-oil exports, and oil exports seem to be the most important source of economic shocks.

In **Egypt**, private consumption expenditure has the lowest volatility compared to other components of real aggregate demand. Compared to consumption, investment and exports are much more volatile, and this is consistent with the experience of other countries, both developed and developing.

Output in **Turkey** exhibits less cyclical fluctuation compared to Iran and Saudi Arabia but it is less stable compared to Egypt, Morocco, and Tunis. Like the other countries in our sample, private consumption is the least volatile and exports and investments are the most volatile components of aggregate demand in Turkey. Investment is less volatile than exports but more than consumption.

In **Saudi Arabia**, private consumption exhibits less volatility compared to the other two aggregates. Consumption volatility relative to GDP is considerably less than other MENA countries studied here. Investment variability is significantly higher than both consumption and GDP, an observation consistent with the experience of other countries in our sample and consistent with the stylized facts of industrial countries. Exports are the most volatile component of GDP, even exceeding the cyclical instability of investment. Excessive instability in export earnings has always been one distinguishing characteristic of commodity or oil-producing countries. As it turns out, it is the case for Iran and Saudi Arabia.

Output in **Morocco** has the least cyclical volatility amongst our six-country sample. Consumption is the least unstable component of aggregate demand.

Investment is the most volatile component, and it is a major factor contributing to cyclical fluctuations. These observations are in line with the "stylized facts" of business cycles in industrial countries. Exports and real government expenditure show about the same degree of volatility, about twice as much as private consumption.

Amongst the components of aggregate demand in **Tunisia**, private consumption has the least degree of instability. Volatility of investment is about twice as high as that of consumption and nearly as much as that of exports. Real government expenditure in Tunis is less volatile than both.

For all the six countries in the sample, cross correlation between inflation and cyclical output and monetary shocks (defined as fluctuations in broadly defined money supply) was calculated. Positive monetary shocks do not have output effects of the same direction in Iran, Saudi Arabia, Tunis, and Turkey. For Morocco, there is a significant and positive correlation between monetary shocks and cyclical output.

MENA Exchange Rate Policies

The crisis that exploded in Turkey at the end of November 2000 is a warning to MENA countries to adopt sound exchange rate policies and put their financial systems in order (see Box 1.2). Turkey's banking system, dominated by state banks, was weak and poorly regulated, its support of modernization and privatization was half-hearted, its currency was overvalued and its current account was in deficit (OECD figures suggest the real exchange rate appreciated by more than 20 percent in 2000 and 2001).

A country cannot simultaneously peg its exchange rate, run an independent monetary policy and keep its capital market open. This is the impossible trinity, and most currency crises result from trying to achieve it. This was the case for the Tequila crisis in Mexico in 1994 and 1995 and now the recent Turkish crisis of 2000 and 2001.

Most MENA countries have opted for exchange rate stability and monetary independence while closing their financial markets to the outside world (Annex Table A1.4). In fact, the market plays little role in determining exchange rates in the region. Out of 22

Box 1.1.
Macroeconomic Stability in Palestine

The Palestinian economy has long suffered under Israeli occupation. There has been little development of the infrastructure or the production base. As a result, Palestinians have had to find jobs in other labor markets, especially Israel, which has employed up to 40 percent of the Palestinian labor force. The gap between gross domestic product (GDP) and gross national product (GNP) is more than 30 percent. Also, the deficit in the Palestinian balance of payments with Israel has been huge.

An atmosphere of optimism followed the signing of the Palestinian Self-Rule Agreements, and in 1994 and 1995 the economy recovered. The Palestinian government set up national institutions, and many of the obstacles and barriers created by the Israeli occupation were eliminated. GDP grew by 7 percent in 1994 and 3.5 percent in 1995.[4] However, in 1996, restrictions on movement and economic blockades by the Israeli army reduced GDP growth to between 1.5 and 0.5 percent.[5] The following year was even worse. Repeated army blockades in 1997 caused growth to drop to as low as 0.5 percent. When such Israeli measures were reduced in 1998 and 1999, large numbers of Palestinians once again began working in Israel and the Palestinian economy rebounded. GDP grew by 4 percent during each of the two years and GNP by 6 percent.

Since the Aqsa Intifada broke out on 28 September 2000, the Palestinian economy has virtually collapsed. The Israeli army re-imposed an economic blockade on the Palestinian territories and restricted travel more tightly than at any point since Israel occupied the land in 1967. This paralyzed much of the economy, and from October 2000 to January 2001, GDP plunged by $907.3 million, or $8.6 million a day.[6] About 130,000 Palestinians working in Israel lost their jobs, costing the economy an estimated $243.3 million. Israel repeatedly shut Palestinian borders with Jordan and Egypt and closed Gaza's international airport, leading to a dramatic slowdown in commerce. Exports fell by 22 percent and imports by 36.3 percent.

Unemployment soared to 39.7 percent in the fourth quarter of 2000 from 8.8 percent in June 2000.[7] Some 31.8 percent of the Palestinians on the West Bank now live below the poverty line, according to World Bank estimates.

Source: Abu- Shokor, 2001.

countries surveyed, only Lebanon, Sudan, Tunisia, Turkey, Yemen, and to some extent Egypt have market-determined exchange rates. Iran, Iraq, and Syria used multiple exchange rates to peg their currencies.[8] Fixing an exchange rate may shield an economy from currency crises, but they are likely to distort them too, while at the same time encourage black markets and corruption, force governments to ration currency and lead people to squirrel their money abroad.

Among the six countries with market-determined exchange rates, Egypt and Turkey have been oscillating between fixed and flexible exchange rate regimes. Sudan, Tunisia and Yemen have a floating (both *de jure* and *de facto*) or managed floating exchange rate regime, while Lebanon has pegged its currency. The fifth column of Annex Table A1.5 shows that most countries with a fixed exchange rate regime peg their currencies to the US dollar.

While this may be sensible for Gulf countries, whose main revenue comes from oil, which is priced in dollars, baskets that includes the euro may be more appropriate for Mediterranean countries, which have a significant share of trade with Europe. The rise of the dollar against the euro was a main reason for the recent appreciation of the region's exchange rates.

Tracking the evolution of the real exchange rate is particularly important because its behavior can help predict a currency crisis. Figure 1.10 shows large appreciations of the real exchange rates of Iran, Egypt, UAE, Turkey and Lebanon. Clearly, the data suggests that the recent crisis in Turkey will add one extra piece of evidence for the relationship between real exchange rate appreciation and currency crisis.[9] Countries with a flexible and market determined exchange rate (Sudan and Tunisia) do not have highly appreciated real exchange rates.

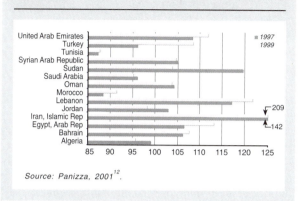

Figure 1.10: Real Exchange Rate Index 1995=100

Source: Panizza, 2001[12].

Although, the United Arab Emirates and Iran have overvalued real exchange rates, these two countries do not have market determined exchange rates and therefore are unlikely to be the subject of a currency crisis. The remaining two countries with an overvalued real exchange rate are Egypt and Lebanon. The exchange rate management policies of these two countries are discussed in boxes 1.3 and 1.4.

One possible benefit to fixed currencies is that they minimize the risk of currency crises. With the exception of Egypt, Lebanon, and Turkey, few MENA countries seem to be vulnerable. On the other hand, pegs limit the action of market forces and generate distortions that hinder economic growth.

External Debt in the MENA Region

Debt service remains a drain on resources despite a gradual decline in total external debt in the region to $203.6 billion in 2000 from $216 billion in 1995, (Annex Table A1.5). The net resource flows to the region increased to $9.3 billion in 2000 from $2.4 billion in 1995 (it had dropped to $2.5 billion in 1999 after a peaking at $14.5 billion in 1998). The increase was mainly due to an increase in net foreign direct investment to $4.5 billion in 2000 from a negative $0.3 billion in 1995.

The improvement can be seen by comparing the region's debts in 2000 to those in 1995. Total MENA debt decreased to 31.2 percent of GNP in 2000 from 37.3 percent in 1995 and to 94 percent of exports from 112.5 percent. Egypt's debt dropped to $30 billion in 2000 from $33.3 billion in 1995, while the cost of debt service fell to 9 percent of exports from 13 percent during the same period. Morocco's debt also decreased to $19 billion from $22 billion within the same period. On the negative side, Lebanon's debt soared to $8.4 billion from $3 billion, while the cost of debt service jumped to 51 percent of GNP from 26 percent. (Annex Table A1.6). The *Global Development Finance Report* of the year 2000 rates a country's ability to service its debt by comparing the debt to GNP and exports. In MENA, it has classified Jordan, Iraq, Syria and Sudan as "severely indebted".

The tendency of developing countries to focus on long-term projects can compound their debt-servicing burden. They are often forced to meet short-term repayment obligations by incurring new debt as they wait for their projects to produce a return in the distant future. To meet rising principal repayments, for example, Qatar had to borrow more in 2001, while Morocco spent privatization revenue. The burden in many MENA countries was reduced when donor countries canceled some debts. More debt may yet be canceled in the future. MENA countries might also reduce their burden by applying greater accountability to their external debt and by intensifying their debt management strategies, some of which have already proven effective.

What Drives Successes and Failures in Fiscal Performance?

Increasing Budget Revenues and Expenditures

Even though their revenue increased by an average 9 percent between 1995 and 1999, Arab governments still face major fiscal challenges (Annex Table A1.7). Shifting to taxes as a source of public funds seems inevitable, but such moves face serious constraints. In Arab countries, tax's share of total revenue increased in the past five years by almost 10 percentage points, growing to 37 percent from 28.6 percent. This was largely at the expense of oil revenue, whose share decreased by almost 9 percentage points (Table 1.1).

Several of the region's countries have been working towards ensuring both efficiency and transparency. Administration has been organized and taxation rates unified to simplify procedures. Tariffs have

Box 1.2.
Macroeconomic Stability: The Case of Turkey

The Turkish economy has gone through a cycle of growth, crisis then reform three times in last two decades. Each cycle had different macroeconomic causes.

As a result of foreign exchange crises from 1977 to 1980, the government put a structural adjustment program in place in January 1980 under the auspices of the World Bank and the IMF. Trade in commodities was liberalized, exports were promoted and prices were reformed with the aim of reducing the state's role in the economy. As a result, the economy surged. In 1988, the economy slowed, prompting the government to open its capital market to global markets the following year. Investors could now borrow short-term money abroad, a source of finance that allowed the public sector to spend more, and the price of imports fell. Growth rebounded from 1989 to 1993.

However, the growth came at a cost. The trade deficit in 1990-93 jumped to 6 percent of GNP from 3.5 percent in 1985-88. Meanwhile, the current account began moving erratically and the budget deficit soared. The economy plunged into crisis in 1994. The government began paying higher real rates of interest on its debt instruments, and foreign capital flowed into the country. At the same time, wages, unexpectedly flexible, fell dramatically. The economy grew with renewed vigor after 1995. The growth, however, was accompanied by severe macroeconomic disequilibrium. The budget and current account deficits, inflation and unemployment were growing, as was social unrest. In August 1998, the financial crisis that began in Asia spread to Turkey. The economy declined in six out of 12 quarters from 1998 to 2000. Government borrowing increased 15 percent, and by 1999 interest payments had risen to 13 percent of GDP. As its debt rose, the government was forced to borrow more money to pay interest. Inflation soared to 72 percent in January 1999.

In December 1999, the Central Bank and the Under Secretariat of Treasury began an IMF-guided program to put the economy back on track. The program aimed to stabilize the lira and reduce inflation to under 10 percent by restricting the growth of the money supply. The currency would be pegged to a basket comprised of one US dollar and 0.70 euros, against which it would be allowed to slide by about 15 percent in 2000. Other elements of the reform program included steps to reduce the government budget deficit, sell state assets, strengthen banks, increase the efficiency of the public sector and build up the central bank's foreign assets.

The program succeeded in the first 14 months: the budget deficit fell, inflation slowed to less than 40 percent and in the whole of 2000 GNP grew 6.5 percent. However, the lira's newly found strength caused the current account deficit to rise to more than 5 percent of GNP. Lower interest rates led a number of banks to use short-term funds borrowed locally and abroad to finance long-term investments. By December 2000, short-term foreign debt had risen to 152 percent the level of the central bank's net foreign reserves, up from 101 percent when the IMF program began two years earlier. The program brought down inflation, but at the cost of less stable banks.

By September 2000, political obstacles had begun blocking privatization, and negative signals emerged.[10] Short-term interest rates surged. By November, many banks were having problems rolling over their short-term debt. They began selling government bonds at fire-sale prices to obtain funds. To help, the central bank expanded the money supply faster than promised to the IMF, but every increase in the money supply was immediately transformed into demand for foreign currency. The central bank's foreign reserves plunged. In early December, the central bank stopped lending altogether and interest rates skyrocketed to 2000 percent. The IMF stepped in with $10 billion, capital flight was temporarily halted, and interest rates fell. But by then the central bank had lost $6 billion in foreign reserves.

In this vulnerable situation, the Prime Minister and the President began feuding, triggering another crisis. On February 19, investors pulled $5 billion out of Turkey, and within three days foreign reserves plummeted by $4.5 billion. On February 22, the central bank was forced to let the lira float, and within six weeks the currency fell against the dollar by 47.7 percent. The economy plunged into recession, with massive lay-offs and increased social unrest.[11]

The damage of the two crises is still being assessed, but commercial banks lost an estimated $10 billion, and the state, which had guaranteed deposits to avoid bank runs, lost between $15 billion and $20 billion. Further, by abandoning the crawling currency peg, the government lost credibility. This has led to self-fulfilling inflationary expectations.

Sources: Yeldan, 2001 and Panizza, 2001.

Table 1.1: Structure of Aggregate Public Budgets for Arab Countries

(Percentages)

	1995	1996	1997	1998	1999
Revenues					
Oil Revenues	57.7	55.2	56.7	48.7	49.0
Tax Revenues	28.6	31.7	30.0	36.8	37.0
Profit and Income taxes	9.0	8.2	7.8	9.7	9.7
Taxes on goods and services	7.0	6.5	6.8	8.5	8.7
Custom tariffs on trade	7.8	6.9	6.0	7.4	7.6
Non-tax revenues	10.6	10.5	10.7	11.2	11.3
Other revenues	3.1	2.5	2.6	3.4	2.6
Expenditures					
Current Expenditures	75.8	76.9	75.9	78.8	80.4
Capital Expenditures	22.5	21.9	22.8	20.0	19.1
Net Lending	1.8	1.2	1.3	1.2	0.5

Source: Unified Arab Economic Report, 2000.

been decreased to encourage trade. In 2001, Egypt expanded its sales tax to include more goods and services with the aim of compensating the imminent loss of income as it lowers its customs barriers. In 2002 it plans to reform the collection of income taxes by lowering the rates it charges on the highest income brackets, then tightening enforcement.

On the expenditure side, total spending in the region increased by almost 10.5 percent from 1995 to 1999. Most of this increase was directed to current spending, whose share grew to 80.5 percent of total expenditure from 76 percent. Capital spending share slid in the same period by almost 3.5 percentage points. Total capital spending dropped to $34.1 billion in 1999 from $36.4 billion in 1995. The decline was especially big in Qatar, where it fell by about 40 percent in the past two years alone; in Libya, where capital expenditure fell by 34 percent between 1995 and 1999; and in Algeria, where it fell 22 percent during the same period.

Expenditures on education, health, wages and subsidies in the MENA region have accounted for an important share of budgetary outlays. MENA countries are not able to keep up with this sizable wage bill and employment increases. Most governments have adopted restrictive wage policies with an aim to contain the wage bill. In the area of health and education, efforts to ensure equal access to health and education in some MENA countries came at the opportunity cost of quality.

Governments have been subsidizing basic foods, energy and other goods and services to reduce poverty. Apart from burdening the budget, the subsidies have not always been effective in targeting the needy, and once in place are hard to remove. However, a number of MENA countries have succeeded in eliminating some subsidies while better targeting others. Governments are aware that new forms of social protection that are more efficient, less costly and better targeted are needed.

MENA Budget Deficits still Persist

In 1999, the combined budget deficit of Arab countries was almost $31 billion, a slight decrease from 1998. This represented almost 5.7 percent of combined GDP, down from 6.1 percent in 1998. Kuwait's deficit soared to 14 percent of GDP in 1999 from 4.8 percent in 1998 after oil revenue plummeted by about 28 percent. Egypt's deficit as a share of GDP increased by about three percentage points after the government boosted spending on giant infrastructure schemes, such as the Toshka desert irrigation project, by 57 percent. In other Arab countries deficits decreased. Yemen's deficit dove to 0.05 percent of GDP in 1999 from 8.33 percent in 1998 after its oil revenue skyrocketed to about 7 percent of GDP. Saudi Arabia's decreased to 8 percent of GDP from 10 percent after oil income leapt by about 30 percent. (Annex Table A1.7).

Mechanisms to Reduce Budget Deficits

A premise that has proven successful in helping explain fiscal performance in a number of countries is the "common pool" problem. This problem is a fundamental dilemma in fiscal policy based on the fact that government expenditures are biased to some social groups, while the funds used for these expenditures are drawn from the pool of fiscal resources that can be used by others. The extent to which socially inefficient policies are avoided

Box 1.3.
Exchange Rate Management in Egypt

In 1991, Egypt successfully implemented an IMF-backed reform program whose centerpiece was tight monetary policy, exchange rate stability and a reduction in the budget deficit. The government on its own initiative pegged its currency, settling eventually on a rate of about 3.4 pounds to the U.S. dollar. Since then, inflation has plummeted to 3 percent in the year that ended 30 June 2000 from 29 percent in 1989.

However, the currency peg has not been as successful. In the late 1990s, pressure increased on the government's foreign reserves, due to a drop in the tourism revenues after the Luxor event. And the government spent more than $6 billion in reserves to support its 3.4 pound peg. Beginning mid-2000, it allowed the pound to slide, first at private money changers, then at banks, until late January 2001, when it again fixed it at around 3.85 to the dollar. It simultaneously cracked down on money changers, fining and even shutting some down for selling pounds too cheaply. Furthermore, the central bank required exchange bureaus to turn over their stock of foreign currency at the end of each day.

Besides the loss of foreign reserves (approximately US$ 1.8 billion during the year 2000), the currency policy has chased away foreign investment and helped drag the stock market to seven-year lows. It also has a cost in terms of currency rationing, distortions and the emergence of a black market, where a dollar has fetched up to 4.88 Egyptian pounds. On the other hand, it has enabled the country to avoid a full-scale currency crisis, a major concern of the government. (In this setting, Egypt is much better positioned than Lebanon (see Box 1.4) to allow a gradual slide of the exchange rate). There have been suggestions that Egypt, instead of pegging the pound against the dollar, fix it to a basket of currencies where the euro is given a large weight. Egypt's monetary policy would be more in line with those of many of its major trading partners.

Egypt is moving towards a more flexible exchange rate, and in November 2001, the Egyptian government gave full independence to the Central Bank of Egypt, making it responsible for setting monetary and credit policy. There has been talk of moving to a currency basket and increasing the flexibility of the price of the pound. However, the fact that the public sector dominates the economy makes inflation targeting difficult to implement. In particular, the four main state-owned commercial banks control more than half of bank deposits. The Central Bank is likely to follow a gradual strategy in targeting both the exchange rate and inflation.

Source: Panizza, 2001.

---

depends on the presence of institutional mechanisms to facilitate coordination and information flows that help social groups and their representatives internalize the marginal costs of the public expenditures that they advocate.

Figure 1.11 charts the average budget deficits of eight MENA countries against the fiscal discipline index[17]. Data from another four countries, outside the region, have been added for comparison. As the diagram indicates, the index is well correlated with the deficits. However, because some expenditure and liabilities are kept off-budget, official data often underestimate deficits or overestimate surpluses. In the absence of better data on deficits and debts, the average rate of inflation reflects the long-term consequence of fiscal imbalances for most developing countries because of the severe constraints on borrowing. Figure 1.12 charts inflation rates against the fiscal discipline index, confirming that low capabili-

ties in fiscal institutions are associated with high macro-economic instability.

The Aggregate Discipline Index is only a starting point for identifying weaknesses in fiscal systems. Examining the constituent components of the systems shows that there are several sources of inadequacy that account for the poor macroeconomic performance among MENA countries, and these sources are discussed below.

Coordination Mechanisms

Countries generally use a combination of four different institutional mechanisms to achieve fiscal discipline. The Aggregate Discipline Index measures the strength of each mechanism and how well they are coordinated in each country. The countries that score low on this index have failed to incorporate any of the four mechanisms in significant ways.

Box 1.4.
Exchange Rate Management in Lebanon

Lebanon pegged its lira to the US dollar after an exchange rate crisis in 1992. In September 1999, the peg was 1507.5 liras to the dollar. In the last three years, this has come under increasing pressure as people lose confidence in the peg and in the government's ability to maintain it, despite its success in reducing inflation in 2000.

One barometer of confidence is the degree of dollarization. By the end of the civil war, the Lebanese kept most of their money in dollar-denominated bank deposits. But by the end of 1997, dollar deposits had fallen to 55 percent of the total. The trend was reversed in 1999-2000 as people lost confidence. Dollar deposits crept back up to 62 percent in 1999 and to 67 percent in 2000. Indeed, for much of 2000 and almost all of 2001, the Central Bank of Lebanon was about the only seller of dollars and buyer of pounds. This determination to support the pound cost Lebanon $2.1 billion in 2000, or about one-third of its foreign reserves.

The government's huge budget deficit and growing mountain of debt is one reason for the lack of confidence. The deficit jumped to 23 percent of GDP in 2000 from an already high 14 percent. The state's debt has risen to 150 percent of one year's GDP, and interest payments comprise 40 percent of all government spending, or 17 percent of GDP.[13] When combined with the country's low economic growth, these figures suggest something will have to break, and people fear it will be the state's tight monetary policy.

Meanwhile, the lira itself is increasingly overvalued as it remains pegged against the dollar, which has risen against the euro, the currency of some of Lebanon's biggest trading partners. The trade deficit grew to 40 percent of GDP in 2000 as importers took advantage of cheap euros. This problem will diminish if the dollar falls, as many people expect it will.

Another reason for declining confidence is the economy's poor performance. In order to defend the peg, the government has hiked up interest rates, throwing the country into recession. This has generated political pressure for an easing of monetary policy. The peg remains highly vulnerable, and a sudden shock could easily generate a currency crisis.

Devaluating the currency would increase international competitiveness by making Lebanese products cheaper abroad. It would also reduce the dollar value of the government's total debt, since 70 percent of it is denominated by the domestic currency. A devaluation is not likely to hurt Lebanese banks either, whose assets and liabilities in dollars generally match those in domestic currency. However, businesses and households may not be so well positioned. A large share of loans to private businesses and almost all mortgages are denominated in foreign currencies. A devaluation would increase the amount of domestic currency and repayment of loans, which could lead to a series of defaults that would hurt both banks and the economy.

Further, if the government chooses to devalue gradually, people will be tempted to convert their liras into dollars as quickly as possible to avoid seeing their savings fall in value. This could lead to a run on short-term pound-denominated bank deposits. Because banks have used these deposits to buy longer-term Treasury Bills, a run on deposits would lead to a cash shortage, drive up short-term interest rates and possibly cause some banks to fail.[14] If the central bank decides to release its monetary brakes and pour funds into the banks, what started as a controlled devaluation could end up as a free fall, with the currency locked in a spiral of inflation and devaluations.

Another, more provocative approach would be to abandon the national currency altogether and adopt the dollar or euro as legal tender. El Salvador recently did this.[15] The idea may seem radical, but the short-term costs would be limited, and it would eliminate currency risk and put interest rates more in line with US levels. Furthermore, since devaluation and inflation would no longer be options, it would motivate the government to improve its finances.[16] Abandoning the domestic currency would also eliminate the currency mismatches that now threaten the stability of the private sector. On the negative side, the policy would prohibit an independent monetary policy.

Source: Panizza, 2001.

The first of these coordination mechanisms is the delegation of authority from the top of the government to make budget decisions. The political systems in MENA countries are highly centralized, and one or a small handful of individuals are in charge of central budget agencies such as ministries of finance or planning and dominate the budget process from design to implementation. Only in the region's three worst economic performers, Iran, Lebanon and Turkey, are central budget agencies relatively weak by international standards, strangely enough.

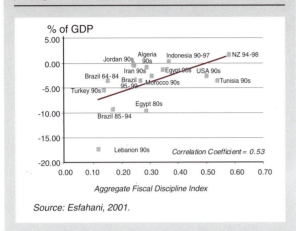

Figure 1.11: Budget Surplus and the Aggregate Fiscal Discipline Index
(Averaged over periods shown)

Source: Esfahani, 2001.

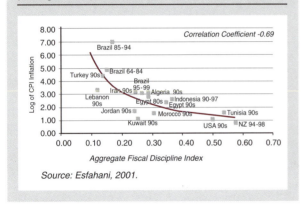

Figure 1.12: Inflation and the Aggregate Fiscal Discipline Index
(Averaged over periods shown)

Source: Esfahani, 2001.

The second mechanism is the degree to which decision makers set total deficit and spending targets before considering budget details. This is related to the first mechanism in that the powerful central budget agencies in most MENA countries draw up agreements in an early stage of the budget process. Morocco and Tunisia are the best at setting targets. Among the poor performers, only Iran employs such a mechanism to any tangible extent. However, even though its use is largely restricted to the legislative stage of the process. Lebanon is particularly weak at it, which has led to bigger deficits (Box 1.5).

The third mechanism is the limit that laws, constitutional clauses and social norms put on spending. Examples include balanced budget requirements or rules that allow governments to borrow only for investment. These constraints are mostly used in economic unions and federal systems to control the spending of member governments. They are rare in MENA countries. This type of constraint may be undermined by creative accounting. In addition, even if loopholes are tightened, such constraints reduce flexibility and prevent governments from using spending as a stabilization mechanism when circumstances warrant.

The fourth and last mechanism is the medium-term macro-programming. This is where the budget-making authorities agree on a plan that can only be altered in a given year provided compensation is made in other years. A few MENA countries follow such plans to some degree, but the programs are relatively primitive and mostly the remnants of investment plans introduced in the 1950s and 1960s. They rarely integrate capital and operational costs into the plans or follow through with compensation when spending exceeds the plan. In the region, Tunisia and Morocco seem to use multi-year planning the most, followed by Algeria, Iran, Egypt and Jordan.

Keeping Spending Under Control

Other aspects of budget-making can affect efficiency. Discipline can be undermined by autonomous growth in parts of the budget and by off-budget spending by organizations such as the military. Many MENA governments have committed themselves to expensive subsidies that guarantee food and energy at low prices. The subsidies often grow out of control, and when governments finance the growing deficits by printing money, the resulting inflation exacerbates the problem. Food and energy subsidies are quite substantial in some MENA countries, like Iran. Generous welfare and pension plans have led to similar problems. Among MENA countries, Egypt and Jordan were able to tackle their problems through fiscal policies reforms.

Public spending outside normal budget channels can also weaken discipline. In Turkey, the legislature often lets the government create special funds with designated sources of finance. Such funds often out-

Box 1.5.
Budgetary Institutions in Lebanon: From Surpluses to Deficits

The growing budget deficits of the 1990s have thrown Lebanese government institutions into crisis. The deficits are a relatively recent phenomenon. From independence in 1943 until 1958, average yearly revenue exceeded spending by more than 30 percent. Deficits became more common from 1959 to 1970 as the state began providing more social and welfare benefits and increased spending. But average revenue nonetheless surpassed spending by more than 1.1 percent during the decade. Deficits became chronic only when the civil war broke out. Revenue fell sharply while spending on salaries, energy and subsidies remained intact.

After the civil war, the deficits persisted, even as revenue rebounded to its pre-war level. Part of the reason was the decentralization of decision-making. The new political system agreed at the Taif peace conference in Saudi Arabia transferred executive power from the president to the council of ministers, a move that undermined the government's ability to restrict spending. The problem was aggravated by the troika formula, which allowed officials to push through new spending without the prior approval of parliament, the main institution that oversees executive spending. As a result, the average deficit between 1990 and 1998 reached an unprecedented 46 percent of spending.

Another reason for recent deficits has been that parts of the budget were made autonomous. The budgets of the Council for Development and Reconstruction (CDR) as well as those of 61 public agencies were excluded from the general budget. In addition, the Court of Accounts, an autonomous financial watchdog, was rendered ineffective and in its annual reports forced to deny claims of waste. Also, the government itself rarely forecasts the operating cost of planned projects, let alone measures these against their benefit.

Budgetary institutions responsible for ensuring fiscal discipline have either deteriorated significantly or were never put in place. The large surpluses before 1970 allowed Lebanon to afford inefficiencies. Now, however, the government has the daunting task of containing the enormous deficits of the 1990s.

Source: Atallah, 2001.

live the purpose for which they were created, draining resources that could be used for higher priority programs within the formal budget. These funds also often run up off-budget debts that they ultimately pass on to the government.

Off-budget spending and debts are particularly a problem in Turkey, Morocco, Lebanon, Iran and to some extent Algeria. Egypt and other countries have reduced the size of the problem by privatizing or commercializing state-owned companies and banks, although they still have far to go. Throughout MENA, governments need to tackle the problem with better regulatory institutions, better assessment of the government's contingency liabilities and greater transparency in the budget.

Lack of Restraints in Governments Budgets

Another problem is the ability of institutions in many MENA countries to alter their budgets during the course of the year. Governments add supplementary budgets or simply disregard allocations and limits. Apart from driving up the deficit, the lack of restraints encourages the various agencies to devote much of their energy competing for their share of the pie throughout the year. The problem is endemic in many MENA countries.

Alarmingly, many MENA policymakers underestimate the problems that the lack of restraints cause, and even perceive it to be beneficial. They view their discretionary power to cut spending during the year as a backup in case revenue falls short or emergencies in other areas require new spending. Maintaining flexibility in the face of fiscal shocks is, of course, a valid concern, especially in countries that lack access to inexpensive finance. Kuwait has responded to the problem by creating a stabilization fund that is built upon when conditions are favorable and drawn from when they are not.

Making the Government Accountable

Budget coordination mechanisms work well when the politicians using them are accountable to the

Economic Research Forum - **17**

public. Unfortunately, this is seldom the case in MENA, where most governments do not release budget data to the public. Budget performance is rarely scrutinized and officials are seldom held accountable when results fall short. Audits focus mainly on financial matters, not on performance.

Accountability tends to be weakest among countries where budget decision-making power is delegated from the top. This concentration of power is likely to diminish as decision-making becomes decentralized and democracy takes root. However, if the delegation mechanism is abandoned without other strong methods replacing it, fiscal discipline may suffer, as the democratization experiences of Iran and Turkey over the past several decades demonstrate.

Social Services Budgets: Public or Private?

Many MENA governments have cut back on social services as structural reform programs impose tighter budgets. The government's involvement is being re-examined in areas that were once taken for granted: primary and higher education, health services, technology acquisition, infrastructure and utilities, environmental protection, social security and pension schemes.

Education and health services are increasingly being financed and delivered by private enterprises. In Lebanon, the private sector has dominated education for years in the absence of the central government. In Jordan, 20 percent of higher education students are enrolled in private institutions, and although previously prohibited, private universities are now being established in Egypt, while private schools at all levels have proliferated. By encouraging the private sector to provide social services, MENA governments will be able to direct more of their resources to those segments of the social sectors that are less attractive to private investor, yet help to meet the needs of the poor.

Performance of the Private Sector

Countries of the MENA region are showing increased commitment to supporting private investment and exports by implementing structural reforms and stabilization efforts aimed at improving the business environment.

In Tunisia, for example, private enterprises account for about 60 percent of total investment by non-financial enterprises, a figure that remained more or less steady throughout the 1990s. Total private investment was 51 percent of total investment in 1999, accounting for 14 percent of GDP. In recent years the Tunisian government has decreased tariff rates as part of its partnership agreement with the European Union, simplified customs procedures, improved its infrastructure, and offered investment and export incentives to the private sector, particularly small and medium enterprises (SMEs), which now dominate manufacturing. The government has given SMEs tax exemptions and established a fund to encourage small information technology firms. In the process, exports are moving away from raw materials to manufactured goods. But private enterprises still face problems in Tunisia. Custom clearance is much slower than in countries such as Morocco. The government still dominates telecommunications. Furthermore, SMEs have more trouble getting credit and attracting investment, suffer longer import procedures and find it hard to take advantage of export promotion programs than do large enterprises.

The *mise à niveau de l'entreprise*, begun in 1996, is a Tunisian government program designed to restructure 2000 enterprises, mainly SMEs, to make them more competitive. It favors the textile and clothing sector. As of February 2000, the restructuring plans of 645 firms had been approved and another 625 were being studied. The program has helped the increase of exports of these enterprises by 45 percent and their employment by 21 percent.

In Morocco, the government has reduced price controls, enacted a new investment code, reformed customs and taxes, worked to adapt training programs to the needs of the market and sold many of its enterprises to private buyers. As a result, the private sector's contribution to GDP increased to 73 percent in 1997, up from 64 percent in 1985. Its share in total exports increased to 75 percent in 1995, up from 60 percent in 1985. The government has a draft price and competition law in Parliament. However, the economy still suffers from slow TFP and low rates of private savings and investment. Moroccan private enterprises still face a shortage of skilled workers, poor infrastructure and an overval-

Box 1.6.
Budget Institutions and Expenditure in Tunisia

Tunisia's experience with alternating periods of growth and stability and of crisis and instability led to difficult adjustments including expenditure cuts and institutional reforms. Part of the instability can be traced to budget policy and institutions. The country has constantly faced a difficult trade off between macroeconomic stability and spending needs in all domains.

In the early 1960s, the Tunisian government expanded education and basic infrastructure while mis-stepping with regard to economic policy and institutional design. The formal stabilization plan applied in 1964/65 was a result of a number of factors, amongst them a government policy that did not allow for enough investment in consumers' goods. This policy also caused the rapid increase in money supply and aggregate demand, leading to an important increase in inflation and foreign payment imbalance, while real per capita hardly increased. At the same time, the legislature was made subordinate to the executive and the ruling party, which allowed it very little input on policy or budgets.

In the 1970s, the government allowed partial liberalization with private sector development, but the economy still remained controlled and heavily protected. The government tried to avoid increases in spending too quickly, particularly on education. It resisted borrowing from the Central Bank to finance the deficit. Nonetheless, oil revenue was rising and the government, which had expanded public projects, eventually lost its financial discipline. Private spending also rose, and GDP climbed by 6 percent a year. The government began borrowing more as its deficit soared, until eventually a crisis erupted.

By 1986/87, the government had no choice but to agree to a stabilization and adjustment program negotiated with the IMF and the World Bank. Much progress was made under the program to restore budgetary discipline. The deficit was reduced sharply to about 3 percent by the end of the 1990s. The deficit was financed mainly by selling government bonds at auctions. The budget was made more comprehensive and hidden spending was reduced.

However, the budget process still falls short. Most expenditure—food, energy and credit subsidies and government salarie —grow autonomously with little government control. Moreover, the budget still does not include all expenditure. Current and capital expenditure are hardly mentioned. In addition, there is little consultation. Business and community leaders are involved to a limited extent only when the government draws up its strategic planning priorities.

With the exception of investment expenditure, only a small part of government expenditure undergoes a systematic and objective analysis or audit. There is little supervision on spending as the budget is implemented. Furthermore, line agencies have no performance indicators. The coming challenge is to ensure that the budget becomes more efficient and a wider base is consulted when it is drawn up and implemented.

Source: Boughzala, 2001.

---

ued local currency. Bureaucracy is also a problem. Land property rights are insecure, getting information is difficult, setting up companies is cumbersome and tax administration and the judicial system are inefficient.

The private sector in Palestine is concentrated in commerce and residential construction. Industry, especially that related to technology, was growing in the two years up to the outbreak of the latest Intifada. Tourism is an area that has great potential and could help generate jobs. The SME sector also holds promise, given the right incentives, and FDI could be forthcoming from the Palestinian diaspora. Present political conditions make it highly unlikely however, that the private sector will be able to grow or to prosper the near future.

Institutional Reforms

The MENA region has felt the impact of globalization, to different degrees reflecting the diversity of political, economic and social conditions prevalent in the area. While there has been very little reduction in the role of the state in any country, the spin-off from liberalization and privatization has prompted a rethink on the basic tenets of public administration. But changes so far introduced in governance are piecemeal and in response to specific needs. For instance, while Egypt's privatization policy should have helped in downsizing the government bureaucracy, high unemployment, fear of social unrest as well as promises made during the parliamentary elections have pushed the government to promise more jobs and better wages in the public sector. Thus, Egypt has committed to allocate about LE32 billion in the new budget for employee remuneration and for the creation of an additional 700,000 jobs. Compelling social concerns, poverty and unemployment have also stood in the way of reform in countries like Jordan. Those reform measures taken in a number of countries have been mainly directed to capacity building, human resources development, financial management, environmental protection, technology transfer, administrative procedure and decentralization.

Under the auspices of the Technical Cooperation Programme (TCP) of the World Bank several countries in the region have improved their systems of administration. For instance, Saudi Arabia's Enhanced Financial System project has helped the computerization of its budget and accounting system. In Oman, TCP helped in conducting studies on the impact of privatization of water and electricity services. The UAE has utilized TCP to upgrade the management of its already better standards of health services, improving management of agriculture and water resources, and strengthening the delivery of services.

In the Gulf region, major efforts are now being made through legislation and regulation to indigenise the labor force in government service. Dependence on foreign labor has been high, prompting governments to adopt improved personnel policies and to create other employment incentives for natives. The impact of this policy has been to lower remittances to countries of the region that have traditionally supplied clerical and specialized personnel to Gulf administrations. The situation will become more acute when similar policies are also adopted by the private sector. A growing awareness of the need for an integrated Arab perspective on regional migration is expected to address this issue and to contribute to a policy that is less contentious.

Decentralization

Decentralizing means giving people more power to make decisions at lower levels of government or outside of government altogether. Lower-level managers are often closer to a problem and have a better idea of what needs to be done. Distributing decision-making power releases people's energy, boosts an economy's productive forces and gives people more power to compete, both locally and internationally.

Despite general awareness of the importance of decentralization, this continues to be a slogan rather than a reality in almost all MENA countries. The state continues to be producer, provider and protector. Privatization has taken away some of the government's power in a few areas. However, much of the privatization has only been partial, with the state continuing to hold the reins of power in the background through minority stakes in companies, indirect stakes through state investment funds and heavy bureaucratic interference.

Reforms to the civil service have so far failed to allow authority to trickle down to lower echelons. On the contrary, reforms are often undertaken to counteract a problems caused by previous liberalization or privatization measures, or are mere window dressing for publicity. In most countries, civil service reform has been pushed by donors without motivation from local governments.

Any hope that elections or other schemes for more representation at the local level might decentralize decision-making has yet to be fulfilled. Where elections are held and officers chosen, dominating bureaucracies have killed the spirit of decentralization. The region's many conflicts have given governments an excuse to postpone administrative changes. Information technology and the communications revolution have given the man on the street more access to information independent of their governments. But at the same time it has given those very same governments greater means to centralize their power and authority.

Nonetheless, there have been a few successes. Iran, Turkey, Tunisia and Jordan have gone ahead with some reforms. Recent elections in Iran appear to have given rural populations more say in local decision-making, but the reform effort has not extended to urban areas, nor has it had any significant impact on power-sharing. Iranian reforms have, however, the distinction of being indigenous, rather than sparked by external assistance and support. Decentralization of authority can take place only with the commitment of the ruling elite, and there are few signs of this happening anytime soon in most MENA countries.

Creating an Enabling Environment

Sound macroeconomic policies, including stability of exchange rates, tight monetary policies and low budget deficits, are needed to attract investment. The lack of effective policies promoting these conditions has encouraged capital to flee MENA countries, notwithstanding that over the last ten years, more than half the region's governments have begun implementing market-based macroeconomic reforms.

On the plus side, almost all MENA countries have vastly improved their investment environment over the past decade. They have offered more incentives, streamlined procedures and allowed private participation greater scope. Countries are also opening up areas that were once a government monopoly. Egypt's new investment law opened previously banned activities to foreign investors. Jordan abolished limits on foreign ownership in the finance, insurance, telecommunications and transport sectors. Some MENA countries offer investors subsidized loans, loan guarantees and subsidies to cover part of their capital, production or marketing costs. They give export credit guarantees, subsidize certain services and offer training. However, surveys suggest incentives don't play as significant a role in attracting foreign investment, as do other factors. These include the quality of the infrastructure, the size and growth rate of the market, a conducive regulatory framework, macroeconomic stability and the cost and quality of labor. In this respect, the record in MENA countries remains uneven.

Institutional support to investors is weaker in MENA than in any other region. MENA countries still suffer from corruption, poor property rights and contract enforcement. Investment laws remain restrictive and the procedures for resolving disputes are deficient. Despite moves to privatize, the public sector still dominates the region's economies. Administration procedures are costly and burdensome, there is insufficient transparency and the judi-

cial system is slow. These weaknesses can only deter investment.

Tariffs and other import barriers are still high compared to other regions. On average, clearing an item through customs in MENA countries can take up to 30 steps and can require several weeks. Nevertheless, non-tarrif-barriers remain the main problem faced by MENA economies, which in many cases are higher than those of export oriented economies in East Asia, Eastern Europe and Latin America. A new emphasis on exports and a de-emphasis of import substitution may encourage governments to re-examine their investment environment as a whole.

Notes

[1] This region includes: Bahrain. Iran, Iraq, Kuwait, Oman, Qatar, Saudi Arabia, UAE and Yemen.

[2] Dani Rodrick, 2000.

[3] Business cycles or fluctuations, defined as deviations of output (or a set of macroeconomic aggregates) from long-run trends, can be caused by various impulses and can be sustained in time through different propagation mechanisms.

[4] Fadle El Naqeb, "The Palestinian Economy and Prospects of Regional Cooperation", UNCTAD, Geneva, July 1998.

[5] The Palestinian Central Bureau of Statistics estimated direct daily losses for each day of Israeli imposed closure in the year 1996 at around $6.1 million.

[6] Before this outburst and according to the United Nations co-ordinator office, the per capita GDP was expected to rise to 2—3 percent and the amount of GDP for the year 2000 was to reach $5,400 million.

[7] About 1,265 thousand persons lost their source of income, representing 40.8 percent of the total Palestinian population of the West Bank and Gaza Strip.

[8] There are often large differences between official rate and market rate. In the case of Syria, for instance, the market rate is approximately 50 Syrian pounds per US dollar and the official rate is approximately 15 Syrian pounds per US dollar.

[9] The sudden devaluation of the Sudanese dinar during 1997-1998 is another example.

[10] Large current account deficits are a classic outcome of exchange-rate-based stabilization policies that generate a real appreciation of the currency. Possible policies for limiting the current account deficit associated with exchange rate stabilization are: (i) a rise in consumption taxes on durables; (ii) to discourage credit booms; (iii) to tax short-term capital inflows (Rodrick, 2000).

[11] By mid-January 2002 the Turkish lira had depreciated by more than 135 percent with respect to its 2001 value.

[12] For all countries excluding Lebanon, Oman and UAE,

the 1990-97 data are from the World Bank's Global Development Finance and World Development Indicators. For the 1997-99 period the data are based on the real effective exchange rate reported in the IFS of the IMF. In the case of Lebanon, Oman and UAE, the real exchange rate was computed using USD, DM and Euro and real exchange rates with a 50% weight assigned to each currency. The same method was used to compute real exchange rate for the 1997-99 period for Egypt, Jordan, Qatar, Syria and Turkey.

[13] For over one year, the government has been attempting to reduce borrowing costs by replacing Lebanese pound debt with foreign currency denominated debt.

[14] It should be said that Lebanese banks are better capitalized and positioned to face a crisis than Turkish banks.

[15] In what follows, the term dollarization will be used to indicate that the country is adopting another country's currency, not necessarily the US dollar.

[16] It should be pointed out that this incentive did not work in Argentina.

[17] The index has been built by averaging the rankings of a variety of institutional aspects, the value of which is between zero and one, with one representing the strongest incentives and opportunities to coordinate and maintain budget discipline.

References

Abu-Shokor, A. 2001. "Macroeconomic Stability in Palestine." Background note for *Economic Trends in the MENA Region*. Cairo: Economic Research Forum.

Arab Fund for Social and Economic Development. 2001. *The Unified Arab Economic Report*. A joint publication by the Arab Fund For Economic and Social Development, The Arab Monetary Fund, the Arab Organization for Petroleum Exporting Countries and the League of Arab States. Abu-Dhabi, UAE.

Atallah, S. 2001. "Budgetary Institutions in Lebanon: From Surpluses to Deficits." Background note for *Economic Trends in the MENA Region*. Cairo: Economic Research Forum.

Boughzala, M. 2001. "Budget Institutions and Expenditure Performance In Tunisia." Background notes for *Economic Trends in the MENA Region*. Cairo: Economic Research Forum.

Economist Intelligence Unit. 2001. *Country Profiles*. Several country reports. London, UK.

Esfahani, H. 2001. "What Drives Successes and Failures in Fiscal Performance? Policymakers vs. Policy-making Institutions." Background note for *Economic Trends in the MENA Region*. Cairo: Economic Research Forum.

Jalali-Naini, A. 2001. "Economic Instability in MENA Countries." Background note for *Economic Trends in the MENA Region*. Cairo: Economic Research Forum.

International Monetary Fund. 2000. *World Economic Outlook*. Washington, D.C.

International Monetary Fund. 2001. *International Financial Statistics*. Washington, D.C.

Nabli, M. 2001. "How Will Current Economic Trends Influence the Developing Markets in the Middle East." Background note for *Economic Trends in the MENA Region*. Cairo: Economic Research Forum.

Ozmuçur, S. 2001. "Economic Prospects for MENA and Forecasts." Background note for *Economic Trends in the MENA Region*. Cairo: Economic Research Forum.

Panizza, U. 2001."Exchange Rate Policies in the MENA Region." Background note for *Economic Trends in the MENA Region*. Cairo: Economic Research Forum.

Rodrik, D. 2000. "Institutions for Higher Growth: What Are They and How to Acquire Them". NBER Working Paper, 7540.

Shehadi, K. 2001." Privatization and Private Participation in Infrastructure in MENA Countries: Trends and Prospects." Background note for *Economic Trends in the MENA Region*. Cairo: Economic Research Forum.

UNCTAD. 2001. *Human Development Report*. United Nations. New York and Geneva.

UNCTAD. 2001. *The Least Developed Countries Report*. New York and Geneva.

Valsan, E.H. 2001. "Institutional Reforms and Decentralization." Background note for *Economic Trends in the MENA Region*. Cairo: Economic Research Forum.

World Bank. 2001. *World Development Indicators*. Washington, D.C.

World Bank. 2001. *Global Development Finance*. Washington, D.C.

Yeldan, E. 2001. "Macroeconomic Instability in Turkey." Background note for *Economic Trends in the MENA Region*. Cairo: Economic Research Forum.

Annex

Table A1.1: Income and Social Development Indicators

| | Population (mn) | ACGR* of Population (%) | | GNP Per Capita | | Inflation | | HDI Rank | Life Expectancy at Birth | Adult Illiteracy (%) | Combined enrollment Ratio (%) |
				$	PPP ($)	GDP Deflator (%)	CPI				
	1999	90-99	99-2015	1999	1999	1990-99	1999	1999	1999	1999	1999
Algeria	30.0	1.8	1.7	1,550	4,753	19.1	2.5	100	69.3	33.4	72
Bahrain	0.6	1.8	-	-	-	-	2.7	40	73.1	12.9	80
Comoros	0.4	0.0	-	350	1,360	-		124	59.4	40.8	36
Djibouti	0.6	1.8	-	790	-	-	2.0	137	51.5	37.4	45
Egypt	62.7	1.8	1.5	1,400	3,303	8.8	3.1	105	66.9	45.5	76
Iran	63.0	1.5	1.7	1,760	5,163	27.0	20.1	90	68.5	24.3	73
Iraq	22.8	2.3	2.0	976^b	-	-	135.0	-	59.01	45.0	49
Jordan	4.7	3.9	2.3	1,500,	3,542	3.5	0.6	88	70.1	10.8	55
Kuwait	1.9	-1.0	2.5	18,205	-	-	3.0	43	76.0	18.1	59
Lebanon	4.3	1.8	1.2	3,700	4,129	24.0	1.0	65	72.9	14.6	78
Libya	5.4	2.1	2.0	5,859^b	-	-	18.0	59	70.3	20.9	92
Mauritania	2.6	2.7	2.2	360^b	-	6.1	4.1	139	51.1	58.4	41
Morocco	28.2	1.6	1.4	1,200	3,190	3.2	0.7	112	67.2	52.0	52
Oman	2.3	3.7	2.2	6.701^b	-	-2.9	0.4	71	70.8	29.7	58
Qatar	0.8	2.9	-	23,500^b	-	-	2.2	48	69.3	19.4	75
Saudi Arabia	20.2	2.5	2.9	6,874^b	-	1.2	-1.4	68	71.3	23.9	61
Somalia	9.4	0.9	-	-	-	-	-	-	46.93	76.02	7
Sudan	29.0	2.2	2.1	330	1,298	66.6	16.0	138	55.6	43.1	34
Syria	15.7	2.6	2.1	970	2,761	8.7	-0.5	97	70.9	26.4	63
Tunisia	9.5	1.5	1.2	2,100	5,478	4.6	2.7	89	69.9	30.1	74
Turkey	64.4	1.4	1.2	2,900	6,126	78.3	64.9	82	69.5	15.4	62
UAE	2.8	4.5	1.9	17,649^b	-	2.4	2.0	45	74.8	24.9	68
West Bank and Gaza	2.8	3.4	-	1,610	-	9.1	5.5	-	71.0	14.01	-
Yemen	17.0	3.6	2.8	370	1,755	26.1	-1.2	133	60.1	54.8	51
Comparator Countries:											
Israel	6.1	2.6	1.6	16,240^b	-	10.7	5.2	22	78.6	4.2	83
Malaysia	22.7	2.2	1.6	3,400	7,963	3.9	2.7	56	72.2	13.0	66
Mexico	96.6	1.5	1.3	4,440	7,719	19.5	16.6	51	72.4	8.9	71
Comparator Regions:											
Low & Middle-Income	5,081.6	1.4	1.2	1,240	3,410						
East Asia & Pacific	1,836.6	1.1	0.8	1,000	3,500	-	-	-	69.2	14.7	71
L. America & Carib.	508.2	1.5	1.3	3,840	6,280	-	-	-	69.6	12.2	74
MENA	290.3	2.0	1.8	2,060	4,600	-	-	-	66.4^a	38.7^a	63^a
South Asia	1,329.3	1.7	1.4	440	2,030	-	-	-	62.5	44.9	53
Sub-Saharan Africa	642.8	2.4	1.9	500	1,450	-	-	-	48.8	40.4	42
World	5,978.0	1.3	1.1	4,890	6,490	-	-	-	66.7	-	65

ACGR: Annual Compound Growth Rate.
Sources: World Bank: World Development Indicators, 2001; World Development Report, 2001; IMF: World Economic Outlook, 2000; International Financial Statistics, 2000; UNCAD: Human Development Report, 2001; The Least Developed Countries 2000 Report;.
Arab Fund: Unified Arab Economic Report, 2000; Economist Intelligence Unit: several country reports, 2001.
Notes: a: figures are for the Arab States only; b: figures are for Gross Domestic Product per capita. 1: figures for 1998; 2: figures for 1997; 3: figures for 1995-2000.

Table A1.2: GDP, Growth and Structure

	GDP 1999		Structure of GDP by Sector (%) 1999								Structure of GDP by Expenditure (%) 1999			
	Current Prices ($ bn)	Av. Growth (%) 1990-99	Agricul- ture & Fishing Industry	Extrac- tive	Manufac- turing	Construc- tion, Energy & Water	Trade & Tourism	Transport & Commu- nication	Financial Services	Public Services	Private Consump- tion	Public Consump- tion	Total Invest- ment	Domestic Saving
Algeria	47.9	-2.8	10.5	28.2	9.0	9.9	11.1	6.8	4.6	12.6	51.2	17.0	27.5	31.7
Bahrain	6.6	4.3	0.9	18.1	12.0	6.5	8.0	7.7	8.7	34.8	55.4	20.8	87.3	-
Comoros[2]	0.2	-	39.0	-	13.0[a]					49.0	14.0	89.0	21.0	-
Djibouti	0.5	2.5	0.8	0.2	2.5	10.6	14.3	21.5	11.6	25.5	63.5	31.9	22.2	-
Egypt	89.0	10.8	16.3	4.2	18.3	7.0	1.2	8.7	20.9	17.0	74.2	10.1	24.1	14.4
Iran	138.9	1.6	21.0	-	31.0[a]	-	-	-	-	48.0	64.0	14.0	18.0	22.9
Iraq	81.9	1.0	32.7	4.7	7.7	3.8	23.8	11.1	7.0	19.8	19.2	61.9	16.7	-
Jordan	7.5	7.2	2.1	3.4	11.8	6.1	9.8	14.6	16.2	21.2	70.7	26.6	22.5	2.6
Kuwait	29.7	5.5	0.4	37.1	12.2	0.0	7.2	5.6	9.3	25.2	50.1	27.3	12.6	22.3
Lebanon	16.5	21.8	7.8	0.0	9.1	10.2	28.8	3.1	6.2	34.9	78.3	30.8	29.1	-12.8
Libya	31.1	-0.6	10.8	24.3	6.6	7.0	13.8	8.9	3.3	25.2	67.0	15.9	18.6	-
Mauritania	0.9	-2.2	22.4	12.0	8.8	5.4	17.5	7.2	5.4	10.4	79.4	12.5	14.4	7.2
Morocco	35.1	3.5	11.5	2.0	17.7	13.3	20.1	5.6	0.0	29.9	66.0	18.8	23.6	20.1
Oman	15.6	3.2	2.6	38.9	4.3	3.8	13.5	7.4	1.3	26.9	48.4	23.8	15.8	-
Qatar	12.2	5.7	0.6	45.0	7.3	6.4	7.2	4.4	10.4	18.0	21.4	26.6	21.4	-
Saudi Arabia	139.2	3.2	6.6	31.3	9.6	9.5	7.2	6.6	4.2	23.2	38.9	29.8	20.3	31.3
Sudan	11.6	-7.1	37.4	1.0	7.4	1.0	7.1	24.0	6.1	16.1	85.7	4.7	16.7	-
Syria	16.8	2.1	24.0	14.6	11.4	4.3	18.6	12.7	4.3	10.2	69.5	11.4	18.8	18.2
Tunisia	20.8	5.7	12.9	3.4	18.2	6.5	14.9	8.0	3.7	19.5	59.4	15.6	27.8	24.4
Turkey	185.7	2.3	16.0	-	24.0[a]	-	-	-	-	60.0	65.0	15.0	23.0	19.6
UAE	52.1	5.0	3.4	25.8	12.5	10.6	13.2	7.2	4.1	22.6	49.7	18.4	28.8	0.0
West Bank & Gaza	4.8	-	6.9[1]	-	16.8[a1]	10.6[1]	-	-	-	58.1[1]	18.8[1]	97.7[1]	26.8[1]	-18.7
Yemen	6.8	-2.8	16.1	31.4	10.4	4.5	8.0	10.9	0.3	15.9	72.4	14.8	20.9	11.8
Comparator Countries														
Israel	100.8	7.5	3.9	-	36.6[a]	-	-	-	-	59.5	60.0	29.0	21.0	11.4
Malaysia	79.0	6.7	11.0	-	46.0[a]	-	-	-	-	43.0	42.0	11.0	22.0	47.3
Mexico	483.7	7.0	5.0	-	28.0[a]	-	-	-	-	67.0	68.0	10.0	23.0	21.9
Comparator Regions														
Low & Middle- Income	6,551.5	4.5	12.0	-	35.0[a]	-	-	-	-	53.0	61.0	14.0	23.0	25.0
East Asia & Pacific	1,894.9	8.3	14.0	-	45.0[a]	-	-	-	-	41.0	53.0	11.0	30.0	36.0
L. America & Carib.	2,052.7	6.8	8.0	-	30.0[a]	-	-	-	-	62.0	66.0	15.0	20.0	19.0
MENA	613.7	4.8	14.0	-	38.0[a]	-	-	-	-	48.0	56.0	20.0	22.0	24.0
South Asia	581.2	4.1	27.0	-	26.0[a]	-	-	-	-	47.0	70.0	11.0	22.0	18.0
Sub-Saharan Africa	324.1	1.0	15.0	-	29.0[a]	-	-	-	-	16.0	68.0	17.0	18.0	15.0
World	30,876.2	4.0	5.0	-	31.0[a]	-	-	-	-	63.0	62.0	15.0	23.0	25.0

Sources: World Bank: World Development Indicators, 2001; World Development Report, 2001.
IMF: World Economic Outlook, 2000; International Financial Statistics, 2000.
UNCAD: Human Development Report, 2001; The Least Developed Countries 2000 Report.
Arab Fund: Unified Arab Economic Report, 2000.
Economist Intelligence Unit: Several country reports, 2001.
Notes: a: whole industrial sector including mining, manufacturing, construction, electricity, gas and water supply. 1: figures for 1998; 2: figures for 1997.

Table A1.3: Fiscal and External Balances

	Fiscal Balance Deficit/Surplus (% GDP)	External Debt		Balance of Payment			Net Private Capital Flows ($ mn)	Official Development Assistance (% GNP)
		($ mn)	NPV[a] (% GNP)	Trade Balance[b] ($ mn)	CA Balance[c] ($ mn)	Overall Balance ($ mn)		
	1999	1999	1998	1999	1999	1999	1998	1998
Algeria	-0.5	37,597	66.0	3,360	20	-2,420	-1,321	0.9
Bahrain	-2.1	na	-	719	-421	26	-	-
Comoros		201[1]	-	-	-	-	-	-
Djibouti	-1.3	280[1]	-	-195	-17	-7	-	-
Egypt	-4.2	28,761	29.0	-9,928	-1,482	-4,027	1,385	2.3
Iran	-5.7	10,357[1]	12.0	300	-1,897	-1,5691	588	0.1
Jordan	-4.2	7,315	110.0	-1,460	405	926	207	5.7
Kuwait	-13.8	na	-	5,568	5,059	925	-	0.0
Lebanon	-14.4	5,410	41.0	-5,083	-3,462	266	1,740	1.5
Libya	0.0	..	-	2,062	800	753	-	-
Mauritania	2.5	1,533	148	23	10.4	-43	3	17.8
Morocco	-2.5	17,548	54.0	-2,555	-269	1,639	965	1.5
Oman	-7.8	3,106	-	2,416	-182	-172	-	-
Qatar	-1.1	na	-	4,962	2,171	2,458	-	-
Saudi Arabia	-7.0	na	-	22,639	-1,701	-8,897	-	0.0
Sudan	-0.7	16,918		-476	-465	115	-	-
Syria	-4.2	18,334	136.0	216	201	259	76	1.0
Tunisia	-1.9	11,652	54.0	-2,145	-436	693	694	0.8
Turkey	-8.4[1]	101,796[1]	49.0	-14,376	-1,364	-	1,641	0.0
UAE	-13.4	na	-	6,335	1,749	1,531	-	-
West Bank and Gaza	6.2	607	-	-	2,864		-	-
Yemen	-0.1	5,137	56.0	26	104	320	-210	5.5
Comparator Countries								
Israel	-2.2.	-		-7,366	-1,881	318		
Malaysia	2.9[1]	45.9	69.0	-64,286	12,606	4,712	-	0.9
Mexico	-1.4[1]	167.0	39.0	-285,444	-14,166	4,278	23,188	0.0
Comparator Regions								
Low & Middle-Income	-3.1[1]	2,563.6	-	38,895	-	-	267,700	0.7
East Asia & Pacific	-3.0[1]	674.7	-	108,578	-	-	67,249	0.5
L. America & Carib.	-4.2[1]	813.4	-	-34,361	-	-	126,854	0.2
MENA	-	208.5	-	9,570	-	-	9,223	0.9
South Asia	-5.1[1]	164.6	-	-15,238	-	-	7,581	0.9
Sub-Saharan Africa	-	216.4	-	-7,586	-	-	3,452	4.1
World	-1.5[1]	-	-	175,177	-	-	-	0.6

Notes: na: not applicable; a. NPV: net present value; b: CA: current account; CA balance excludes official transfers; c: trade balance includes merchandise trade only.
1: figures for 1998.
Sources: World Bank: World Development Indicators, 2001; World Development Report, 2001.
IMF: World Economic Outlook, 2000; International Financial Statistics, 2000; Balance of Payments Statistics;. Arab Fund: Unified Arab Economic Report, 2000.
Economist Intelligence Unit: Several country reports, 2001.

Table A1.4: Exchange Rate Arrangements in the MENA Region

	Market Versus Official	Multiple Exchange Rates	Type of Exchange Rate (IMF)	Fixed to	Type of Exchange Rate (de facto from LYS)		
					1997	1998	1999
Algeria	Official	NO	Managed float		NA	NA	Float
Bahrain	Official	NO	Fixed	USD	Fixed	Fixed	Fixed
Comoros	Official	NO	Fixed	EURO	Inconclusive	Fixed	Fixed
Djibouti	Official	NO	Super Fixed (Currency Board)	USD	Inconclusive	Inconclusive	Inconclusive
Egypt	Market/Official	NO	Fixed until mid-2000, managed float from mid 2000 to January 2001, managed peg from January 2001	USD	Inconclusive	Inconclusive	Inconclusive
Iran	Official	YES	Fixed	NA	Inconclusive	Inconclusive	Inconclusive
Iraq	Official	YES	Fixed	NA	NA	NA	NA
Jordan	Official	NO	Fixed	USD	Inconclusive	Inconclusive	Inconclusive
Kuwait	Official	NO	Fixed	Basket of currencies	NA	NA	NA
Lebanon	Market	NO	Fixed	USD	Fixed	Fixed	Fixed
Libya	Official	NO	Peg with band	SDR	Fixed	Float	Float
Mauritania	Official	NO	Managed float		Dirty Float	Float	NA
Morocco	Official	NO	Fixed	Basket of currencies	Float	Float	Float
Oman	Official	NO	Fixed	USD	Fixed	Fixed	Fixed
Qatar	Official	NO	Fixed	USD	Fixed	Fixed	Fixed
Saudi Arabia	Official	NO	Fixed	USD	Fixed	Fixed	Inconclusive
Sudan	Market	NO	Managed float		Crawling Peg	Dirty Float	Float
Syria	Official	YES	Fixed	NA	Inconclusive	Inconclusive	Inconclusive
Tunisia	Market	NO	Monetary targeting		Float	Float	Crawling Peg
Turkey	Market	NO	Crawling peg until February 2001,	USD and EURO	Float	Float	Fixed
			then floating		UAE	Official	NO
UAE	Official	NO		USD/SDR	Inconclusive	Fixed	Inconclusive
Yemen	Market	NO	Fixed Floating		Dirty Float	Float	Float

Source: IMF International Financial Statistics and Levy Yeyati and Sturzenegger (2000). No information available for Somalia and West Bank and Gaza. Inconclusive means that Levy Yeyati and Sturzenegger were not able to classify these countries.
Notes: The first five columns of the table were built using information from the International Financial Statistics of the IMF and report the various countries' official exchange rate arrangements as of January 2001. The last three columns report the countries' de facto exchange rate arrangements derived by Levy Yeyati and Sturzenegger: "Classifing Exchange Rate Regimes: Deeds vs Words," mimeo, Universidad Torquato di Tella, Buenos Aires.

Table A1.5: Summary Debt Data for the Middle East and North Africa
($ billion)

	1990	1995	1997	1998	1999	2000
TOTAL DEBT STOCKS (EDT)	183.8	216.0	216.5	217.0	208.5	203.6
Long-term debt (LDOD)	137.6	165.1	166.5	173.4	155.0	151.6
Public and publicly guaranteed	136.1	161.8	157.4	167.5	151.1	146.8
Official creditors	81.0	117.7	113.2	117.0	105.0	99.5
Private creditors	55.1	44.1	44.1	50.5	46.1	47.3
Private nonguaranteed	1.5	2.3	9.1	5.9	3.9	4.8
Use of IMF credit	1.8	2.2	2.9	3.0	2.9	2.5
Short-term debt	44.4	48.8	47.1	40.6	50.6	49.4
NET RESOURCE FLOWS	**10.1**	**2.4**	**17.4**	**14.5**	**2.5**	**9.3**
Net flow of long-term debt	(0.7)	(0.6)	10.5	2.8	(3.0)	0.5
Public and publicly guaranteed	(0.7)	(1.6)	4.9	1.6	(2.2)	(0.1)
Official creditors	1.4	(2.2)	0.7	(1.9)	(1.9)	(1.9)
Private creditors	(2.1)	0.6	4.2	3.5	(0.3)	1.8
Private nonguaranteed	0.0	1.0	5.7	1.2	(0.8)	0.7
Foreign direct investment (net)	2.5	(0.3)	2.6	6.6	1.5	4.5
Portfolio equity flows	0.0	0.2	1.5	0.9	0.7	0.9
Grants	8.3	3.2	2.8	4.2	3.3	3.4
NET TRANSFERS	**3.6**	**(5.6)**	**9.1**	**5.8**	**(6.3)**	**(0.2)**
Interest on long-term debt	5.2	6.8	7.0	7.2	7.2	7.2
Profit remittances on FDI	1.3	1.3	1.4	1.5	1.6	2.3
NET TRANSFERS ON L-T DEBT	**(6.0)**	**(7.4)**	**(10.1)**	**(4.4)**	**(10.2)**	**-**
Public and publicly guaranteed	(5.7)	(8.2)	(10.8)	(5.3)	(9.2)	-
Official creditors	(1.0)	(6.1)	(8.4)	(6.3)	(6.2)	-
Private creditors	(4.7)	(2.1)	(2.4)	1.0	(3.0)	
Private nonguaranteed	(0.1)	0.9	0.7	1.0	(1.0)	-
Debt indicators						
Debt/GNP (%)	45.7	37.3	29.4	37.7	34.9	31.2
Debt/Exports of G&S (%)	112.5	133.4	114.6	134.6	111.5	93.8
Debt service/Exports of G&S (%)	14.9	15.0	10.5	14.5	13.7	10.9
Interest/Exports of G&S (%)	5.3	6.0	5.1	5.9	5.1	4.7
Short-term/Total debt (%)	11.5	22.6	21.8	18.7	24.3	24.3
Concessional/Total debt (%)	24.2	26.0	27.1	27.5	28.2	29.3

Source: Global Development Finance, World Bank, 2001.

Table A1.6: Debt Data for Selected MENA Countries, 1999
($ billion)

	Algeria	Egypt	Jordan	Lebanon	Morocco	Oman	Syria	Tunisia	Yemen
TOTAL DEBT STOCKS	28,015	30,404	8,947	8,441	19,060	3,603	22,369	11,872	4,610
Public and publicly guaranteed	25,913	25,998	7,546	5,568	17,284	1,768	16,142	9,487	3,729
Private nonguaranteed debt	0	112	28	671	1,593	0	0	772	0
Use of IMF credit	1,906	0	498	0	0	0	0	76	409
Short-term debt	195	4,294	875	2,202	183	1,835	6,227	1,538	473
NET RESOURCE FLOWS	-1,797	1,814	501	1,965	-26	-390	55	968	297
Net flow of long-term debt	-1,855	-564	97	1,630	-438	-475	-93	510	148
Net foreign direct investment	7	1,065	158	250	3	60	91	350	-8
Portfolio equity flows	3	550	11	3	91	11	0	0	0
Grants	48	763	234	82	317	14	57	108	157
NET TRANSFERS	-3,710	-1,401	90	1,320	-1,403	-173	-362	374	400
DEBT INDICATORS									
Debt/Exports of G&S (%)	199	158	163	…	150	49	385	123	118
Debt/GNP (%)	61	34	113	51	56	…	149	59	75
Debt service/Exports of G&S (%)	38	9	12	…	24	10	6	16	4
Interest/Exports of G&S (%)	13	5	6	…	9	2	4	6	2
Short-term debt/Total debt (%)	1	14	10	26	1	51	28	13	10
Concessional/Total debt (%)	12	74	45	7	32	16	67	22	74
Memo:									
Gross National Product (GNP)	45,739	90,144	7,918	16,486	34,024	…	15,019	20,040	6,171

Source: Global Development Finance, World Bank, 2001.

Table A1.7: Fiscal Position of MENA Budgets
($ billion)

	Revenues			Expenditures			Deficit or Surplus (%of GDP)		
	1997	1998	1999	1997	1998	1999	1997	1998	1999
Arab Countries	171,797	146,228	147,789	184,043	177,357	178,787	-12,246 (-2.32)	-31,129 (-6.13)	-30,999 (-5.74)
Algeria	16,057	13,186	14,277	14,912	15,027	14,525	1,145 (2.39)	-1,841 (-3.89)	-248 (-0.52)
Bahrain	1,809	1,474	1,770	2,142	1,784	1,909	-333 (-5.24)	-310 (-5.01)	-139 (-2.09)
Djibouti	156	155	169	178	162	175	-22 (-4.35)	-6 (-1.18)	-7 (-1.25)
Egypt	19,033	20,071	21,553	19,720	20,897	25,296	-687 (-0.91)	-826 (-1.00)	-3,743 (-4.19)
Jordan	2,284	2,396	2,516	2,503	2,898	2,831	-219 (-3.13)	-501 (-6.86)	-315 (-4.22)
Kuwait	14,584	11,837	9,197	12,915	13,051	13,281	1.669 (5.56	-1,214 (-4.79)	-4,084 (-13.76
Lebanon	2,438	2,935	3,228	6,320	5,215	5,607	-3,882 (-26.11)	-2,281 (-14.11)	-2,379 (-14.43)
Libya	14,097	13,837	10,653	14,097	13,827	10,653	0 (0.00)	0 (0.00)	0 (0.00)
Mauritania	303	290	261	247	250	238	56 (5.22)	41 (4.14)	23 (2.45)
Morocco	8,601	8,736	10,347	9,616	9,359	11,223	-1,015 (-3.04)	-623 (-1.75)	-876 (-2.49)
Oman	5,896	4,801	4,674	6,001	5,778	5,885	-104 (-0.66)	-977 (-6.90)	-1,211 (-7.75)
Qatar	4,050	4,181	3,873	4,972	4,678	4,009	-922 (-8.16)	-497 (-4.84)	-136 (-1.11)
Saudi Arabia	54,873	37,762	39,321	59,085	50,682	49,024	-4,211 (-2.87)	-12,920 (-10.06)	-9,703 (-6.97)
Sudan	689	822	856	826	880	939	-138 (-1.30)	-58 (-0.46)	-83 (-0.71)
Syria	4,150	4,120	4,157	4,704	4,816	4,860	-555 (-3.34)	-696 (-4.34)	-703 (-4.18)
Tunisia	5,500	6,328	6,130	6,225	6,419	6,525	-726 (-3.83)	-91 (-0.45)	-395 (-1.88)
UAE	15,307	11,630	12,609	17,540	19,461	19,608	-2,233 (-4.43)	-7,830 (-16.53)	-6,999 (-13.42)
Yemen	1,970	1,676	2,196	2,040	2,175	2,199	-70 (-1.05)	-499 (-8.33)	-3 (-0.05)

Source: Unified Arab Economic Report, 2000.

CHAPTER TWO

FINANCIAL AND CAPITAL MARKETS, PRIVATIZATION AND FDI

Financial Markets Hit by Turmoil

The 1994 Mexican crisis and the 1997 Asian crisis shifted the focus of structural adjustment programs in developing countries to financial markets. These are vital for financing investment at a time when many developing countries are increasingly encouraging the private sector. More and more private capital is moving across borders, both from rich countries to emerging markets and between emerging markets themselves. However, an exception has been the MENA region, where the net inflow of international investment and foreign capital actually fell over the past year.

Even before the September 11 terrorist attack on the US, the world was facing an economic downturn. The world financial markets were slowing down, specially in the US and in Japan. The MENA region was particularly hurt in 2001 by the financial turmoil in Turkey, the slowdown in the US economy and the political uncertainty after the second Intifada erupted in September 2000. The September 11 attack and the military campaign against Afghanistan have compounded the uncertainty. The slowdown of the US and European economies reduced demand for MENA's exports and slowed the flow of new investment into the region. Stock markets performed badly, and will continue to do so, given the overall worsening capital and financial markets situation. It is still not clear how and when the financial and capital markets will recover, but there is a reasonable prospect that a recovery will begin during the first half of 2002.

For the MENA region to overcome its difficulties, governments should continue their financial reforms, encouraging the private sector and attracting capital and direct investment. Most governments have, by and large, decreased their dependence on indirect tools of monetary policy, liberalized interest rates and given banks greater freedom to expand their activities and introduce new financial instruments. Some governments have opened their insurance markets and stock brokerage to the private sector, though the state still dominates. Yet despite the positive developments, MENA financial markets remain far behind those of Asia and Latin America, reflected in the fact that Arab countries account for only about 0.25 percent of the world insurance industry.

On the other hand, the assets and capital of MENA banks have been increasing. However, these banks are still considered small when compared to their counterparts abroad. Of the world's 500 largest banks by capital, only 26 were Arab, for example.[1]

Banking and Financial Markets in MENA

The MENA region's financial and monetary performance has varied from country to country in the past few years, even though most governments have had similar goals: to decrease intervention, rely on market mechanisms for allocating resources, reform institutions, make monetary policy more efficient and open banking to more competition.

MENA monetary policies have aimed mainly to maintain stable exchange rates and keep money supply tight while liberalizing interest rates. Most

Economic Research Forum - **31**

MENA governments are adopting indirect monetary tools while relying more on market forces. State banks still dominate most MENA economies, but governments have been opening up the sector to foreign banks and there has been pressure to merge banks, especially smaller ones. The new international competition has been forcing insulated local banks to adapt, and most have introduced new technology, though sometimes slowly.

Total bank deposits increased 4.6 percent in 1999 to $304.9 billion, up from $291.4 billion in 1998, reflecting an increased confidence in the banking sector. Lebanon and Jordan had the highest deposit ratio, both exceeding 100 percent of one year's GDP (Table 2.1).

Table 2.1: Total Bank Deposits as Percent of GDP in Selected MENA Countries

Country	1998	1999
Egypt	68.4	68.3
Jordan	101.0	111.1
Kuwait	96.7	82.3
Lebanon	159.8	177.0
Morocco	52.7	57.1
Saudi Arabia	49.3	47.2
Tunisia	38.8	38.6
Turkey	20.9	28.0

Source: The Unified Arab Economic Report, 2000 and the IFS, July 2001.

Tunisian banks lent a greater percentage—93 percent—of their total credit to private borrowers in 1999 than did any other MENA country. Oman was second at 92 percent (Table 2.2). Turkey's lending to the private sector dropped from 70 percent in 1997 to 45 percent in 1999, reflecting the financial crisis that the country is facing.

In many of the region's countries, a handful of large local banks control most bank assets, with many small and relatively weak competitors fighting for leftovers. International competition has already begun squeezing their profit margins. Local banks have traditionally relied on lending for their income while neglecting retail banking, fee-based activities and other potential areas for growth. This is a high-risk strategy in the absence of strictly-enforced regulations on creditworthiness, particularly in the case of very large borrowers. In some countries such as Egypt, lending has favored larger at the expense of smaller clients.

Table 2.2: Credit to the Private Sector
(as a share of total banking credit)

Country	1997	1998	1999
Egypt	59	63	65
Jordan	92	90	89
Kuwait	52	56	58
Lebanon	57	55	55
Morocco	58	60	64
Saudi Arabia	56	59	58
Tunisia	9	10	13
Turkey	70	57	45

Source: The Unified Arab Economic Report, 2000 and the IFS, July 2001.

In the GCC, local banks, though reasonably well capitalized and soundly managed, often need outside help to provide the vast sums needed to finance the region's infrastructure, hydrocarbon and industrial projects. GCC banks have yet to develop structured finance, derivatives, commodity hedging and other specialized financial services. Saudi Arabia, Oman and other countries have committed themselves to liberalize under World Trade Organization agreements. This may result in their opening up banks to as much as 100 percent foreign ownership. This should encourage competition and expand the range of services offered.

Key Monetary Policy Developments in MENA

Egypt over the last four years experienced a series of economic shocks. In November 1997, the tourism industry was temporarily wiped out after the terrorist attack in Luxor. At about the same time, the price of oil, also a major revenue earner, was falling, the Asian finance caused foreign investment and Suez Canal revenue to shrink, while the decline in oil revenue in the Gulf reduced worker remittances. As a result, demand for the Egyptian currency plunged.

Rather than let the exchange rate slide, the government chose instead to support the pound, first by spending foreign reserves, then later by tightening the money supply and restricting imports. As a result, the economy slowed down, and by some accounts even slipped into recession. The problem was compounded by government overspending, especially on huge infrastructure projects such as the Toshka irrigation scheme in the country's south, financed by bank borrowing which crowded out private borrowing. Beginning in May 2000, the government finally began letting the pound slide in small increments. The crises have taken their toll, and reforms, though still underway, slowed considerably. The government may be prepared to consider the shift to a new system based on a trade weighted currency basket biased towards the euro (Box 2.1). In November 2001 a presidential decision declared the independence of the Central Bank, making it fully responsible for managing monetary policy.

Among Mashreq countries, a stable dinar and low inflation continued to be the main monetary goals in **Jordan**. The Central Bank of Jordan recently cut interest rates and commercial bank reserve requirements, which in turn prompted a sharp increase in both the dinar and foreign currency liquidity. A slowdown in the economy and imports of cheap foodstuffs from Europe helped keep inflation low in 2000.

In **Iraq**, fiscal and monetary policies remained unpredictable and determined by political expediency. The government controls most financial transactions, although a vast black market in foreign currency has emerged despite periodic crackdowns. Though the Central Bank of Iraq issues and manages currency, supervises banks and buys and sells foreign exchange, the state-owned Rafidain Bank, the biggest commercial bank, often acts for the state in other functions.

Lebanon continues to run huge budget deficits, and government debt has expanded to alarming proportions. The government is finding it increasingly hard to borrow locally or abroad, and interest rates are soaring, with little sign of relief. Banque du Liban, the central bank, continues to maintain the currency's peg to the dollar and keep monetary policy tight. However, as the government's financial problems grow, it will come under increasing pres-

sure to let the lira slide. Already, people are moving out of liras and into dollars in the expectation of a devaluation (Box 2.2). In order to overcome this crisis, the government can still sell its Eurobonds to the domestic commercial banks and it can also speed up the privatization of the telecommunication projects.

Syria, under its new leader, has been encouraging the private sector. It has permitted private banks to operate and is considering floating the currency. However, the interest rate is still fixed at 7 percent regardless of inflation or liquidity conditions. The government has committed itself to removing controls on its distorting system of interest rates and reducing direct control over monetary policy. The pace of reform is nevertheless expected to be very slow. Weak economic growth will likely keep inflation in check despite the increased government spending begun in 2000.

Among North African or Maghreb countries, the government of **Algeria** continues to keep spending in check, and Banque d'Algerie, the central bank, is working to rein in monetary policy to prevent the dinar from falling and keep inflation low. Helped by lower international interest rates and strong oil prices, the central bank reduced interest rates in 2000 in the hope of stimulating growth, though at the risk of fueling inflation. The discount rate of 7.5 percent was decreased to 6 percent to encourage growth. Treasury bill rates were also lowered. Banks followed suit, with commercial lending rates now fluctuating between 8 percent and 10 percent. In the meantime, the government continues to privatize, deregulate and restructure.

However, its plans to sell off state assets have been slowed by red tape and corruption, and the country's macroeconomic situation remains fragile. Growth is still below the 6 percent to 7 percent needed to bring down unemployment.

In **Morocco**, Bank Al-Maghreb, the central bank, has maintained a tight monetary policy. As a result, inflation is low and the exchange rate is relatively stable. A poor harvest and an increase in the price of oil imports have not yet pushed prices up significantly, although this could change as the economy recovers and if world commodity prices rise. The currency basket used for pegging the dirham is weighted 60 percent against the euro and 40 percent against the US dollar. Some 60 percent of exports are priced in euros, while oil imports are paid for in dollars. Exporters want the dirham devalued, and there is concern Moroccan exports will be hurt if the euro strengthens against the dollar. However, the government is concerned a devaluation would increase the cost of servicing its external debt, encourage demands for salary rises and discourage domestic and foreign investment. Banks remain healthy, but non-performing loans have increased to 14.2 percent of total loans and some state-owned banks are undercapitalized.

Banks in **Tunisia** suffer from weak capital bases and an alarming level of non-performing loans. The government, which owns the four biggest commercial banks and two of the largest development banks, has begun merging a number of its banks to strengthen their balance sheets and improve management. Foreign banks will be able to compete in Tunisia beginning in 2001 under agreements with the World Trade Organization and the European Union. Compared to industrialized countries, Tunisia's insurance sector is undeveloped, with premiums equal to less than 2 percent of GDP. The government controls four of Tunisia's 20 insurance companies, and foreigners own five. The biggest state-controlled company accounts for one-third of the total insurance market. Insurance sector reform is part of the economic policy of Tunisia in the coming five years.

Among **Gulf Cooperation Council** (GCC) countries, Bahrain, Qatar, Saudi Arabia and the United Arab Emirates and Oman, backed by their substantial oil income, peg their currencies against the dollar. Kuwait similarly fixes its dinar against a basket of currencies that gives the dollar a heavy weight. As a result, interest rates in these countries have tracked the recent declines of US interest rates.

The **Bahraini** economic approach will focus on consolidating Bahrain's position as the free trade and services hub of the Gulf region. Its organized regulatory structure is helping persuade foreign financial and commercial firms to base their operations in the country. The Bahrain Monetary Agency, the central bank, will continue to maintain the dinar's peg to the US dollar. Interest rates in Bahrain will

have to follow those prevailing in the US. Given the currency peg, the government is forced to rely on fiscal policy to influence economic conditions. The government will continue to encourage foreign businesses to use Bahrain as a regional operational base and offers incentives to international firms to establish manufacturing ventures. There is also a move towards privatization.

In the **UAE**, the main focus of monetary policy would be to control inflation and protect the currency peg to the dollar, especially since oil prices and greater spending on new infrastructure projects may fuel inflation. As US interest rates have fallen, local rates will follow suit, reflecting the UAE risks as oil revenues falls. The profits of UAE banks plunged 21 percent in 1999 to $926.4 million, due to low oil prices, weak re-export markets and bad loans.

Saudi Arabia Monetary Agency and **Oman** Central Bank will face difficulty in maintaining their local currencies pegged against the US dollar. Local interest rates will fall, following those of the US, reaching their lowest level in 2002. Serious efforts are being undertaken by the Omani government to diversify the economy away from oil and related activities.

Yemen agreed to IMF and World Bank reform programs in 1995. A $350-million Poverty Reduction and Growth Facility, due to expire in October 2000, was extended until the end of the year 2001 and possibly longer. Higher oil revenue threatens to undermine the Central Bank of Yemen's target of bringing inflation, running at about 15 percent at the end of 2000, down to a single digit.

Iran in 2000 passed a new law regulating foreign investment, sparking interest among foreign companies in the promising oil and gas sector. Nevertheless, many people in the country are still hostile towards foreign businesses, making other, less promising sectors even less attractive. The Central Bank of Iran has targeted the fiscal year 2002 for the introduction of the new, unified foreign exchange regime.

MENA's Capital Markets Emerge

A new capital markets law in the mid-1990s and the sale of a series of state companies on the Cairo and Alexandria Stock Exchanges sparked a revival of share trading in **Egypt**. In 1994, Egypt's stock market was one of world's best performing, skyrocketing 157 percent in US dollar terms. The market climbed another 42.5 percent in 1999, with foreigners entering the market in increasing numbers. Foreigners accounted for 27.4 percent of all purchases by value in 1999, compared to 18 percent in 1998, while their share of sales declined to 17.3 percent from 22 percent. However, in 2000 the pace of privatization slowed and the central bank devalued the pound by 6.4 percent in August, 2001, followed by a further 9.6 percent by early January 2001. Meanwhile, investors have shown more confidence in the stock market and in fixed income securities, which have been responsible for 50 percent of the total stock turnover since the September attacks.

The Amman stock exchange in **Jordan** fell 30 percent in 2000, due partly to concern over the Palestinian uprising which broke out in late September in the neighboring West Bank, but also to a general economic slowdown and the reluctance of listed companies to release information to investors. The central bank recently relaxed its monetary policy, but this does not yet appear to have helped the market.

The Beirut Stock Exchange in **Lebanon** has been disappointing since January 1996, when the first three construction materials companies were listed and share trading began for the first time since the end of the civil war. Investors were initially optimistic. Solidere, the company rebuilding downtown Beirut, listed on the exchange in 1997 after having traded on the secondary market, a move that boosted the value of shares listed on the bourse to $2.6 billion from $1.8 billion. Several banks and other companies subsequently joined, bringing the number to 12. However, after intense activity in late 1997, interest in the market has lessened, with weekly trade rarely exceeding $2 million in 2000. The benchmark Beirut Stock Exchange share index slipped 0.6 percent between June and September 2000, while year-on-year market capitalization fell by 7.2 percent to $2.6 billion. There is a general feeling that share prices are manipulated. The lack of confidence among investors and Lebanon's broader economic problems pushed trading volume down by 8.5 percent over the year.

In **Morocco**, the Casablanca Stock Exchange's general index fell 15.3 percent in 2000 and the Upline Securities Index of leading stocks dropped 19.6 percent. The market recently introduced an electronic quotation system, a central depository and clearing house for settlement, and new market guarantees. The stock market watchdog, the Conseil des Valeurs Mobilieres, is working to improve transparency and crack down on bourse members who breach the rules.

In **Tunisia**, beginning in the mid-1990s, a series of reforms to the Tunisian stock market have increased transparency and boosted confidence. Tunindex, the market's official index of 34 companies, climbed 20 percent in 2000, after the country's buoyant economy pushed up the earnings of blue-chip stocks and improved bank results. Foreign investors bought more shares. However, the stock market has fallen again in June 2001 and continued to fall until August. On September 13th the Tunindex registered a 10.2 percent fall in its level at the start of the year. Despite the expected economic growth and low inflation rates, the stock market is held back by the relatively small number of listed companies.

Among **GCC** stock exchanges (see Annex Table A2.1), higher oil prices and a new capital markets law boosted the market in **Saudi Arabia**, with the all-share NCFEI index advancing 10 percent in 2000, an increase greater than that of any of the previous five years. The **Bahrain** Stock Exchange's index of 41 companies slid 18 percent in 2000. The **Kuwait** Stock Exchange index fell 6.8 percent during 2000 to 1337.8 as of January 2, 2001. However, it recovered in 2001 to more than 1800, only to fall by 11 percent after the September suicide attacks in the United States. The number of companies listed on the Kuwaiti market has increased and the government now allows foreigners to buy shares. **Qatar** is expected to introduce a new law that will allow foreigners to invest on the Doha Securities Market, beginning initially with GCC citizens and expatriates living in Qatar. The **United Arab Emirates**' first official stock exchange, the Dubai Financial Market, opened in March 2000 after years of anticipation. Trade so far has been slow, with average daily volume below one million dirhams and about 30 transactions per day.

A stock market was established in **Iraq** in March 1992, but trade has been minimal. **Syria** has been considering introducing its own stock market.

The Istanbul Stock Exchange boomed in late 1999 and early 2000 after **Turkey** signed a stand-by agreement with the International Monetary Fund. However, the euphoria soon dissipated. The country's still unsolved economic problems prompted investors to transfer between $6 billion and $7 billion out of the country, and by August 2000 the ISE index had crashed to 12,711 from its peak of 19,577 in January 2000. Nonetheless, an increase in the number of initial public offerings has boosted the supply of stocks on the market, and there is continued optimism that the government will continue to privatize.

MENA Governments Work to Sell Their Assets

The MENA region has not fared well in privatization in the last few years, but it may be on the verge of an improvement in 2002 and beyond. Privatization and private participation in infrastructure (PPI) have been slow in the MENA region, though it has been growing.[2] Before 1996, PPI in the MENA region was barely 0.5 percent of the total of such transfers in all developing countries. Since then, the percentage rose to 3.4 percent in 1998 and 3.5 percent in 1999. From 1991 to 1998, privatization proceeds in MENA countries averaged a mere 2.7 percent of the total, amounting to US$2.4 billion in 1999 (Table 2.3).

PPI was not much higher in 2000. MENA governments collected less than one percent of the $200 billion dollars governments around the world earned from selling their assets, including infrastructure assets. However, there is reason to believe that privatization will slowly pick up in the near to medium term (Figure 2.1). High budget deficits, especially in oil-poor countries, stagnant foreign direct investment and deteriorating infrastructure have pushed privatization and PPI to the top of MENA country agendas. Both Jordan and Morocco in 2000 passed new privatization laws designed to make the sale of government assets less cumbersome. In Jordan, the Executive Privatization Commission replaced the Executive Privatization Unit and was given a broader mandate.

Table 2.3: Private Participation in Infrastructure (PPI)
(in billion $)

Region	1995	1996	1997	1998	1999
MENA	0.1	0.4	5.3	3.5	2.4
Sub-Saharan Africa	0.8	2.1	4.5	2.4	2.9
Latin America	19.4	28.8	51.1	71.0	36.3
South Asia	7.6	6.1	7.1	2.3	4.0
East Asia & Pacific	23.4	33.4	38.8	9.5	14.1
Total	59.9	82.3	121.9	100.2	68.5
MENA (share in %)	0.1	0.4	4.3	3.4	3.5

Source: The Unified Arab Economic Report, 2000 and the IFS, July 2001.

Figure 2.1: Total Privatization Proceeds 1990-98

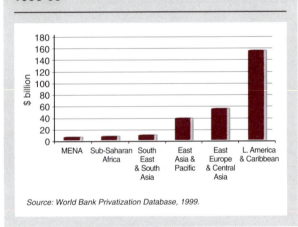

Source: World Bank Privatization Database, 1999.

PPI in Selected MENA Countries

Over the last decade, the most progress in turning infrastructure over to private businesses was made in countries where stock markets were relatively well developed, such as Egypt, Morocco, Tunisia and, more recently, Jordan (Box 2.1). Other countries have also recently begun moving to sell infrastructure assets. Oman has sold new power projects and is preparing to sell stakes in its telephone company and its main airport. The United Arab Emirates has let private businesses move into the power sector. It awarded the operation of more than 70 sewage pumping stations run by the Abu Dhabi Municipality, representing about three-quarters of the system, to private companies. Qatar sold Qatar Telecom. Jordan sold 40 percent of Jordan Telecommunications Co. to a consortium led by France Telecom.

Governments have announced their intention to sell more than $100 billion in assets, but so far have actually sold only about 10 percent.[3] If transfers of infrastructure assets and operation are added, the portfolio becomes much bigger. Future power systems in Saudi Arabia alone are expected to require investments of more than $100 billion (Figure 2.2).

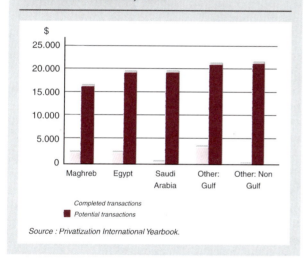

Figure 2.2: Completed vs. Potential Transaction MENA, 1999

Source : Privatization International Yearbook.

Some 58 percent of total privatization proceeds in developing countries came from foreign investors in 1998. On this, 93 percent was foreign direct investment and the rest portfolio investment. According to the World Bank, foreign investors (direct and portfolio investors) contributed to 58 percent of total privatization proceeds in the developing world. In 1998, FDI rather than portfolio sales was the main source of foreign revenue raised through privatization accounting for 93 percent of the total. In 1998, the flow of portfolio equity to developing countries fell to almost half its 1997 level, while the flow of FDI increased (Figure 2.3).

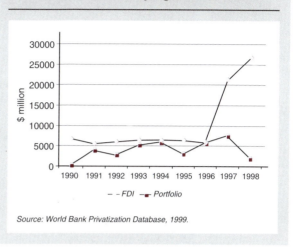

Figure 2.3: Foreign Investments in Privatization in Developing World, 1990-98

Source: World Bank Privatization Database, 1999.

Selling MENA's Telephone Companies

MENA governments have been reluctant to give up their telephone monopolies. However, the rapid pace of technological innovations and the phenomenal international telecom market growth have made it impossible for the state-owned operators to keep up with these changes. In Lebanon, for example, the high-speed ISDN technology, almost 10 years old, is only now being introduced on the market.

Countries in other regions began opening their telecommunications market to private enterprise in the early 1990s. Between 1990 and 1999, there were over 500 telecommunications projects in developing countries that involved the private sector. These brought in $243 billion in investment commitments. Of these, only $4.5 billion, or less than 2 percent of the total, were in the MENA region. It is only recently that MENA governments began committing themselves to selling their telecommunications. However, after telecommunications, media and technology stocks were trounced in international stock markets in 2000, they will be harder than ever to sell.

One of the few advantages of delayed telecommunications privatization is that it allows governments to learn from other countries' experiences. Before privatizing, governments need to have a clear policy.

Box 2.1.
Privatization in Jordan

Jordan has made significant strides toward a greater private sector role in the economy. The government:

- Awarded management of the Greater Amman Water and Wastewater Networks to France's Suez Lyonnaise des Eaux.
- Sold 33 percent of Jordan Cement Factories to France's Lafarge in October 1998 for $102 million.
- Sold 40 percent of Jordan Telecommunications Company to a joint venture comprising France Telecom, the National Bank of Kuwait, Saudi Arabia's National Commercial Bank and Jordan's Arab Bank. The joint venture paid $508 million.
- Plans to sell a stake in Royal Jordanian Airlines. A number of foreign airlines have expressed interest.
- Is preparing to sell the Central Electricity Generating Company (CEGCO), the Electricity Distribution Company (EDCO) and the Irbid Electricity Company (IDECO) in 2002.
- Is reviewing strategies for private participation in the Amman Queen Alia International Airport, the Aqaba port and other transportation infrastructure.

Source: Shehadi, 2001.

A timetable for rapid sales should be set, the social responsibility of private operators laid out and the role of telecommunications authorities defined. Governments need to enact new laws to establish independent regulatory institutions and end legal monopolies. Without such a policy, investors will place a high price on political risk, which they will then pass on to consumers.

Governments are best off when they sell their assets by means of a transparent and competitive process. The criteria for companies wanting to buy telecommunications licenses, and the details of the subsequent selection process, should be made public. The same is true when the shares of telecommunications companies are sold. Thus prepared, governments should move ahead quickly with privatization. Giving state owned operators a few years to restructure or upgrade their services has seldom worked. Only competitive pressure to offer the best quality of service at the lowest possible price will give Arab citizens the telecommunications infrastructure they need.

Getting Privatization Right

Privatization removes an important tool at the hands of governments to maintain political control, and for this reason, they have preferred to move cautiously. Technocrats often promote the sale of state assets, but rarely does the leadership give it the necessary political backing. One example where it did is in Jordan, where King Abdullah's intervention led to the successful sale of the state telecommunication company.

Privatization contributes to growth and creates jobs. In Yemen the sale of hotels and agricultural enterprises produced a remarkable number of new jobs. Because of its visibility, foreign investors often view privatization as a indication of a government's commitment to economic reform. And yet, the small private sector in most MENA countries is often crowded out by the government, and companies are usually owned by families.

When privatizing, governments often take decisions based more on their perceptions than on data collected through research. Governments usually insist on retaining a degree of control after the sale, often preserve monopolies and often allow the old management to keep their jobs. Governments are reluctant to deal with overstaffing and often cite this as a reason not to proceed. Egypt and other countries have successfully worked around the problem with a combination of attrition and early retirement programs. Yet some state companies simply aren't worth preserving. Others may need to increase their prices to stay in business, which is unpopular with consumers, who often accuse the government of a breach of their social contract.

There is a strong demand for state assets among investors. However, governments have tended to overprice their assets, like in Qatar and Egypt, or have hindered foreign investors from buying assets with both formal and informal barriers. Nonetheless, an increasing volume of successful sales indicates that problems are being overcome (Figure 2.4).

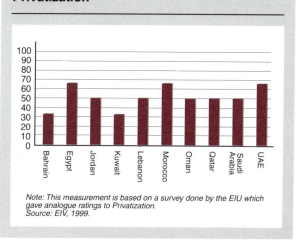

Figure 2.4: Measure of Commitment to Privatization

Note: This measurement is based on a survey done by the EIU which gave analogue ratings to Privatization.
Source: EIV, 1999.

Key Efforts on the Privatization Front

In **Egypt**, law 203 of 1991 removed 314 public-sector enterprises from the control of government ministries and placed them under 16 government holding companies—now down to 10—paving the way for their sale. A 75 percent stake of Nasr City Housing and Development Co. was sold on the stock exchange in May 1996, making it the first major sale. Several other companies followed later in the year. However, the pace slowed down in 1997 after the better performing companies were sold. Less attractive companies faced massive overstaffing, huge debts and large unsold inventories. Apart from the sale of several of the country's big cement companies, privatization since mid-1999 was confined mainly to liquidations and the sales of small firms to their employees. As a result the total revenue raised by privatization remains at LE15.8 billion as of end of June 2001. There are still 191 public sector firms to be privatized.

Many enterprises remain off limits, including EgyptAir, the Egyptian General Petroleum Corporation and the Suez Canal, and were not included among the 314 initial offers. Among those that were offered, no more than 40 percent of certain "strategic" sectors such as pharmaceuticals and flour mills will be sold. Meanwhile, the government has relaxed its ban on the sale of utilities. The sale on the stock exchange of a 20 percent stake in the state telecommunications monopoly, Telecom Egypt, projected for late 2000, was postponed indefinitely after telecommunications stocks plunged in world markets, and the government is now looking for a large international investor to buy a 35 percent stake. The government is also looking to sell a number of companies working in the oil industry and has approved the sale of parts of the gas distribution network.

Of 314 Egyptian companies originally slated for sale, majority stakes in 37 had been sold on the stock exchange by mid-2000 and minority stakes sold in 16. Another 24 had been sold directly to large investors, 12 had been leased and 30 sold to employee federations.

New ministerial appointments and the adoption of a new telecommunications law in August 2000 gave privatization a boost in **Algeria**. However, little progress was made otherwise. In August 2001, a license for a second GSM license was awarded to Egypt's Orascom Telecom Holding. The pace of privatization is expected to pick up in 2002.

Turkey sold more than $6 billion state assets in 2000, more than it did during the entire previous ten years. The government on 14 December 2000 announced a new tender to sell Turk Telecom and passed a new telecommunications law in May to speed up the sale. It now aims to sell both it and Turkish Airlines in 2002. The country hopes to sell $3 billion to $4 billion in 2002. Among other assets slated for sale are sugar refineries, cigarette factories, mining operations and parts of the petrochemicals company Petrokimya Holding, or Petkim, which is owned 96 percent by the government.

Urged on by the International Monetary Fund, **Tunisia** in 2000 published a list of 41 companies to be sold, but by end of March 2000, only 22 firms had been privatized. The government said the combined assets of the 41 companies was 1.84 billion Tunisian dinars. However, a number of companies the gov-

Table 2.4: Proceeds from Privatization in MENA
(in billion $)

Country	1990-98
Algeria	9.3
Egypt	2,048.9
Jordan	63.8
Morocco	1,938.9
Oman	60.1
Tunisia	514.6
Turkey	4,616.4

Source: World Development Indicators, 2000, World Bank.

ernment had previously earmarked for privatization appeared neither on the official list of companies sold nor on any other list. Lists, for the first time, included the financial sector, with the Union Internationale de Banque, with assets of about 1.38 billion dinars, and an insurance company, Lloyd Tunisien. Health care companies were also included for the first time.

Only about one-half of the 114 state enterprises identified for privatization in **Morocco** in 1993 have been sold. The privatization program has stagnated partly because of lengthy parliamentary debates over which assets to sell. However, a 35 percent stake in Maroc Telecom was sold in late 2000 and the government plans to sell two new licenses in early 2002 to operate fixed-line national telephone networks. The government meanwhile has committed itself to other major sales. Parliament approved the sale of Banque Centrale Populaire (BCP), the country's largest state-owned bank, but no date has yet been announced. The sale of up to 40 percent of Royal Air Maroc (RAM) was postponed until 2002 to allow the company to improve its earnings after poor results in 1999 and 2000. Other companies in line for privatization include Credit Immobilier et Hotelier (CIH), Banque Nationale de Development Economique (BNDE), which is a state development bank with a large portfolio of outstanding long-term debt, three agricultural companies, the state tobacco company, a textiles firm and a car-assembly plant.

The government also intends to pool its holdings in 287 companies in which it owns less than 20 percent into a privatization fund, which would then be sold on the stock exchange.

FDI Grows Worldwide

Worldwide FDI has continued to grow between 1999 and 2000 with a growth rate of 18 percent. Foreign investors built factories, bought local companies, developed local marketing networks and invested abroad in other ways at a rate faster than the rate at which international trade expanded. This growth record is expected to decrease for the year 2001 due to the global slowdown and the greater risks perceived after the September 11 event.

A report by UNCTAD identified 63,000 transnational corporations (TNCs) in 1999. They had 690,000 foreign affiliates, up from 450,000 in 1998. The gross product, or value added, of these affiliates was around $3 trillion, while the gross product of all TNC systems, including the parent companies, was around $8 trillion.

The gross product of foreign affiliates of TNCs alone account for 10 percent of global GDP. The sales by foreign affiliates have grown faster than world exports of goods and services. The ratio of total FDI stock to global GDP has grown twice as fast as that of total world imports and exports, showing that cross-border production, alongside trade, is leading increasingly to global interdependence.

In 1990, only 20 percent of foreign direct investments flowed to developing countries. By 1999, this had increased to more than 30 percent, equal to $1.44 trillion. Foreigners invested $208 billion in developing countries in 1999, representing 24 percent of all global FDI for that year.[4] Investments in Asian and Pacific countries represented 51 percent of all inflows to developing countries and 60 percent of the total FDI stock in developing countries.

FDI Moves Slowly into MENA Countries

The MENA region, despite some limited improvements, appears to be still lagging behind on its FDI performance within the context of dramatic changes taking place in this new world investment scene.

Box 2.2.
FDI: Important for Many Reasons

From 1993 to 1998, some 84 percent of all private investment flows to developing countries were direct investments. Private flows alone account for about 85 percent of all resource flows to developing countries, making FDI the main source of funds for these countries.

Foreign capital increases a country's output or productivity by engaging unemployed resources or making better use of existing resources. The increased output and productivity act as a catalyst for local investment.

FDI stimulates the development and dispersion of technology, as the foreign investor transfers techniques and skills to its local affiliate. These skills then generally spill over to other companies and institutions in the local market, and are often the missing resource that countries need to expand their access to international markets and to develop areas in which they have a comparative advantage. FDI also leads to the transfer of important capital goods and intermediate inputs. It can even help a country develop new comparative advantages, as was the case with the electronics industry in Southeast Asia.

FDI is a mutually advantageous relationship. In addition to helping the host country, it also allows transnational corporations to expand their output and markets, and ultimately their profits.

Source: Hafsi, 2001.

Compared, for example, to the countries of South, East and Southeast Asia, MENA countries have had a hard time attracting FDI.[4] Investment in Algeria, Iraq, Sudan and other countries has been frightened away by political turmoil. Yet even stable countries have been slow to increase investments from abroad, despite new laws designed to encourage FDI (Annex Tables A2.2 and A2.3).

Egypt did reasonably well in the last five years. The inflow of FDI in 2000 was about $1.2 billion, boosting total stock to $19 billion, the highest in the region after Saudi Arabia. However, the inflow was still only equivalent to 6 percent of gross domestic product, well below the average for all developing countries, and even that of Africa as a whole.

The flow of FDI into **Tunisia** was equivalent to 13 percent of gross domestic product, slightly above the average for all developing countries. At $11.6 billion in 2000, the total stock of FDI in Tunisia has decreased from $12 billion in 1999. Net foreign investment, both direct and portfolio, exceeded $800 million in Tunisia in 2000 and is expected to rise to as high as $1 billion by 2002. Energy-related industries, textiles and government companies on sale appear set to attract the biggest share of FDI.

FDI into **Morocco** was equivalent to only 4 percent of gross domestic product, which, as with Egypt, was

also well below the average for all developing countries. Total stock was $5.8 billion in 2000. In 1999, FDI inflows jumped to $847 million from $329 million in 1998. In 2000, inflows dropped dramatically reaching $201 million, discouraged by the drought that attacked the country.

Investors, deterred by UN sanctions, withdrew a net $100 million of investments from **Libya** in 1999. This was less than the $152 million withdrawn in 1998. The climate is expected to improve following the suspension of sanctions in April 1999 and as the Libyan government eases its restrictions on foreign investments. Most investment has been in hydrocarbons, a tendency that is expected to continue.

In West Asia, **Saudi Arabia** has performed best. It attracted $1 billion in investments in 2000 after several years of dis-investment before 1997. This brought the total stock of FDI in the country to $28.8 billion in 2000. Saudi Arabia seems to be reaping the benefits from an overhaul in its investment regulations and interest in the oil industry.

Turkey attracted FDI of $982 million in 2000 and Jordan $300 million. **Bahrain**, **Lebanon** and the **UAE** also attracted significant investment. In 1995 there were 92 TNCs and 351 affiliates[5] based in **Oman**. The figures are even higher in Bahrain and the UAE. However, **Yemen** experienced significant dis-investment, possibly for reasons of perceived instability.

However, overall, the ratio of the flow of investment to GDP of Middle East countries compares poorly to that of other developing regions. Further, few Middle Eastern countries made significant direct investments abroad. Egypt invested around $271 million and Kuwait around $254 million in 2000. The total stock of outward FDI from the MENA region stands at $10 billion, with Bahrain, Kuwait, Libya, Saudi Arabia and Turkey accounting for most of it.

The region has also been slow to negotiate investment agreements between themselves. MENA countries accounted for only a handful of the 1,856 bilateral treaties and 1,982 double taxation treaties announced in 1999. Members of the Arab League signed a multilateral investment treaty, and most members of the Organization of the Islamic Conference have signed a similar one. However, they are too general to significantly affect FDI flows in the region.

Is MENA a Good Place to Invest?

Investors tend to put their money in places where there is a sound legal framework, government incentives and a conducive economic environment. They want to minimize risk. The investment climate varies throughout the MENA region, with each country having reached different levels in various factors that investors deem important.

The UAE, Turkey, Tunisia, Oman, Morocco, Egypt and Bahrain have reasonably good **societal** attractiveness. But despite an acute awareness among policy makers of the need for foreign investment, a portion of the political elite and of the population in some MENA countries is wary of foreigners in general and foreign investment in particular. Because of this basic problem, attempts to improve the attractiveness of other factors are bound to be less effective than they would be otherwise.

As for **infrastructural** attractiveness, the MENA region does well on technical infrastructure. Most countries are reaching acceptable levels, even in electricity and telecommunications. But foreign investors believe most MENA countries have neglected the managerial aspects of government services. Despite significant improvements, this discourages foreign investors in Morocco and Egypt especially. Most countries have been improving their scores and streamlining their bureaucracies. One example is in build-operate-transfer contractual arrangements. In Saudi Arabia, a recent FDI law established the General Investment Authority, a one-stop shop to speed up approval for foreign investors' projects. In addition, both Iran and Kuwait have moved to allow foreign participation in the oil industry.

As for **productive** factors, most MENA countries fare well in raw materials and energy, are average in human resources and lag behind in technology. But the human capability factor is problematic, posing an obstacle to investors in some countries of the region. The level of education, for example, is known to be usually high, but the attitude is sometimes suspicious. A more positive attitude is most likely to emerge with an improved situation in Palestine and more settled conditions in countries such as Algeria. However, with recent harsh Israeli policies in the occupied Palestinian territories, a stagnant peace process and tension following the September 2001 suicide bomb attacks in the United States, distrust of foreign agendas may yet again be on the rise.

Governability is still seen as a major problem everywhere, but there have been interesting improvements. Although the legitimacy of many governments is fragile, the arrival of popular leaders in Algeria and Morocco has improved the situation in North Africa. MENA societies, with few exceptions, are in transition and lack consensus on which direction political development should take. Investors hope the instability that has plagued the countries of the region may be coming to an end. This does not necessarily require transformation of these countries into democracies. Authoritarian Southeast Asia countries have generally had good governability, with a reasonable consensus among their elites and legitimacy among the population.

Finally, as for **competitiveness**, MENA region countries have been doing well. Most have successfully conducted or are conducting forceful economic restructuring programs. They have liberalized their FDI rules and procedures significantly and provided generous incentives to potential investors. However, most governments in the region have been slow to reform their bureaucracies. As a result, foreign investment, though on the increase, is still below its potential. North Africa's score, especially that of Egypt, Morocco and Tunisia, has steadily improved since it hit a low in 1995. It is still however unclear, how FDI inflows to the region will react to the global economic slowdown especially after the September event. Preliminary figures suggest that a minimum of 5 percent of FDI will be lost in the MENA region.

It is clear that much needs to be done to attract more investors to the region. In 1996, the profits that affiliates of American TNCs earned in developing countries were 50 percent higher than those earned elsewhere. In 1993, the rate of return of FDI was around 26 percent for affiliates in Africa, 15.3 percent for West Asian including Middle East countries, and 15 percent for Latin America, as compared to an average of 8.7 percent for developed countries. Yet despite the high returns in developing countries, investors are still staying away. MENA countries must increase their attractiveness, and governments must concentrate their efforts on improving all of the factors that will draw investors into the region.

How to Improve the Investment Climate

The level of FDI depends mainly on two actors: the investor and the agency that manages the investment environment—generally the government. Investors are not all alike. Each has its own specific agenda and strategy. Some may be more comfortable in more hostile environments; others thrive only with stability. Some, by the very nature of their industry, are oriented toward the short term and are thus less sensitive to governability and more sensitive to incentives. Others look more to the longer term. For the latter, the nature of the industry and the character of a specific firm making the investment tend to be more important.

In the short term, MENA policy makers must do a better job at identifying which companies are likely to be attracted to the specific cultural and political environments in their countries. Once the companies are identified, policy makers should consider

what types of incentives, if any, might be offered. In the longer term they must try to improve the basic factors that affect the attractiveness of FDI. A major task is to demonstrate to elites, local media and the general population the positive impact of FDI on regional economies in a globalizing world. This will make the task of introducing simpler procedures and clearer regulations easier, and help resolve conflicts more constructively. More work is needed to lead to an environment that is open to change and that will free commercial, technological and cultural exchanges.

Measuring Risks in MENA Countries

The ICRG is a composite index that measures credit risk based on 22 components. It gives a value of zero for the greatest level of risk and 100 for the lowest. According to the ICRG index, the level of risk in MENA countries has been increasing, going from 70.5 in 1998 to 68.5 in December 2000.[6] This was due perhaps to the volatility of oil prices and to increased political tension in the region, especially after the outbreak of the Aqsa Intifada in Palestine in September 2000. On the other hand, the indices of both the Institutional Investor and Euromoney registered a decrease in risk during the same period (Table 2.5).

The MENA region's risk ratings compare well with the world average and with other low -and middle-income regions. Kuwait and the United Arab Emirates enjoy the lowest risk in the region by all standards and compare favorably with high-income groups. Iraq and Sudan have the region's highest risk.

Sovereign ratings measure the ability and willingness of governments to meet their financial obligations. The main rating agencies are Standard & Poor's, Moody's and Fitch. The agencies use somewhat different notations in their ratings, although all three assign a "triple-A" for debt that is considered to carry the least risk, then move down the alphabet as risk increases. However, in the case of local short-term debt, Fitch assigns a rating of "F1" for the lowest level of risk, followed by "F2" and F3", then "B", "C" and "D". Most MENA countries are doing reasonably well among rating agencies (Table 2.6).

Table 2.5: Credit Risk Ratings of MENA Countries, 1998 and 2000

	ICRG Risk Rating		Institutional Investors Ratings		Euromoney Credit-worthiness Rating	
	Dec.		Sept.		Sept.	
	1998	2000	1998	2000	1998	2000
Algeria	56.5	59.0	25.8	33.1	26.3	37.7
Egypt	70.8	69.3	43.2	51.0	43.1	56.4
Iran	69.5	68.5	29.3	27.0	23.4	40.6
Iraq	45.8	47.0	7.0	12.6	6.8	9.0
Kuwait	78.3	80.3	57.4	64.4	77.7	73.3
Lebanon	56.3	61.0	31.8	36.8	34.1	46.8
Libya	64.3	66.8	28.6	31.5	21.6	19.3
Morocco	72.5	67.8	42.2	47.3	41.0	55.1
Oman	75.0	78.3	53.4	54.9	61.5	66.2
Saudi Arabia	73.0	76.0	55.7	57.0	63.7	68.3
Sudan	43.3	49.5	7.2	8.7	7.1	25.5
Syria	70.5	69.3	24.5	23.1	24.4	39.0
Tunisia	72.5	72.5	49.0	54.5	45.7	57.5
Turkey	52.3	55.5	37.8	46.8	38.5	52.7
UAE	78.3	80.0	61.8	66.3	79.4	75.6
Yemen	67.0	63.5	-	-	-	-
Low & Middle income	64.0	63.3	28.6	28.0	25.6	35.0
MENA	**70.5**	**68.5**	**34.3**	**39.3**	**37.2**	**46.3**
East Asia & Pacific	66.7	67.0	32.9	39.8	27.5	38.4
Europe & Central Asia	65.9	66.2	33.8	30.3	23.7	36.9
Latin American & Caribbean	62.8	69.5	33.7	40.1	36.3	45.6
South Asia	62.8	60.4	25.7	27.6	21.0	33.8
Sub-Saharan Africa	60.8	58.8	18.5	17.9	20.2	28.6
High Income	83.3	81.8	80.4	87.2	91.3	89.7
World	67.7	67.8	35.3	37.0	29.0	38.8

Source: World Development Indicators, 2001.
Notes: ICRG is a composite index based on 22 components, scaling from 0 to 100, the higher the index the lower the risk.
2. Institutional Investor rating measures the credibility of investing in a country, scaling from 0 to 100, the higher the index the lower the risk.
3. Euromoney ratings measures the creditworthiness of a country, scaling from 0 to 100, the higher the index the lower the risk.

Rating Agency Rankings

Standard & Poor's has given Egyptian long-term foreign debt a "BBB-" rating, its lowest investment grade rating. However, it warned in July 2000 that the rating may be lowered sometime in the following three years if the government did not speed up privatization, cut its budget deficit and make its monetary policy more flexible. Fitch also gives Egypt its lowest investment grade rating, while Moody's rating is one notch below investment grade.

Jordan was given a lower ""BB-" long-term foreign debt rating by Standard & Poor's. This is due to a GDP growth forecast of 3.5 percent in 2001 (which is low in per capita terms) a government deficit forecast of more than 6 percent for 2001 and a high debt burden, estimated at 126 percent of GDP. On the positive side are Jordan's commitment to economic reforms and a relatively low inflation rate. Moody's similarly cited the heavy foreign debt burden and low growth when it assigned Jordan a "Ba3" rating.

Standard & Poor's warned in May 2001 that it may reduce Lebanon's "B+" long-term foreign debt rating unless the government did something to curb its growing debt burden. At the same time it cut the country's credit rating for Lebanese pound-denominated bonds to "B+" from "BB-". In February 2001, Fitch lowered its rating on foreign currency debt to "B+" from "BB-", four notches below investment grade.

Kuwait's "A" rating is the highest among MENA countries. According to Standard & Poor's, the high rating is due to the country's huge oil reserves, its estimated $60 billion in foreign assets and its track record of prudent macroeconomic policies. Working against Kuwait are the continued military threat from Iraq and the large government role in the economy.

Moody's warned in April 2001 it may reduce Turkey's "B1" rating for foreign currency loans, already four notches below investment grade, even lower because of a loss in confidence in the country's financial markets and soaring borrowing costs after the country allowed the currency to fall about 40 percent in February. Standard & Poor's and Fitch have also assigned non-investment grade ratings to Turkey.

Table 2.6: Selected MENA Countries Ratings

| | Local Currency | | | | | Foreign Currency | | | | | |
| | LT debt | | | ST debt | S&P Outlook | | LT debt | | ST debt | | S&P |
	S&P	Moody's	IBCA	S&P		S&P	Moody's	IBCA	S&P	IBCA	Outlook
Egypt	A-	Baa1	A-	A-1	-ve	BBB-	Ba1	BBB-	A-3	F3	-ve
Jordan	BBB	Ba3		A-3	Stable	BB-	Ba3		B		+ve
Kuwait	A+	-		A-1+	Stable	A	Baa1		A-1		Sable
Lebanon	BB-	B1	BB	B	Stable	B+	B1	BB-	B	B	Stable
Morocco	BBB	-		A-3	Stable	BB	Ba1		B		Stable
Oman	BBB+	Baa2		A-2	Stable	BBB	Baa2		A-3		Stable
Qatar	A-	-		A-2	+ve	BBB+	-		A-2		+ve
Tunisia	A	Baa2		A-1	Stable	BBB	-		A-3		Stable
Turkey	B	-	BB	C	Watch Neg	B	B1	BB-	C	B	Watch Neg

Notes: Figures from S&P are for April, 2001; figures for Moody's are for January, 2001 and figures for IBCA are for end 2000.
Source: Word Development Indicators, 2001; Standard & Poor's Credit Week April, 2001; and Fitch IBCA Country reports. 2000.

EIU Business Environment Ranking

The Economist Intelligence Unit's Business Environment Index measures the quality or attractiveness of the business environment in 60 countries, including six in the Middle East.[7] It is based on how conducive to business a country is in ten separate categories: political environment, macroeconomic environment, market opportunities, openness to free enterprise and competition, foreign investment policy, foreign trade and exchange controls, taxes, financing, labor markets and infrastructure. Each category in turn is compiled from a number of indicators that reflect a country's performance over the previous five years and its expected performance over the following five years. About half the indicators are quantitative, drawn from national and international sources, while the other half are qualitative, drawn from a range of sources and business surveys.[8] Except for Israel, every MENA country measured by the Economist Intelligence Unit lags behind most other countries in the world (Table 2.7). These forecasting figures were calculated before the September 11 event, and it is expected that they will decrease from 0.5 to 0.75 percentage point in the forecasted period 2001-2005.

Table 2.7: MENA Business Environment Rankings

| | Overall Ranking (out of 60 countries) | | Value of the Index (scores out of 10) | |
	1996-2000	2001-05	1996-2000	2001-05
Israel	25	24	6.75	7.63
Egypt	39	44	5.44	6.07
Saudi Arabia	40	42	5.43	6.13
Turkey	43	46	5.35	6.02
Algeria	57	57	4.02	5.07
Iran	60	60	3.24	4.16

Source: EIU, Country Forecast Reports, 2001.
Notes: 1: The index takes the values from 0 to 10, where 0 denotes the worst performance and 10 denotes the best performance.
2: The index is calculated for 60 countries.

The outlook of the business environment in **Algeria** is improved for the 2001 to 2005 period. The civil war hurt the country's rating in the 1990s, and now that the violence has declined the government is freer to work on reforming the economy. The macroeconomic index for the coming five years is better than the previous five years, although it has not improved as much as in other countries (Table 2.8). The government has committed itself to increasing the role of private businesses in the economy, a move that pushed up the private enterprise index. The government is working to reduce trade barriers and is expected to enhance trade relation with the EU, hence the improvement in the trade index. It also streamlined taxes, with income tax divided into five bands ranging from 10 percent for the lowest income group to 40 percent for the highest income group. Corporate income tax is now set at a flat rate of 30 percent.

Egypt's attractiveness is expected to improve in the five years, though not as quickly as that of other countries. Egypt's political environment is expected to remain stable. However, a lack of transparency and a cumbersome bureaucracy are expected to keep institutions inefficient. Meanwhile, the macroeconomic environment is actually projected to deteriorate. Although the signing of an agreement to liberalize trade with the European Union improved the outlook in the trade and currency exchange controls category, other emerging markets have been liberalizing trade even faster. A proposed new labor law designed to loosen wage regulations, plus moves to make it easier for employers to hire foreign workers, have boosted Egypt's outlook in the labor market category.

Even though **Iran** has borrowed very little from abroad and has successfully attracted some foreign investment, it still ranks last among the 60 countries

Table 2.8: MENA Business Environment Index by Ranks and Values 1996-2000 and 2001-05

	Algeria		Egypt		Iran		Israel		Saudi Arabia		Turkey	
	1	2	1	2	1	2	1	2	1	2	1	2
Political env.	52	51	37	39	56	47	36	35	43	43	41	44
	(3.9)	(4.1)	(5.1)	(5.5)	(3.3)	(4.7)	(5.3)	(6.1)	(4.5)	(5.1)	(4.7)	(4.9)
Macroeconomic env.	30	42	24	44	53	39	38	32	19	37	59	60
	(7.1)	(7.5)	(7.8)	(7.6)	(4.9)	(7.6)	(6.7)	(8.0)	(8.4)	(7.8)	(2.7)	(3.1)
Market opportunities	42	48	49	51	36	40	39	43	32	22	30	31
	(4.8)	(5.3)	(4.3)	(4.7)	(5.3)	(5.5)	(5.1)	(5.6)	(5.7)	(6.8)	(5.8)	(6.3)
Private enterprise policy & competition	52	56	44	46	58	59	22	20	33	33	34	41
	(3.5)	(4.1)	(4.4)	(5.5)	(2.4)	(3.5)	(6.9)	(8.0)	(5.8)	(6.9)	(5.5)	(6.1)
Policy to FDI	55	52	22	27	60	60	2	2	55	56	30	39
	(4.4)	(5.5)	(7.8)	(7.8)	(2.1)	(3.3)	(9.4)	(9.4)	(4.4)	(4.9)	(7.2)	(7.2)
Trade & exchange controls	56	50	46	51	60	60	29	11	36	39	36	29
	(3.8)	(6.6)	(4.9)	(6.6)	(2.1)	(2.7)	(7.2)	(8.9)	(6.1)	(7.2)	(6.1)	(8.3)
Taxes	58	51	31	32	60	60	18	20	28	31	24	40
	(2.7)	(5.3)	(5.6)	(6.2)	(2.5)	(3.0)	(6.6)	(6.8)	(5.7)	(6.2)	(5.9)	(5.9)
Financing	59	59	41	41	59	60	24	17	41	44	34	34
	(1.8)	(3.3)	(4.8)	(5.9)	(1.8)	(2.5)	(7.0)	(8.9)	(4.8)	(5.5)	(5.5)	(6.6)
Labor markets	57	55	48	42	58	57	21	19	59	59	48	47
	(4.8)	(5.3)	(5.4)	(6.2)	(4.3)	(4.7)	(6.3)	(7.0)	(3.9)	(4.5)	(5.4)	(6.0)
Infrastructure	50	53	38	42	48	50	19	19	32	33	37	33
	(3.5)	(3.7)	(4.4)	(4.8)	(3.7)	(4.2)	(7.1)	(7.8)	(5.1)	(5.7)	(4.8)	(5.7)
Overall	57	57	39	44	60	60	25	24	40	42	43	46

Notes: 1 is the period 1996-2000 and 2 is the period 2001-2005.
The index takes the values from 0 to 10, where 0 denotes the worst performance and 10 denotes the best performance.
Source: EIU, Country Forecast Reports, 2001.

in the EIU's Business Environment Index. The country is expected to introduce structural and fiscal reforms in the next few years, including a new exchange rate regime, a relaxing of import restrictions and a cautious reform of domestic banking rules, moves that should improve the macroeconomic environment. Iran is preparing legislation and working to improve the business environment in an attempt to attract foreign investment in hydrocarbons. Nonetheless, it is still expected to have the worst foreign investment environment of all countries in the index in the coming five years. Iran's trade relations with other countries are starting to improve, especially with Arab countries and the European Union, and the current account is expected to be in surplus. However, tariffs remain high and the currency is not freely convertible.

Israel's business environment is expected to improve in the next five years. This pushed its ranking up one step to make it the 24th best country on the list. The government has continued to reform the economy even as the political environment remains unstable. Inflation was brought down to 1.2 percent in 2000, helping to improve the country's ranking in the macroeconomic index for the coming five years. Political uncertainty, a lack of natural resources, the economy's small size and a slowdown in economic growth over the past few years pulled down its ranking in the market opportunities category. Israel is the second most attractive country for foreign direct investment on the EIU list. An improvement in capital accounts, together with efforts to deregulate foreign exchange controls, boosted the country's outlook in the category of foreign trade and exchange controls to 11th place from the previous 29th place. The government is expanding trade agreements, especially with EU countries.

Even though **Saudi Arabia** is expected to improve the overall attractiveness of its business environment in the next five years, it nonetheless fell two steps to 42nd place among the 60 countries on the EIU list, based on its slow pace of reform and liberalization. The macroeconomic outlook is clouded by the economy's heavy reliance on oil exports for revenue and the uncertainties of international demand for oil. Unemployment among Saudi citizens and a deteriorating infrastructure are expected to contin-

ue to be a problem. However, the kingdom's outlook in the remaining categories is steady or improving. The government is expected to liberalize trade and adopt policies to attract foreign direct investment. A key improvement will be Saudi Arabia's accession to the World Trade Organization, expected in 2004.

Turkey's outlook in the overall business index fell to 46th place from its previous 43rd place, due mainly to its poor macroeconomic performance. The macroeconomic outlook is the worst among all 60 countries, especially after the crisis of February 2001, when the currency plummeted 30 percent against the dollar. Turkey ranks well in terms of market opportunities, and its liberalization of current and capital accounts since 1990 and its customs union agreement with the European Union, which came into force in 1996, have improved the outlook for foreign trade and exchange controls. Its reluctance to reform taxes pushed down its ranking in this category to 40th place from its previous position at number 24.

Global Competitiveness and MENA Countries

The World Competitiveness Report for 2000 includes four Middle Eastern countries. Its Growth Competitiveness Index (GCI) measures factors that contribute to growth in per capita GDP. It is a minor revision of the Competitive Index used in previous reports and is calculated from the average of three newly created indices: the Economic Creativity Index, the Finance Index and the Openness Index.

Table 2.9: MENA Countries Overall Ranking in the Growth Competitiveness Index (1995-2000)

	1995	1996	1997	1998	1999	2000
Egypt	27	29	28	38	49	42
Israel	23	24	24	29	28	19
Jordan	41	28	43	34	40	47
Turkey	40	42	36	40	44	40

Notes: 1: In 2000, the index used three indices: Economic Creativity, Finance and Openness which combine factors used in previous reports.
Sources: The Global Competitiveness Report, 1995 to 2000, World Economic Forum, Davos Switzerland.

The Economic Creativity Index combines several aspects of innovation, technology transfer and diffusion. It is based on a survey with questions on innovation, technology transfer, the ease of starting up new businesses and the availability of finance. The Finance Index and Openness Index are calculated from a mix of survey and macroeconomic data.

The Middle Eastern countries included in the GCI improved their overall ranking in 2000, except for Jordan, whose rank deteriorated by seven places to 47 (Table 2.9). The low ranking reflects Jordan's poor performance in each of the three indices that make up the Growth Competitiveness Index. Egypt, on the other hand, jumped seven places as a result of improvements both in economic creativity and in finance, even though it ranked a low 55 in openness. Turkey's ranking also improved, boosted by its high score of 29 in the Economic Creativity Index. Turkey's rank in the Openness Index was also a respectable 36. However, the financial and exchange rate crisis that rocked the Turkish economy pushed its rank in the Finance Index to a low 54 for the year 2000.

The Current Competitiveness Index is compiled from a survey of 4,000 businessmen from 58 countries, who are questioned about two broad dimensions of micro-economic competitiveness: the sophistication of company operations and the quality of the micro-economic business environment. The index revises the previous year's Micro Competitiveness Index to include factors that enhance productivity and current economic performance. (Table 2.10).

Egypt's and Israel's position in the Current Competitiveness Index improved over the three years, while Jordan's declined and Turkey's did not change. Egypt's rank increased due to an improvement in company operation and strategy and in the business environment. Turkey's overall ranking improved in 2000. Jordan's lower ranking reflects a need for further reforms to the economy.

Table 2.10: The Current Competitiveness Index

	Egypt			Israel			Jordan			Turkey		
	98	99	00	98	99	00	98	99	00	98	99	00
Overall	40	43	39	21	20	18	32	32	35	29	31	29
CCI Company Operation & Strategy	47	49	44	21	18	13	42	44	46	26	33	28
Quality of the Business Environment	35	42	39	20	20	20	32	28	35	29	32	29

Sources: The Global Competitiveness Report for the years 1995 to 2000, World Economic Forum, Davos Switzerland.

Notes

[1] Only 26 Arab banks are ranked among the world largest 500 banks in terms of their capital (*The Banker*, July, 2000).

[2] PPI is defined as either the sale or transfer of infrastructure assets or their operation to private businesses or the investment by private businesses in new infrastructure.

[3] World Bank staff estimates.

[4] The comparison holds also against Mexico or the leading countries of Latin America.

[5] In all the figures presented in this note, TNC's affiliate refers to three realities: (1) an entity incorporated in the country in which the TNC owns more than 50% of the shareholders voting power; (2) an entity incorporated in the country in which the TNC owns at least 10% but less than 50% of the voting power; and (3) an entity wholly-owned by the TNC and not incorporated in the country.

[6] The index is on a scale of 0 to 100, with higher values denoting lower risk.

[7] Those countries are: Algeria, Egypt, Iran, Israel, Saudi Arabia and Turkey.

[8] The rankings of the index are calculated in several stages. First, each of the 70 indicators is scored on a scale from 1 (very bad for business) to 5 (very good for business). A weighted average of the indicators scores are taken in each category to derive the category score. These are adjusted, using a linear transformation, to produce index values on a 1—10 scale. An arithmetic average of the ten category index values is then calculated to obtain the business environment score for each country, again on a scale of 1—10.

References

Al-Mashat, R. 2001. "Financial Markets in the MENA Region." Background notes for *Economic Trends in the MENA Region.* Cairo: Economic Research Forum.

Al-Shroogi, M. 2001. "What Are the Emerging Investment Opportunities in Banking?" Background notes for *Economic Trends in the MENA Region.* Cairo: Economic Research Forum.

Arab Fund for Social and Economic Development. 2001. *The Unified Arab Economic Report.* A joint publication by the Arab Fund For Economic and Social Development, The Arab Monetary Fund, the Arab Organization for Petroleum Exporting Countries, and the League of Arab States. Abu-Dhabi, UAE.

Economist Intelligence Unit. 2001. *Country Profiles.* Several country reports. London, UK.

Economist Intelligence Unit. 2001. *Country Forecast.* Several country reports. London, UK.

Hafsi, T. 2001. "Foreign Direct Investment in the Middle East and North Africa Regions: An Overview." Background note for *Economic Trends in the MENA Region.* Cairo: Economic Research Forum.

International Monetary Fund. 2000. *World Economic Outlook.* Washington, D.C.

International Monetary Fund. 2001. *International Financial Statistics.* Washington, D.C.

Kandil, M. 2001. "Globalization and Arab Financial Markets in the Twenty-first Century." Background notes for *Economic Trends in the MENA Region.* Cairo: Economic Research Forum.

Speakman, J. 2001. "Privatization in the MENA Region." Background note for *Economic Trends in the MENA Region.* Cairo: Economic Research Forum.

UNCTAD. 2001. *World Investment Report: Promoting Linkages.* New York and Geneva: United Nations.

World Bank. 2001. *World Development Indicators.* Washington, D.C.

World Economic Forum. 1996, 1997, 1999, 2000 and 2001. *Global Competitiveness Report.* Geneva, Switzerland: World Economic Forum.

Annex

Table A2.1: Market Capitalization in Selected MENA Countries, 1990-2000

	Market Capitalization				Turnover Ratio[a] ($ bn)				S&P/IFC Investable Index[b]		Listed Domestic Companies		
	1990	1998	2000	April 2001	1990	1998	2000	April 2001	1999	2000	1990	1997	2000
Egypt	1.7	24.3	28.7	28.7	...	22.3	34.7	1.1	24.2	-45.6	573	650	1076
Jordan	2.0	5.8	4.9	5.0	20.0	11.6	7.7	0.8	-3.6	-24.5	105	139	163
Kuwait	...	25.8	18.8	...	...	...	32.8	...	...	...	...	74	76
Lebanon	...	2.9	1.58	...	...	...	6.7	...	-18.0	-18.6	...	9	12
Morocco	0.9	15.6	10.8	10.0	...	10.1	9.2	0.7	-7.8	-19.1	71	49	53
Oman	1.06	7.1	3.4	3.07	12.3	21.3	14.2	3.07	7.2	7.2	55	114	131
Saudi Arabia	48.2	42.5	67.1	69.6	...	26.9	27.1	2.9	42.3	42.3	59	70	75
Tunisia	0.53	2.2	2.8	...	3.3	6.8	23.3	...	16.8	9.0	13	34	44
Turkey	19	33.6	69.6	52.1	42.5	154.9	206.2	17.6	254.5	-51.2	110	257	315
UAE	...	...	28.2	...	...	...	...	...	...	...	...	...	53

Source: The World Bank Development Indicators 2001.
Notes: a: Turnover Ratio= value of shares traded as % of capitalization.
b: S&P/IFC Investable index= % change in price index.

Table A2.2: FDI inflows by Host Region and Economy, 1989-2000
(millions of US$)

Host Region/ Economy	1989-94 (Av.)	1995	1996	1997	1998	1999	2000
World	200,145	331,068	384,910	477,918	692,544	1075,049	1270,764
Developed economies	137,124	203,462	219,688	271,378	483,165	829,818	1,005,178
Developing economies	59,578	113,338	152,493	187,352	188,371	222,010	240,167
Africa	3,952	4,694	5,622	7,153	7,713	8,971	8,198
North Africa	1,533	1,209	1,214	2,359	2,299	2,530	2,616
Algeria	12	5	4	7	5	7	6
Egypt	741	598	636	891	1,076	1,065	1,235
Libya	76	-107	-135	-82	-152	-128	-a
Morocco	352	335	357	1,079	329	847	201
Sudan	-5	-a	-	98	371	371	392
Tunisia	358	378	351	366	670	368	781
Asia	37,659	75,293	94,351	107,205	95,599	99,728	143,479
West Asia	2,181	-2	2,892	5,488	6,580	936	3,427
Bahrain	237	431	2,048	329	180	448	500
Iran	-23	17	26	53	24	33a	36a
Iraq	1	2a	..	1a	7a	-7a	-a
Jordan	6	13	16	361	310	158	300a
Kuwait	-4	7	347	20	59	72	16
Lebanon	10	35	80	150	200	250	180a
Oman	119	29	60	65	101	21	62a
Qatar	48	94a	339 a	418 a	347 a	144 a	303 a
Saudi Arabia	502	-1,877	-1,129	3,044	4,289	-782	1000 a
Syria	98	100	89	80	80	91	84 a
Turkey	708	885	722	805	940	783	982
UAE	90	399 a	301 a	232 a	253 a	-13 a	100 a
Yemen	300	-218	-60	-139	-266	-329	-201
South, East and S-E Asia	35,078	73,639	89,406	98,507	86,004	96,224	137,348
Indonesia	1,524	4,346	6,194	4,677	-356	-2,745	-4,550
Malaysia	3,964	5,816	7,296	6,513	2,700	3,532	5,542

Source: World Investment Report 2001, UNCTAD, Promoting Linkages, UN, Geneva and New York.

Table A2.3: FDI Inward Stock, by Host Region and Economy 1985, 1990, 1995, 1999 and 2000 *(millions of US$)*

Host Region/ Economy	1985	1990	1995	1999	2000
World	893,567	1888,672	2937,539	5196,046	6314,271
Developed economies	546,281	1,397,983	2,051,739	3,353,701	4,210,294
Developing economies	347,237	487,694	849,376	1,740,377	1,979,262
Africa	24,830	39,427	60,898	88,771	95,381
North Africa	8,952	15,259	24,337	32,021	33,347
Algeria	1,281	1,316	1,377	1,400	1,407
Egypt	5,703	11,043	14,102	17,770	19,005
Libya	..	..	..	..	..
Morocco	440	917	3,034	5,647	5,848
Sudan	76	54	53	893	1,285
Tunisia	6,876	7,259	11.038	12,075	11,566
Asia	241,266	328,232	580,697	1,118,416	1,261,776
West Asia	241,266	328,232	580,697	1,118,416	1,261,776
Bahrain	399	552	2,403	5,408	5,908
Iran	2,427	1,686	1,944	2,079	2,115
Iraq	..	..	..	..	..
Jordan	493	615	627	1,471	1,771
Kuwait	33	26	12	510	527
Lebanon	34	53	138	818	998
Oman	1,200	1,721	2,208	2,455	2,517
Qatar	77	55	435	1,684	1,987
Saudi Arabia	21,828	22,500	22,423	27,845	28,845
Syria	37	374	915	1,255	1,338
Turkey	360	1,320	5,103	8,353	9,335
UAE	482	751	1,769	2,542	2,645
Yemen	283	180	1,882	1,089	888
South, East and S-E Asia	212,873	297,282	535,348	1,046,724	1,183,952
Indonesia	24,971	38,883	50,601	65,188	60,638
Malaysia	7,388	10,318	28,732	48,773	54,315

Source: World Investment Report 2001, UNCTAD, Promoting Linkages, UN, Geneva and New York.

CHAPTER THREE

EXPORT COMPETITIVENESS: WHERE THE REGION STANDS

Low but Intensified Product Diversification

The expansion of transportation and high-speed communication networks throughout the world has increased the export opportunities of Middle East and North Africa (MENA) producers. It has also increased competition for the region's producers by helping companies in other countries and regions export to world markets as well. Countries in the MENA region occupy a place midway up the ladder of comparative advantage. It is being squeezed from above by the more advanced developing countries, such as those in East Asia, whose labor is more skilled and whose industries are more capital intensive. On the other hand, it is being squeezed from below by countries such as China and India, with their large supply of unskilled labor.

Countries that export a wide range of products are better equipped to weather shocks that affect their overseas markets. The Export Diversification Index assigns a value of zero to the most diversified economies and a value of one to the least. Many of the more diversified economies of the MENA region were able to widen the range of their export products even further during the last decade. From 1985 to 1997, Oman, Tunisia, Egypt and Syria showed the greatest improvement, followed by Jordan, Morocco, and Qatar (Table 3.1). However, these countries all lag behind Turkey, which has the most diversified export base in the region. Oil producing countries such as Libya, Saudi Arabia, Oman, Kuwait and Algeria, which weren't very diversified to begin with, didn't improve much during the decade.

With the exception of Turkey, Tunisia, and Jordan, half the exports of MENA countries are concentrated in a few commodities, agricultural or raw materials and minerals. The major export is crude petroleum and petroleum products. But Qatar exports gas, Jordan fertilizers, Sudan and Syria cotton and Sudan and Morocco vegetables. Their dependence on a few exports makes them more vulnerable to price fluctuations.

Table 3.1: Export Diversification Index

	Including Oil		Excluding Oil	
	mid-1980	mid-1990	mid-1980	mid-1990
Algeria	0.57	0.59	0.68	0.72
Bahrain	--	0.56	--	0.55
Jordan	0.35	0.26	0.36	0.27
Kuwait	--	0.59	--	0.63
Libya	0.88	0.78	0.78	0.71
Morocco	0.30	0.23	0.30	0.23
Oman	0.91	0.74	0.33	0.27
Qatar	0.71	0.64	0.41	0.34
Saudi Arabia	0.77	0.75	0.57	0.57
Sudan	--	0.35	--	0.35
Syria	0.55	0.58	0.52	0.30
UAE	--	0.36	--	0.36
Tunisia	0.43	0.26	0.26	0.27
Turkey	0.16	0.16	0.16	0.16
Egypt	0.57	0.32	0.43	0.33
Yemen	--	0.90	--	0.35

Note: -- not available; Herfindahl index of concentration is used.
Source: Hadad, 2001, computations based on UNCOMTRADE data, 2000.

Other countries export significant amounts of manufactured products. Bahrain exports aluminum, Oman cars, the UAE aluminum and garments, Egypt and Tunisia, textiles and garments. Turkey ranks among the top ten developing countries for exports of manufacturing alongside China and South Korea. In 1997-1998, it was exporting 26 out of 70 leading developing countries manufactures.

Are MENA Countries Climbing the Technology Ladder?

The types of products that MENA countries export have changed over the past decade (Table 3.2). Some countries that exported mainly primary products, such as Algeria, Libya, Syria and Yemen, have scarcely diversified toward manufactured products

Table 3.2: Technological Composition of MENA Exports
(percent share in total exports)

	Primary Products	Resource-based Manufactures	Low Technology Manufactures	Med. Technology Manufactures	Hi Technology Manufactures	Other Transactions
1985						
Algeria	60.1	39.3	0.1	0.5	0.0	0.0
Bahrain	54.4	10.9	11.8	22.0	0.6	0.2
Jordan	43.7	10.3	13.7	16.6	14.4	1.3
Libya	88.8	10.1	0.0	1.2	0.0	0.0
Morocco	44.5	30.6	15.9	8.5	0.4	0.0
Oman	93.8	0.7	0.4	3.3	1.2	0.6
Qatar	72.2	11.0	5.2	11.4	0.1	0.1
Saudi Arabia	82.7	13.6	0.6	2.9	0.1	0.0
Syria	61.6	26.4	7.8	4.0	0.2	0.1
UAE	22.3	15.0	16.1	33.0	5.6	7.9
Tunisia	48.2	14.1	22.2	14.0	1.1	0.4
Turkey	27.0	15.9	38.6	17.1	1.2	0.3
Egypt	74.7	15.4	8.8	0.4	0.3	0.4
Yemen	9.6	90.3	0.0	0.1	0.0	0.0
1997						
Algeria	81.2	17.7	0.2	0.7	0.0	0.0
Bahrain	56.1	12.5	13.1	16.7	1.5	0.1
Jordan	39.0	19.8	8.2	26.5	5.9	1.1
Libya	78.6	18.1	1.6	1.7	0.0	0.0
Morocco	35.1	30.0	22.4	12.2	0.3	0.1
Oman	76.9	5.7	2.6	11.8	1.6	1.4
Qatar	67.4	10.5	7.9	13.9	0.3	0.1
Saudi Arabia	74.5	18.0	1.6	5.7	0.2	0.4
Syria	80.2	10.0	8.3	1.1	0.2	0.2
UAE	35.6	14.9	33.4	15.7	0.3	0.1
Tunisia	11.3	19.0	51.3	15.1	3.3	0.0
Turkey	13.9	14.4	48.4	18.2	4.1	1.1
Egypt	31.4	34.4	26.8	5.5	1.6	3.3
Yemen	92.5	5.6	0.6	0.9	0.1	0.0

Note: Shares may not add up to 100 due to rounding.
Source: Hadad, 2001, author's computations based on UNCOMTRADE data, 2000.

at all. Most countries, however, have gradually moved away from primary products towards those manufactures with greater technological input. Turkey and Tunisia are ahead of the others, with primary products accounting for less than 15 percent of exports. Morocco, Egypt, and UAE have also reduced their share of primary goods to 30 to 35 percent of all exports. A number of countries that exported mainly primary exports in 1985 diversified into medium-technology manufactures without increasing their low-technology manufactures first.

Re-exports Gain; Geographic Diversification Remains Low

Some countries, particularly some in the Gulf Cooperation Council, are diversifying their exports by way of re-exports. This has allowed them to move away from primary exports and has reduced their risk to price fluctuations. However, competition within GCC countries for the regional re-export market has been rising.

Countries that export to a small number of countries are more vulnerable to changes in demand than are countries whose export markets are diversified. Overall, MENA countries' export markets are not diverse. Over half the region's exports go to industrial countries, mainly in Europe. For many MENA countries, this reflects historical and political ties. For example, Morocco and Tunisia tend to export to France, Turkey to Germany, Egypt to the United States. Syria in the mid-1980s exported to Eastern Europe, but by the mid-1990s had shifted more to France and neighboring Turkey.

A geographic diversification index, in which zero represents the most diversified and one the least diversified, shows that Egypt, Turkey, Tunisia, and Jordan had the most diversified export markets in 1997 (Table 3.3). Kuwait, Qatar, Saudi Arabia and Libya had the least. Excluding oil, GCC countries such as Bahrain, Oman and the UAE were well diversified, while Saudi Arabia was not. The destinations of Syria's non-oil exports were more diverse than those of its oil exports. Only a few MENA countries, such as Algeria, Jordan, Oman, Syria and Egypt, significantly expanded their markets over the course of the decade. Oman, which previously exported mainly to the UAE and the United States, switched its main markets to Japan and other East

Asian countries, including Thailand and China, markets that few MENA countries had previously tapped. Turkey has been penetrating the Russian and US markets. Morocco's exports on the other hand went increasingly to France and Spain, while Tunisia's went increasingly to France, Italy, and Germany.

Table 3.3: Geographic Diversification Index

	Including Oil		Excluding Oil	
	mid-1980	mid-1990	mid-1980	mid-1990
Algeria	0.41	0.34	0.46	0.37
Bahrain	--	--	0.28	0.27
Jordan	0.32	0.24	0.32	0.24
Kuwait	--	0.95	--	0.90
Libya	0.37	0.42	0.38	0.39
Morocco	0.29	0.33	0.29	0.33
Oman	--	0.36	--	0.41
Qatar	0.70	0.64	0.32	0.30
Saudi Arabia	--	0.51	--	0.57
Sudan	0.25	0.30	0.25	0.30
Syria	0.44	0.36	0.41	0.29
UAE	--	--	--	0.23
Tunisia	0.36	0.38	0.35	0.37
Turkey	0.29	0.26	0.29	0.26
Egypt	0.30	0.24	0.26	0.23
Yemen	0.32	0.37	0.32	0.33

Note: -- not available; Herfindahl index of concentration is used.
Source: Hadad, 2001, computation based on UNCOM-TRADE data, 2000.

Intra-regional Trade is Higher When Oil is Excluded

The high concentration of MENA's exports to a few markets is due mainly to its abundance of oil, most of which goes to industrialized countries. When oil is excluded, Algeria's and Egypt's exports still go mainly to developed countries. However, the big oil-producing countries send most their non-oil exports to other countries within the region, especially those of the GCC, which generally export to one another. Syria's non-oil exports go to Lebanon and Saudi Arabia, while Yemen's go to Saudi Arabia and Bahrain. In fact, 30 percent of all non-oil exports go to other countries within the region, compared to 7 percent when oil is included. Intra-regional trade varies among countries. Oil producers trade overwhelmingly abroad: in 1997, only 8 percent of Saudi Arabia's exports went to and only 6 percent of its imports came from the region. Among non-oil producers, 47 percent of Jordan's exports went to the region, 45 percent of Lebanon's and 20 percent of Syria's.

Export Competitiveness

The Revealed Comparative Advantage Index

The RCA index provides an indication of the potential for expanding exports and reflects the products that might have an advantage in export markets based on the factors of production that a country possesses. The highest RCAs for most countries of the region are in raw materials and mineral fuels. Jordan, Morocco, Syria, Turkey and Egypt, which are not major oil exporters, tend to have comparative advantages in food and live animal products. Jordan, Morocco, Qatar and Tunisia have an edge in chemical products. Morocco, Tunisia, Turkey and the UAE have potential in more advanced manufacturing (miscellaneous manufacturing). Egypt and the UAE also have a comparative advantage in material-based manufacturing which is typically labor intensive. While Egypt is abundant in low-skill labor, UAE exports rely on foreign workers for such products. A real worry is a virtual absence of comparative advantage in products that require a high level of skills.

The Intra-industry Trade Index

Because many MENA countries are rich in raw materials, they have had little incentive to diversify and expand their industries. Intra-industry trade (IIT), or trade in similar goods between countries, is one way to measure the degree of diversity, specialization and technical sophistication of a country's industry. Overall, the MENA region scores low. Its average IIT index rating was 0.18 for 1997 (Table 3.4). This compares to 0.88 for industrial countries, as measured for the years between 1992 and 1994, and 0.52 for the South American trading bloc

Mercosur, whose per capita income is similar to MENA's. IIT increased for most MENA countries between 1985 and 1997, with the notable exception of Syria. MENA countries with the highest IIT index tend to be non-oil exporters such as Jordan, Tunisia, and Turkey. Among GCC countries, Bahrain and Oman have a high IIT rating, mainly on account of re-exports. Some MENA countries have lower IIT ratings in trade with the world as a whole, as opposed to trade with other countries in the region. This means that these MENA countries trade more with each other in similar goods than they do with the world at large, and thus have similar levels of industry specialization. For these countries, intra-regional trade provides an opportunity to compete more effectively in intra-industry trade.

Table 3.4: Intra-Industry Trade Index (IIT)

| | IIT with World | | | IIT with Region | | |
	1985	1997	Period Average	1985	1997	Period Average
Algeria	0.01	0.04	0.05	0.04	0.08	0.08
Bahrain	0.21	0.24	0.23	0.08	0.07	0.07
Jordan	0.30	0.33	0.31	0.07	0.14	0.14
Kuwait	0.20	0.12	0.16	0.21	0.16	0.18
Libya	--	--	0.03	--	--	0.09
Morocco	0.12	0.17	0.17	0.05	0.16	0.11
Oman	0.16	0.49	0.32	0.10	0.11	0.13
Qatar	0.09	0.12	0.13	0.04	0.05	0.05
Saudi Arabia	0.13	0.17	0.13	0.13	0.08	0.10
Sudan	--	0.02	0.01	--	0.03	0.01
Syria	0.09	0.08	0.09	0.10	0.11	0.08
UAE	--	--	0.20	--	0.17	0.16
Tunisia	0.20	0.32	0.29	0.17	0.20	0.15
Turkey	0.35	0.37	0.32	0.01	0.02	0.03
Egypt	0.04	0.18	0.13	0.07	0.21	0.14
Yemen	--	0.07	0.04	--	0.17	0.09

Note: start year and end year vary for countries according to data availability; IIT index is based on Grubel and Lloyd and is weighted average of IIT at 3-digit SITC; period average is simple average.
Source: Hadad, 2001; computations based on UNCOM-TRADE data, 2000.

Regional Integration: Should Intra-MENA Trade Increase?

Intra-regional trade can be measured against specific numerical targets or against the level of trade one might expect by comparison to others countries with similar economic characteristics. By either measure, the level of intra-MENA trade is low. This indicates that regional schemes for economic integration have not been successful. Intra-MENA trade is also low compared to that of countries in other regions.

Why is Regional Integration Desirable?

Every MENA country belongs to at least one regional integration scheme. These range from cooperation on specific projects to the removal of all trade barriers. In general the schemes reflect both political and economic imperatives: MENA politicians have declared regional integration to be an important goal. It was commonly assumed that integration would enable member countries to overcome the barriers of small size and the lack of human and physical capital, and to break colonial ties.

A political argument in favor of MENA integration is that regional integration can calm tensions. A high flow of trade between two countries increases the costs of conflict and thus reduces its probability. In post-war Europe, the formation of the European Economic Community was viewed as such a way of guaranteeing peace, especially between France and Germany.

An economic argument is that trade barriers between MENA countries reduce the incentive for international firms to locate in the region. It would make more sense for them to locate in a low-cost country outside the region, perhaps in southern Europe, where, because of trade agreements between the Europe Union (EU) and individual MENA countries, they would have access to the entire region.

How Intra-MENA Trade Compares to Other Regions

Commerce between MENA countries is tiny compared to their trade with countries outside the region. In 1998, only 2.95 percent of all goods entering or leaving MENA countries came from or went to another MENA country. This figure has remained roughly constant for more than two decades. In contrast, more than 40 percent of MENA's trade in 1998 was with the European Union. For Maghreb countries, the European Union accounted for more than 60 percent of total trade.

Intra-regional trade as a share of total trade is more than 20 times higher in the European Union and more than 15 times higher in the North America Free Trade Association (NAFTA) than it is in MENA. Moreover, trade among Southern Cone countries increased by 15 percentage points during the 1990s and among NAFTA countries by 10 percentage points, while intra-MENA trade actually decreased.

Among obstacles to intra-regional trade are bad transportation and communications infrastructure, non-convertible currencies, poor economic policies and political instability. On this front, a 1 percent improvement in a country's transportation and telecommunication infrastructure boosts its ability to export by about 3 percent and its ability to import by between 0.6 and 1 percent. Similarly, the ease of buying and selling a country's currency helps trade. Intra-regional trade increases by almost 2 percent for each percentage point reduction in the premium paid for a currency on the black market. Adopting structural adjustment programs and creating an economic and institutional environment conducive to foreign direct investment also helps, as does a reduction in political tension.

The Potential for Increased Intra-MENA Trade

Since the mid-1980s, many MENA countries implemented policies designed to liberalize their economies. During these years, their exports to Europe, their major trading partner, have moved toward more sophisticated goods such as electrical equipment and electronics and away from traditional goods such as food and agriculture. This suggests that further measures to promote openness and competition would improve the performance of MENA enterprises, and that the final barriers protecting companies from foreign competition should be removed.

Political tensions hinder intra-regional trade. However, this is counterbalanced by the notion that intra-regional trade makes conflict more expensive. As trade helps to improve economies and standards of living, people have more to lose. Moreover, some political tension is often the result of poverty and poor economic performance. Tension may well be reduced if increased intra-regional trade is allowed to foster regional economic growth.

Policies designed to promote trade are often expensive in the short term, especially in terms of lost jobs, while their benefit is long term. In addition, although the overall net benefit to the economy of more liberal trade is positive, some people will inevitably lose while others gain. The potential losers might seek to block the liberalization process. Hence, measures to smooth the transition are desirable, and mechanisms should be found to redistribute the benefits of increased openness.

The Future of Regionalism in the Arab World

Greater economic integration in the Arab world has consistently been a stated goal of public policy and a yardstick for evaluating the achievements of Arab nationalism in the post-independence era. The quest for economic integration since the 1960s lay behind the launch of numerous regional initiatives aimed at deepening trade and investment links between Arab countries. Reflecting this change, the proportion of regional trade in total Arab trade has doubled between 1970 and 1990. Despite this progress, proponents of regionalism in the Arab world remain pessimistic about the prospects of further regional integration in the future. Underlying the pessimism of the 1990s are concerns about the impact of globalization, the emergence of powerful regional trading blocks and the signing of free-trade agreements between several Arab countries and countries outside the region. The absolute and relative size of intra-Arab trade remains low compared to that of other regions in the world. Regional trade actually declined in the 1990s despite the move towards more open trading regimes in several Arab countries.

Recent Trends in Intra-Arab Trade

Exports to other Arab countries comprised only 8 percent of all Arab exports in 1998 (Table 3.5). This compares unfavorably with other regions. Intra-regional trade as a share of total trade between

Andean Pact countries in South America was nearly 50 percent higher than in the Arab countries, while that between European Union countries was seven times higher. Moreover, the share of intra-Arab trade only increased to 8 percent in 1998 from 5 percent in 1970. During the same period, intra-regional trade increased to 11 percent of total trade from 2 percent among Andean Pact countries, to 25 percent from 11 percent among the Southern Cone countries and to over 50 percent from 36 percent among members of NAFTA.

Table 3.5: Direction of Arab Trade, 1998

	1970	1975	1980	1985	1990	1995	1998
All Arab countries	5.2	4.9	4.5	7.8	9.4	6.7	8.2
Andean Pact countries 1/	1.7	3.6	3.5	3.1	4.0	11.3	11.4
Australia & New Zealand	6.1	6.1	6.4	7.0	7.6	9.9	8.6
Southern Core Countries 2/	11.4	11.1	14.3	6.7	10.6	21.6	25.5
East Asian Economies 3/	19.2	21.3	22.4	20.7	20.7	26.4	22.2
NAFTA 4/	36.0	34.6	33.6	43.9	41.4	46.2	51.0
European Union	59.5	57.7	60.8	59.2	65.9	62.4	56.8

Notes : 1: Colombia, Ecuador, Peru and Venezuela.
2: Argentina, Brazil, Chile, Paraguay and Uruguay.
3: China, Indonesia, Japan, Korea, Malaysia, the Philippines, and Thailand. Data exclude exports by Taiwan Province of China.
4: Canada, Mexico and United States.
Sources: IMF Direction of Statistics Yearbook, various editions; Fund staff calculations.

Arab intra-regional exports totaled US$12 billion in 1998. Of this, about 60 percent went to GCC countries and another 25 percent to Mashreq countries (Table 3.6). The proportion of trade within the four subgroups is significantly higher than overall intra-Arab trade. Nearly two-thirds of the exports of Maghreb countries to the Arab world went to other Maghreb countries, three-fourths of the GCC's Arab exports went to other GCC countries and one-third of the Mashreq's Arab exports went to other Mashreq countries.

58 - *Economic Research Forum*

Table 3.6: Indicators of Intra-Arab Trade, 2000

Exports to:	Arab Countries	Maghreb Countries	Selected GCC Countries	Mashreq Countries	Other Countries
	(Intra-regional exports, in billions of US dollars)				
Arab countries, Of which:	12.0	1.6	7.5	2.6	0.3
Maghreb	2.0	1.0	0.6	0.4	0.0
GCC	6.8	0.1	5.3	1.2	0.2
Selected Mashreq	2.6	0.5	1.2	1.0	0.0
Other Arab	0.6	0.0	0.4	0.0	0.1
	(Intra-regional exports, as percent of exports to world)				
Arab countries, Of which:	8.2	4.9	7.7	22.7	12.5
Maghreb	1.4	3.1	0.6	3.3	0.0
GCC	4.6	0.4	5.5	10.2	7.5
Selected Mashreq	1.8	1.4	1.2	8.6	0.1
Other Arab	0.4	0.0	0.4	0.6	4.9
	(Intra-regional exports, as percent of exports to Arab countries)				
Arab countries, Of which:	100.0	100.0	100.0	100.0	100.0
Maghreb	16.7	63.2	7.7	14.7	0.1
GCC	56.6	7.6	71.4	44.9	59.9
Selected Mashreq	21.8	29.1	15.6	37.7	0.8
Other Arab	4.9	0.1	5.2	2.7	39.3

Source: IMF Direction of Trade Statistics, 1998 Yearbook.
Notes: Country groupings are:
Maghreb: Algeria, Libya, Mauritania, Morocco, Tunisia.
GCC: Bahrain, Kuwait, Oman, Qatar, Saudi Arabia, United Arab Emirates.
Selected Mashreq countries: Egypt, Jordan, Lebanon, Syria, Sudan.
Other countries: Djibouti, Somalia, Yemen.

Why Arabs Don't Trade More With One Another

The policies of Arab governments discourage trade within the region. With the notable exception of GCC countries, which maintain relatively open trade regimes, most Arab countries impose major trade barriers. The average import tariff for the region as a whole is higher than that of any other region except Africa. Non-tariff barriers include restrictive licensing, outright import bans, state trade monopolies, restrictive foreign exchange allo-cation and multiple exchange rates. Differences in overall economic strategy in general also discourage intra-Arab trade.

At the same time, structural factors in the Arab world tend to encourage inter-regional rather than intra-regional trade. The resources in Arab countries are broadly similar, as are the goods they produce, lessening the potential benefits from trade. Likewise, the lack of a diverse industrial base limits opportunities for trade based on product differentiation. High transport, communications and other costs of trade also constrain intra-Arab trade. Arab countries are spread out geographically and the terrain between them is often difficult. Maghreb countries, for example, are closer to Europe than to the rest of the Arab world. Finally, differences in per capita income tend to dampen intra-Arab trade. Richer Arab countries prefer the high-quality goods produced by industrial nations. Income levels, while by themselves not an impediment to trade, can be when coupled with the homogeneity of the export base among many Arab countries.

The Status of Intra-Arab Trade

Intra-Arab trade is less than what would be consistent with the economic fundamentals of geography, income and trade barriers. Empirical analysis shows that this is particularly striking in the case of GCC and AMU countries, where trade agreements have failed to promote significant integration among members. Arab trade with the rest of the world is also low, for both oil and non-oil exporting countries. Indeed, there is considerable scope for increased trade with the rest of the world as well as within the region itself. Distance, trade barriers and differences in income and economic size all appear to hinder trade. For example, transport costs between Arab countries are higher not only because of distance, but also because of closed borders and poor infrastructure.

Research suggests that Arab countries would benefit from the liberalization of their trade, possibly in the context of greater regional integration. Freer trade would boost growth not only by allowing regional producers to benefit from economies of scale, but also by encouraging foreign direct investment and deepening capital markets. There have been a number of recent initiatives to encourage regional integration. In 1998, 14 Arab countries established the Greater Arab Free Trade Agreement (GAFTA) under which tariffs will be reduced for participating members by 10 percentage points annually, with the target of free trade by 2007. Considerable room also exists for the growth of Arab trade with the rest of the world. Recent agreements in the Southern Mediterranean basin will encourage greater trade with Europe.

Box 3.1.
Regionalization and Trade Opening:
A Focus on the Mediterranean Countries

Trade between countries bordering both sides of the Mediterranean tends to be higher than would be expected, considering their trade with other parts of the world and given their overall trade potential (Table 1). This is true among the three Maghreb countries, especially with Morocco and Tunisia, which tend to direct their trade towards southern EU members and which have little trade, for example, with eastern European countries. It is also true among countries in the south-east Mediterranean, which tend to direct their trade toward one another, although Turkey, Egypt, Syria, Lebanon and Jordan, unlike the Maghreb, also have high trade intensities with eastern European countries. In addition, trade between Southern Mediterranean countries, with the exception of Turkey, and northern EU countries is relatively low.

This is due partly to geographical proximity as well as cultural and historical affinities. But it is also due to political ties and trade policies and to the specialization of each country. Countries that produce similar products tend to have less incentive to trade with one another. Countries with similar levels of per capita income also tend to trade more with one another.

The intensity of trade between southern European countries and southern Mediterranean countries has decreased since 1980 from its previous high level. This is partly because relatively closed developing countries tend to cluster their trade toward a very few trading partners. As these countries develop and open up, they tend to branch out to other countries, even as they continue to trade at high levels with their earlier trading partners. Within southern Mediterranean countries, trade remained high. This is partly because their economies were increasingly specialized and tended to complement one another. However, in many cases it was due to the easing of political tensions between neighbors.

In the eastern Mediterranean, Syria, Jordan and Lebanon used to trade intensively with eastern European countries. They gradually reduced this relative preference to the benefit of their neighbors. The intensity of their trade with southern European countries meanwhile didn't increase.

Many Asian countries seem to have used their ability to import from their neighbors as a springboard to export beyond the region to industrialized countries, particularly in their earlier stages of development. This model doesn't apply to southern Mediterranean countries, which tend to export more intensively to their neighbors rather than import from them. Developing Mediterranean countries lack the competitiveness to export outside the region. They remain very dependant on the EU market and above all on markets in the southern EU countries, where they benefit from low transportation costs.

One measure of an economy's openness is the Economic Freedom Openness Indicator (EFOI). According to this indicator, Mediterranean countries have liberalized since 1980 at roughly the same pace as the world as a whole. In 1997, Mediterranean countries scored an average 6.4 on the index, compared to an average 6.6 for the world as a whole.

A second measure is the Trade Discrimination Indicator (TDI). This measures the concentration of a country's trading partners. A small number of partners indicates that tariff or non-tariff barriers are barring access to foreign suppliers. The greater the obstacles, the fewer the suppliers who can afford to bear the imports costs, even if there is no explicit discrimination. Mediterranean countries score fairly well under this measure. Trade discrimination decreased by more than 20 percent on average, with little difference between Mediterranean and non-Mediterranean countries.

However, some countries scored differently under the two measures. The openness of Portugal, Greece, Israel, Egypt and Morocco grew less quickly under the EFOI than under the TDI, while that of Algeria grew more under the TDI.

There is some fear that the expansion of regional trading blocs may be at the expense of world trade. However, there seems to be little link between openness and regionalization in the Mediterranean region. Those countries that rely on their neighbors as trading partners may be doing so because their products are not good enough to attract demand in countries further away. In general, regional free trade agreements or other regional trade agreements can be promoted as a first step toward overall opening for Mediterranean countries.

Source: Guillaume Gaulier and Deniz Ünal-Kesençi, 2001.

Table 1: Relative Bilateral Trade Intensities, 1995-97

	North EU	South EU	South Medit.	Israel	CEEC & Ex-Yug.	Rest of the World
South EU15	1.4	2.7	2.0	1.1	1.5	0.4
South Med	0.8	2.6	3.8	0.7	1.2	0.5
Morocco	0.8	3.6	1.8	0.1	0.8	0.4
Tunisia	1.0	3.8	2.9	0.0	0.6	0.2
Algeria	0.6	3.3	4.5	0.0	0.8	0.4
Turkey	1.3	1.3	5.0	1.6	2.0	0.6
Egypt	0.8	1.8	3.6	2.7	1.5	0.6
Syria-Lebanon-Jordan	0.6	1.7	5.1	0.1	1.4	0.9

Notes: Relative intensity indicator is calculated for total bilateral trade (exports plus imports). A ratio above corresponds to an intensive bilateral trade and symmetrically a ratio below corresponds to a low intensity.
Source: Guillaume Gaulier and Deniz Ünal-Kesençi. 2001. Author's calculations from CHELEM data base CEPII.

MENA Water Resources and Free Trade

A mountain of literature, from hydrology and engineering to international relations and economics, has dealt with the problem of the looming water shortages in the MENA region. Proposed remedies include more desalination plants, improved distribution and irrigation networks, pricing schemes that reflect water scarcity and new legal arrangements to divide rivers and acquifers. Trade policy has rarely been considered, even though free trade is one of the best known and most efficient ways of allocating scarce resources. When it is mentioned, it is usually in the context of the direct trade of water through a pipeline. Free trade, however, can help alleviate shortages in other ways.

Fresh water is an important input in many products, particularly agricultural. The import and export of many goods in effect transfer significant amounts of concealed water resources across borders. For example, because cotton growing requires enormous amounts of water, countries that import cotton are essentially importing the water resources that went into its production. Though less obvious, the same is true for clothing and textiles, whose production requires cotton and, by extension, water resources. Thus it is possible to transfer water resources, if not the water itself, across borders, embodied in traded merchandise.

Turkey is a country that exports large amounts of agricultural and non-agricultural goods that require significant amounts of water to make. These exports can be viewed as hundreds of millions of tons of water in disguise. Moreover, given that Turkey is relatively better-endowed with fresh water than its customers in Middle East, these exports appear to be compatible with the notion that, with free trade, countries with relatively abundant supplies of a particular factor of production tend to export those commodities that use that factor more intensively.

A sample was taken of the comparative advantage of 13 tradable sectors in 11 countries to measure how important water was in the production of exports. The measurements were rough, because the data in many of the countries is not always reliable. The results show that the exports of most of the countries sampled, including Iran, Israel, Jordan, Kuwait, Lebanon, Saudi Arabia and Syria, are not significantly affected by the amount of water required to produce them. This implies either that these countries export goods that contain more water input than is warranted by their scarce water supplies, or that other factors are at work that are more important than water.

There is a lot of evidence showing that countries in the survey indeed distort trade in a way that in effect causes their scarce water resources to be transferred abroad. This might be because governments pro-mote the export of commodities that need a lot of water to produce, such as agricultural goods and industrial goods like textiles and clothing, or restrict their import. However, further study is needed to back this up.

Despite the lack of conclusive evidence, it is safe to say that freer trade would encourage water-rich countries to specialize in products that are water intensive, and prompt water-scarce countries to specialize in products that need less water. Such a system, by making more efficient use of water, might help resolve water-related conflicts, especially if complemented with a regional grid of water pipelines to enable direct exports and imports of water.

Trade Options for the Palestinian Economy

The current Palestinian trade regime was laid out in the 1994 Paris Protocol, which grants preferential access for Israeli goods to the Palestinian market and vice versa. The system, which formalizes the *de facto* customs union in place since Israel occupied the West Bank and Gaza Strip in 1967, gives Israel control over access to external markets and the power to set the level of import duties, standards requirements and other trade policies.

The system has not served the Palestinian economy well. In 1998, Palestinians paid an average customs duty of 17 percent on imports from countries other than Israel. On top of this, trade has been made more expensive because of Israeli restrictions on movement. Israel has continually limited, and often cut off entirely, Palestinian vehicles, goods and people moving between Gaza, the West Bank and Jerusalem and within the West Bank itself through a highly complex system of checkpoints and permits. As a result, Palestinian consumers pay inflated prices for foreign goods, while Israeli products have gained an artificial advantage in the Palestinian market.

Movement restrictions have also hindered the development of the Palestinian economy as a whole. About 80 percent of all goods came from outside the Palestinian territories in 1998. Of these, 75 percent originated in Israel while the other 5 percent came from other countries, mainly the United States and the European Union, both of which have signed free trade agreements with Israel. The geographical distribution of exports has been even more one-sided. More than 95 percent of all Palestinian exports were sold to Israel. In 1998, only about one percent of imports came from and about 3 percent of exports went to the Arab world.

Supposing the Palestinians Could Choose

It is hoped that at some point the Palestinians will be able to reach a political agreement with Israel that will allow them to determine their own trade and tax policies. In such a case, the Palestinians would have to decide what type of trade regime would best serve their needs—then have the political will to implement it. From a strictly economic point of view, the most rewarding system would be one that lowers the domestic price of imported goods and helps develop competitive markets.

One measure of gains in welfare is to compare how much a household would have to pay to consume the same quantity of goods before and after any proposed reforms. The less the better. Two extreme scenarios are explored here.

The first scenario is the continuation of the current free trade relationship with Israel, but on the basis of the removal of restrictions on the movement of people and goods, the unrestricted ability to import through Palestinian ports of entry and the elimination of any extra import taxes imposed by the Palestinian government. This regime would require the Palestinians to agree with Israel on rules of origin and to introduce mechanisms to enforce these rules.

The second scenario is complete free trade, or, in other words, the elimination of all tariffs on imports from all origins, including Israel. This would require the Palestinians to give up their customs union with Israel, including their preferential access to the Israeli market.

Either option would require that the Palestinians put a customs administration in place. The Palestinian government in both cases would also have to expand its value-added tax to replace the lost revenue from import duties, which in 1998 accounted for more than one-sixth of total tax revenue.

A recent technical report by two World Bank economists concluded that the benefits under either of the two options were roughly the same. The elimination of tariff and other import barriers would increase the purchasing power of households by about 6 percent. However, once the rules of origin were imposed, the gains from a customs union with Israel would be cut in half to 3 percent. Likewise, if preferential access to the Israeli market were lost as a result of opening the Palestinian market to all countries, the gains would also be reduced to 3 percent.

In both cases, the lower price of imports would not only benefit consumers, but also producers as inputs became cheaper. Imports from Israel would become less competitive compared to imports from other origins, increasing the variety available in the Palestinian market. Competition in the Palestinian economy would increase, forcing a more efficient use of resources. Some sectors would shrink while others expanded. Overall gains in productivity would likely generate a significant increase in real wages and return on capital without jeopardizing the competitiveness of Palestinian exports.

There would be other longer-term costs and benefits not included in the analysis. Among the costs would be the transitional cost of reallocating resources, notably labor, as the economy shifted and protected industries contracted. However, the benefits would likely outweigh the costs. Among these would be a lower cost of investment and a potentially greater rate of return. Real wages would likely increase, encouraging more people to seek jobs. An increased diversification in the origin of imports would lead to a larger variety of accessible inputs, helping producers increase productivity. New markets would be opened, creating opportunities to sell new products to new customers. Goods with lower standards than those required to enter Israel would become available, further expanding the variety of inputs available to producers. Trade flows with Israel and the rest of the world be put in better balance, therefore reducing the dependency of the Palestinian economy on economic shocks occurring in Israel, as well as its vulnerability to disruptions caused by Israeli security concerns.

Box 3.2.
Liberalization and Joining The WTO: The UAE Case

During the oil boom period from 1975 to 1984, the United Arab Emirates' gross domestic product (GDP) grew to 104.5 billion dirhams in 1984 from 39.6 billion dirhams in 1975, an average annual growth of 16.4 percent. During the decline in oil prices from 1985 to 2000, GDP grew to 223.0 billion dirhams in 2000 from 101.9 billion dirhams in 1985, an annual growth of 7.4 percent a year. In the last 15 years, the share of oil in GDP dropped to 34 percent from 43.8 percent as the government sought to diversify the economy.

The UAE has a liberal trade policy and lets the private sector take the lead. Apart from a few exceptions, particularly on chemical and pharmaceutical products, import duties are, on average, only about 4 percent. The country imposes no non-tariff import barriers, no foreign exchange controls and no taxes or restrictions on exports, and allows companies to import a large number of foreign workers. Apart from providing a number of incentives for exports and a large amount of money for the education and training of local citizens, the government generally has only a regulating role.

The UAE has always advocated the free movement of goods and services across regional and international borders. Prior to joining the WTO some studies were carried out to investigate the economic implications of UAE membership. These concluded that the benefits would outweigh the costs.

Because of its liberal trade policy and its low tariffs, the UAE had little difficulty adjusting when it joined the WTO in March 1996. It will not be required to reduce its average tariff rate below the present 4 percent. In fact, for some agricultural and manufactured products it may raise its tariffs to as much as 15 percent should it choose to. However, tariffs on chemical and pharmaceutical products should be reduced to a maximum 10 percent by 2011 from their current high rates. The UAE must tighten trademarks, patents, copyrights and other intellectual property rights and is currently amending its laws. It is also training government and private-sector employees on WTO rules.

In a second round of WTO talks, the UAE hopes to negotiate a gradual liberalization of its financial, business, insurance, telecommunications and other services over a period of 10 to 15 years. It is not required to liberalize its services sector under the present accord.

It hopes to provide more investment incentives under a new foreign investment law that would allow foreigners to own more than the 49 percent of companies to which they are currently limited.

Source: Amerah, 2001.

Egyptian Exports: The Exporters' Point of View

Some 45 Egyptian exporters were surveyed to see how much help they felt the government was giving them in their attempts to penetrate foreign markets, and if this help had improved over the past decade. The four areas covered were export promotion agencies, regulations and infrastructure, the quality of Egyptian labor and the potential benefits of the trade agreement Egypt signed in mid-2001 with the European Union. General conclusions can be drawn.

Exporters think export promotion agencies are ineffective, especially those run by the government. They rarely depend on them to gather information on foreign markets, to market their products or to provide specialized services such as those related to standards and quality. This is especially true among the more experienced exporters. However, exporters believe there is nonetheless a need for such agencies, particularly in promoting exports to the European Union, and would like them to expand their agenda to act as business brokers.

The government has improved the duty drawback system in the last decade. However, exporters feel it should be extended to indirect exporters to enhance the subcontracting scheme between large exporters and small and medium enterprises. Customs procedures, though still cumbersome, have improved and import tariffs lowered. Laws and regulations are better than before, but enforcement remains weak. The quality of telecommunications, electricity, postal services, banking, insurance, air transport and maritime services, all vital to exporters, has improved. However, the cost of these services has increased.

Different types of skilled labor and management have become increasingly available over the last decade, with the exception of highly skilled labor, the cornerstone of any successful exporting scheme. Exporters complain that they often train workers at great expense, only for them to quit their jobs soon afterwards. They nonetheless recommend that training centers be run more and more by private business rather than by the government.

Exporters believe the trade agreement between Egypt and the European Union will improve access to the EU market, though they are uncertain as to how. Most exporters, except those of textiles and ready-made garments, are still unfamiliar with issues such as rules of origin. They are neutral concerning European competition law and see no urgency in its application in Egypt. Those who export to the United States believe that EU standards are not complicated, while those exporting mainly to Africa and the Arab world believe they constitute a major obstacle.

Morocco and the EU Free Trade Agreement

Morocco and the European Union in 1996 signed a partnership agreement under which a free trade area for manufactured goods will be established over a 12-year transition period, with the status of agriculture and fishing products to be negotiated later. The agreement is part of a wider European project aimed at setting up a free-trade area with Mediterranean countries by the year 2010. The European Union has signed similar agreements with Tunisia, Israel, Palestine, Jordan, Egypt and Lebanon and is negotiating others with Algeria and Syria. The agreements go beyond the strictly commercial accords signed in the 1960s and 1970s in that they also entail financial, economic and technical cooperation, social and cultural exchange and political dialogue, with a focus on security.

The Impact of Agreement

So far, the impact on Morocco at the macro level, has been an increase in imports that is slightly faster than the increase in exports. Hence there was a small increase in the trade deficit. EU imports are increasing quite strongly, while those from the rest of the world have diminished. Both GDP and the demand for labor are dropping by 1.5 to 2 percent per year, but private consumption has remained steady due to the lower price of imports. Investment has fallen by 10 percent. Government revenue fell by 12 percent after customs revenue was cut by more than half.

At the micro-level, industries that exported before the agreement, being used to competition, have been developing production and foreign trade better than others. As expected, protected industries have been more vulnerable than exposed ones and have suffered. Their losses have mounted as they face more competition. Investment in construction has been falling even as the sector opens up to more competition.

Recommended Economic Policies

Tax revenues must be increased, perhaps by improving collection, to compensate for the loss of customs. The budget deficit must not be allowed to grow to the point where government borrowing crowds out private borrowing. The recent fall in the level of investment must be met by increased saving, by both the private and public sectors. In addition, the government should consider devaluing the dirham as a possible means of making local industry more competitive. Textile and clothing makers, Morocco's main exporters, have been calling for such a step for more than a year. The dirham was indeed devalued by 5 percent in April 2000.

Export Strategies that Raise Competitiveness

In order to achieve higher export competitiveness and diversification, several policies need to be implemented. Countries should try to attract foreign direct investment. Trade barriers need to be lowered, ideally under the framework of the World Trade Organization (WTO). Saudi Arabia, Lebanon, Syria and other MENA countries that are not yet members of WTO should speed up their membership. The Euro-Mediterranean partnership, the Greater Arab Free Trade Area and other regional coordination arrangements currently being negotiated or implemented need to be pursued with greater vigor. Finally, governments need to continue

Economic Research Forum - **65**

to invest in education, especially secondary education, to upgrade the skills of the workforce.

References

Al-Atrash, Hassan and Tarik Yousef. 2000. "Intra-Arab Trade: Is It Too Little." IMF Working Paper 00/10. Washington: International Monetary Fund.

Amerah, M. 2001. "Trade Liberalization and Accession to WTO, The UAE Case. Background paper to *Economic Trends in the MENA Region.* Cairo: Economic Research Forum.

Astrup, Claus and Sebastien Dessus. 2001. "Trade Options for the Palestinian Economy: Some Orders of Magnitude." Background paper to *Economic Trends in the MENA Region.* Cairo: Economic Research Forum.

El-Erian, Mohamed, and Stanley Fischer. 1996. "Is MENA a Region? The Scope for Regional Integration." IMF Working Paper 96/30. Washington: International Monetary Fund.

El-Imam, M. 1990. *Arab Economic Integration Between Two Decades.* Al Mustaqbal Al Arabi, No. 138, August.

El-Naggar, Said (ed.). 1992. *Foreign and Intratrade Policies of the Arab Countries.*Washington: International Monetary Fund.

Gaulier, Guillaume and Deniz Unal-Kesençi. 2001. "Regionalization and Trade Opening: A Focus on the Mediterranean Countries." Background paper to *Economic Trends in the MENA Region.* Cairo: Economic Research Forum.

Ghoneim, Ahmed. 2001. "The Egyptian Exporting Community and the Institutional Setup: Assessment of the Last Decade's Developments and Perspectives for the EU-Med Partnership." Background paper to *Economic Trends in the MENA Region.* Cairo: Economic Research Forum.

Haddad, Mona. 2001. "Export Competitiveness: Where Does The Middle East & North Africa Region Stand?" Background paper to *Economic Trends in the MENA Region.* Cairo: Economic Research Forum.

Hamdouch, B. 2001. "The Impact on Morocco of the Free Trade Agreement with the EU." Background paper to *Economic Trends in the MENA Region.* Cairo: Economic Research Forum.

Hamdouch, B. and Chater, M. 2000. "Impact des Accords de Libre-échange Euro-Méditérrannéens. Cas du Maroc." Rapport Final, FEMISE.

IMF. *Direction of Trade Statistics Yearbook*, various issues.

Sayan, Serdar. 2001. "Could Free Trade Lead to a More Efficient Use of Scarce Water Resources in the MENA Region?: An Innovative Application of the Heckscher-Ohlin Framework." Background paper to *Economic Trends in the MENA Region.* Cairo: Economic Research Forum.

Sekkat, Khalid. 2002. "Intra-regional Trade Evolution, Opportunity and Challenge." Background paper to *Economic Trends in the MENA Region.* Cairo: Economic Research Forum.

UNCTAD. 2002. COMTRADE Database.

Yousef, Tarek. 2001. "Regional Trade and Global Economic Integration in the Middle East, 1970-1995." Background paper to *Economic Trends in the MENA Region.* Cairo: Economic Research Forum.

CHAPTER FOUR

THE TRANSITION FROM THE OLD TO THE NEW ECONOMY

There is no question that the world economy is very different today than it was only a decade ago. But what looms large for debate is what will be the future consequences of all the economic changes. The pace of technological change is increasing the importance of research and development and knowledge-based industries. Information technology industries are changing the nature and location of economic activity as they create new products and new markets. The new technologies are accessible and relatively inexpensive, but they are also changing rapidly.

The Middle East will face a dramatically different environment in the next decade compared with the 1980s and 1990s. Competition is intensifying and the basis of success is changing. But unfortunately Middle East economies remain concentrated in resource-based activities and have made few advances into the "new economy." A transition strategy that builds on the experiences of other regions is needed to move the region ahead.

The advantages of new technology won't be seen regionally unless changes are made in institutions, infrastructure and certain value systems. The potential for the Middle East to catch up exists, but it can only be realized by countries that develop strong social capabilities—for example those that manage to mobilize investment, education and research and development activities in the right direction.

Absence of Innovation-intensive Manufacturing Activity

With only a few exceptions, the MENA region has lagged behind other regions in promoting technological development, which often means shifting investment into research and development.

Turkey stands out for having diversified towards higher value-added manufacturing activity, particularly in the area of electronics and communication equipment as well as pharmaceuticals (Table 4.1).

Kuwait is a representative case of oil-exporting countries in the region, where petroleum-refining dominates manufacturing. Refining activities account for 76 percent of Kuwait's total manufacturing output in 1997, only slightly down from 77 percent in 1990 (Table 4.2).

In Egypt between 1990 and 1995 petroleum-refining rose to the top rank, taking the place of spinning and weaving activities. Otherwise the top ten ranking manufacturing activities remain largely unchanged (Table 4.3).

The share of high-tech exports as a percentage of total exports in selected MENA countries provides evidence of the lag in technological development. These shares look meager when compared to other regions (Table 4.4).

The low number of patent applications in the MENA region is another indicator of the absence of a culture of innovation that is a prerequisite to new-economy type manufacturing activity (Table 4.5).

By now, a transition strategy should be clear. The culture of innovation in countries like Japan, Malaysia and others in Southeast Asia can be used as a framework and adapted to suit the Middle East's special conditions. The failure of the Soviet

Economic Research Forum - **67**

Table 4.1: Turkey's Top Ten Ranking Manufacturing Activities (% of total manufacturing output)

	1990	Rank	1997	
Petroleum refineries	12.45	1	9.70	Petroleum refineries
Spinning, weaving, textiles	8.64	2	9.60	Spinning, weaving and finishing textiles
Iron and steel basic industries	8.02	3	8.07	Motor vehicles
Motor vehicles	6.03	4	7.03	Iron and steel basic industries
Wearing apparel, except footwear	4.13	5	5.55	Wearing apparel, except footwear
Petroleum and coal products	3.73	6	2.63	Machinery and equipment, except electrical
Machinery and equipment except electrical	3.03	7	2.27	Food products not elsewhere classified
Tobacco manufactures	2.90	8	2.19	Radio, TV & comm. equipment
Cement, lime and plaster	2.61	9	2.14	Vegetable and animal oils and fats
Synthetic resins, plastic & man-made fibres	2.51	10	2.05	Drugs and medicines

Source: Calculated from UNIDO 2001 data base on CD-ROM.

Table 4.2: Kuwait's Top Ten Ranking Manufacturing Activities (% of total manufacturing output)

	1990	Rank	1997	Kuwait Output
Petroleum refineries	77.46	1	75.88	Petroleum refineries
Non-metallic mineral products	3.67	2	2.97	Non-metallic mineral products.
Wearing apparel, except footwear	1.9	3	1.64	Structural metal products
Bakery products	1.37	4	1.47	Wearing apparel
Fertilizers and pesticides	1.24	5	1.36	Fertilizers and pesticides
Structural metal products	1.22	6	1.31	Bakery products
Cement, lime and plaster	1.02	7	1.12	Plastic products
Furniture and fixtures	1.01	8	1.01	Jewellery and related articles
Soft drinks & carbonated waters	1.00	9	1.00	Food products
Food products not elsewhere classified	0.89	10	0.98	Cement, lime and plaster

Source: Calculated from UNIDO 2001 data base on CD-ROM.

economies and the irrelevance of other systems such as that of Brazil also help show the types of policies and institutions to be avoided. There are no short cuts to a successful transition, and many issues need to be tackled simultaneously and aggressively.

Science and Technology

To understand why the region has failed to venture towards new economy manufacturing, it is impor-
tant to analyze the region's achievements in science. The evidence presented here is based on UNESCO data on research and development in the natural sciences.

Table 4.6 includes information contained in the 1996 and 1998 World Science Reports (WSRs) of UNESCO on science inputs and outputs. It is supplemented by other sources in ten regions in the early 1990s.

Table 4.3: Egypt's Top Ten Ranking Manufacturing Activities (% of total manufacturing output)

Egypt	1990	Rank	1997	Egypt
Spinning, weaving & finishing textiles	12.52	1	15.63	Petroleum refineries
Petroleum refineries	10.92	2	8.58	Spinning, weaving and finishing textiles
Grain mill products	6.57	3	5.09	Iron and steel basic industries
Iron and steel basic industries	6.43	4	5.05	Grain mill products
Bakery products	4.20	5	3.99	Cement, lime & plaster
Non-ferrous metal basic industries	3.25	6	3.53	Drugs and medicines
Drugs and medicines	3.17	7	3.36	Non-ferrous metal basic industries
Fertilizers and pesticides	2.88	8	2.84	Sugar factories and refineries
Soap, perfumes, cosmetics, toiletries	2.58	9	2.61	Vegetable & animal oils & fats
Cement, lime and plaster	2.53	10	2.57	Bakery products

Source: Calculated from UNIDO 2001 data base on CD-ROM.

Table 4.4: High-Technology Exports (% of manufactured exports)

	1992	1994	1996	1998
Malaysia	37.05	43.80	43.94	54.49
Korea, Rep.	19.52	25.03	26.06	26.77
Hong Kong	16.02	17.79	19.06	20.61
Israel	11.66	12.95	16.95	19.74
China	5.77	7.71	11.69	14.53
Oman	1.10	1.18	2.59	..
Kuwait	6.10	..	1.90	..
Bahrain	..	0.95	1.74	..
Tunisia	1.65	1.53	1.73	2.21
Turkey	1.12	1.63	1.60	2.15
Saudi Arabia	0.05	0.07	0.74	..
Egypt	..	0.32	0.50	0.17
Algeria	1.28	0.82	0.37	..
Morocco	..	2.11	0.35	..
Jordan	1.01	7.82		

Source: World Bank, World Develoment Indicators on CD-ROM 2001.

Table 4.5: Number of Patent Applications in Selected MEAN Countries

Patent applications, nonresidents	1996	Patent applications, residents	1996
Korea, Rep.	45,548	Korea, Rep.	68,446
China	41,016	China	11,698
Turkey	19,668	Israel	1,363
Israel	12,172	Egypt	504
Hong Kong	2,059	Turkey	367
Saudi Arabia	810	Morocco	90
Egypt	706	Iraq	68
Morocco	237	Algeria	48
Algeria	150	Tunisia	46
Tunisia	128	Hong Kong, China	41
Libya	23	Saudi Arabia	27
Iraq	18	Libya	12

Source: World Bank, World Develoment Indicators on CD-ROM 2001.

This analysis relies on two criteria, Research and Development Personnel and Gross Expenditure on Research and Development (GERD). According to the UNESCO data, the Arab region fares relatively well on the overall size of research and development personnel. But on GERD, the region performs miserably, with just 0.2 percent of GDP compared to the world average of 1.4 percent. It ranks the lowest among the ten regions surveyed. It is lower than Sub-Saharan Africa, which is considerably poorer. Arab scientists, it appears, are starved for resources. This is a chief reason why scientific output in the region is low.

Two basic classes of indicators of scientific output

Table 4.6: Basic and S & T Indicators by Region

Region	R&D personnel, 1992			GERD, 1994		
	Thousands	% of world	Per 1000 people	Billion (PPP$)	% of world	Per capita (PPP$)
Arab States*	166	3.8	0.7	1.9	0.4	8
Israel**	20	0.5	3.7	1.3	0.3	243
North America	1014	23.4	3.6	178.1	37.9	624
Oceania	49	1.1	2.3	6.0	1.3	283
CEE (1)	286	6.6	2.2	4.4	0.9	34
Western Europe	785	18.1	1.8	130.2	27.7	296
CIS (2)	453	10.4	1.6	11.8	2.5	42
Asia (excluding Arab states)	1226	28.3	0.4	125.1	26.6	41
Sub-Saharan Africa	177	4.1	0.4	2.3	0.5	5
Latin America	159	3.7	0.3	9.2	2.0	20
World	4334	100	0.8	470.4	100	88

*In the 1996 WSR: Arab States were part of the North Africa and Middle and Near East region, and were excluded using data from the 1995 and 1997 HDRs.

**In the 1998 WSR: Israel was excluded from Western Europe using its percentages to Western Europe in 1992.

(1) Central and Eastern European Countries

(2) Commonwealth of Independent States

Source: UNESCO World Science Reports.

are used internationally: publications (derived from the Science Citation Index) and patents granted. UNESCO reports on patent registration sources in Europe and the United States.

The Arab region shows a modest share of scientific publication, but vanishes from the international map of patent registration (Figure 4.1). This indicates a lack of a strong institutional foundation. It's easier for an individual to publish than to produce a patent, and publishing is often required for promotion within academic institutions. Another indicator is the productivity of scientific activity in the region. Figure 4.1 compares scientific productivity, measured by publications relative to population, research and development personnel, GERD and GDP, as a percentage of the world average.

The Arab region's publication productivity, relative to GERD, is above average. In fact, according to this indicator the Arab region ranks higher than North America, Western Europe and Asia. It appears that valuable individual productivity is being squandered because of a dearth of resources. The Arab region's

Figure 4.1: Arab States' Share (%) of the World Total, Basic and S & T Indicators

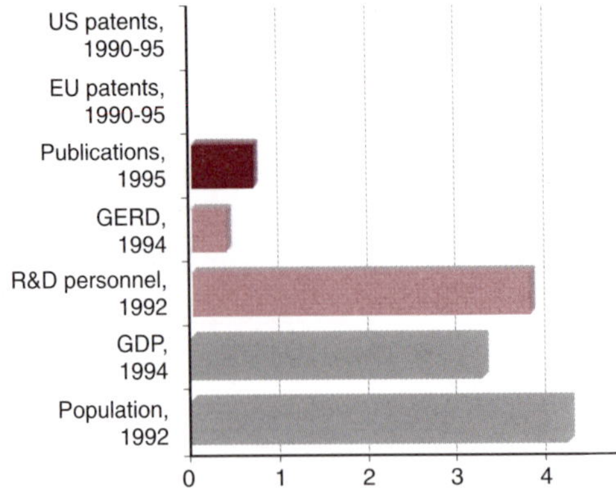

Note: GERD is Gross Expenditure on R&D.
Source: UNESCO, 1998.

relatively higher publication productivity represents a waste of potential and is an indicator of the extensive

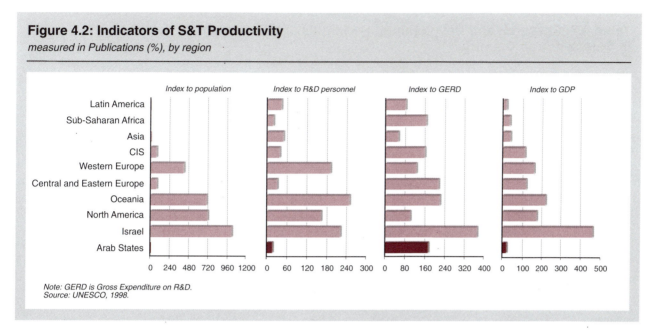

Figure 4.2: Indicators of S&T Productivity
measured in Publications (%), by region

Note: GERD is Gross Expenditure on R&D.
Source: UNESCO, 1998.

brain drain of Arab scientific talent to other regions.

But relative to research and development personnel, the Arab region's publication productivity ranks lowest among the ten regions (Figure 4.2). It is slightly lower than Sub-Saharan Africa. With the exception of publications per unit of GERD, science productivity in the Arab region is considerably lower than the world average. On all indicators of scientific productivity considered, the Arab region is roughly comparable to the much poorer Sub-Saharan Africa. The data shows that Arab wealth is quite ineffective in this respect.

Diversity among Arab Countries

So far, we have pooled Arab countries into a single Arab region. But within the region there is considerable diversity. A 1998 regional study sponsored by the UNESCO Cairo office provides data on research and development personnel and expenditure in 18 Arab countries. Table 4.7 provides information derived from this source as well as others.

The table shows that the conditions of science vary tremendously among Arab countries. A specimen of five countries, representing different types, is shown in Figure 4.3.

Egypt and Saudi Arabia dominate the basic resource base, Egypt with the largest population in the region and Saudi with the greatest GDP. Although in absolute terms Saudi Arabia has spent a considerable sum on research and development, it has a small base of research and development personnel—smaller than Morocco, which is significantly poorer. Egypt has an overall edge in science inputs, with close to 60 percent of research and development personnel, considerably more than twice its population share. Egypt also has a larger level of

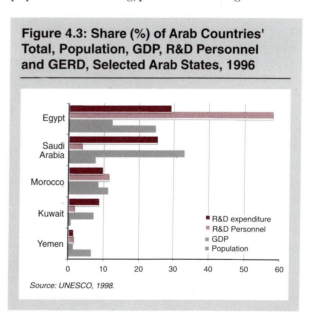

Figure 4.3: Share (%) of Arab Countries' Total, Population, GDP, R&D Personnel and GERD, Selected Arab States, 1996

Source: UNESCO, 1998.

Table 4.7: Research and Development Personnel and Expenditure in Selected Arab Countries

State	R&D personnel				R&D expenditure (Million US $)			
	1992	1996	1996/ 1992 (%)	1996 (%)	1992	1996	1996/ 1992 (%)	1996 (%)
Algeria	2082	2588	124.3	4.0	33.6	35.6	105.9	4.5
Bahrain	105	143	136.2	0.2	1.9	3.7	192.8	0.5
Egypt	27499	37073	134.8	58.0	156.3	227.5	145.6	29.1
Iraq	2011	2840	141.2	4.4	33.1	27.6	83.2	3.5
Jordan	1053	1471	139.7	2.3	15.1	20.6	136.6	2.6
Kuwait	878	1130	128.7	1.8	47.2	67.1	142.2	8.6
Lebanon	417	444	106.5	0.7	5.8	7.5	128.4	1.0
Libya	691	903	130.7	1.4	13.4	16.9	126.3	2.2
Mauritania	432	509	117.8	0.8	3.7	4.3	116.2	0.5
Morocco	6354	7329	115.3	11.5	70.6	74.9	106.0	9.6
Oman	190	382	201.1	0.6	5.9	10.8	182.4	1.4
Qatar	74	74	100.0	0.1	4.3	5.5	127.0	0.7
Saudi Arabia	1878	2421	128.9	3.8	131.1	196.1	149.6	25.1
Sudan	2634	2047	77.7	3.2	8.8	10.0	114.1	1.3
Syria	1840	2105	114.4	3.3	14.7	24.2	164.8	3.1
Tunisia	794	1132	142.6	1.8	16.5	28.9	175.2	3.7
UAE	179	313	174.9	0.5	10.8	10.9	100.8	1.4
Yemen	1043	1041	99.8	1.6	6.6	10.3	155.6	1.3
Total	**50154**	**63945**	**127**	**100**	**579**	**782**	**135**	**100**

Source: Qasem, 1998.

gross expenditure on research and development than Saudi Arabia. The difference in resource endowment between Egypt and Saudi Arabia illustrates how benefits could accrue from a regional collaboration in science and technology.

Morocco is more balanced, with both its resource base and science inputs in the range of 10 percent of the region totals. Kuwait is distinguished by higher levels of research and development personnel to population as well as research and development expenditure relative to GDP. At the other extreme, Yemen is representative of the least developed countries in the region. It has a relatively large population and a small presence of research and development personnel and a low level of gross economic output and research and development gross expenditure.

The study also shows there has been only limited improvement over time. According to the 1998 UNESCO study, the number of scientific research and development personnel in Arab countries grew by 6 to 7 percent per year between 1992 and 1996, more than twice the rate of population growth. The numbers of research and development personnel was maintained or increased. Countries that outperformed the average include Oman, UAE, Tunisia, Iraq, Jordan, Bahrain, Egypt and Libya. Except for Egypt, this entire group started with a small base. Sudan, Yemen, Qatar and Lebanon fared below average in augmenting the population of research and development personnel. In Sudan there has been considerable decline.

Gross expenditure on research and development has risen by close to 9 percent per year in the region. However, because the population is growing by about 3 percent, real per capita GERD has most likely fallen. The relatively small countries of Bahrain, Oman and Syria fared better in this category. Expenditure in Iraq declined. The UAE, a rich country, maintained its level.

The lack of funds going into research institutions reflects the low status of science in Arab societies.

Trade Liberalization and Innovation
A Case Study of Turkish Industry

The degree of innovation in companies will play an important role in the industrialization of developing countries. In this section, ways in which Turkish manufacturing firms pursued innovation since trade liberalization began in 1980 are examined. Turkey's development strategy was based on import-substitution from 1960 to 1980. It then switched to more outward-oriented policies that involved promoting exports as well as liberalizing imports.

The Technology Development Foundation of Turkey surveyed 1,297 Turkish manufacturers to determine their level of innovation. The survey identifies whether or not a firm introduced an inno-

---

Box 4.1.
Arab Industry Can Enter the New Economy

1) Arabs need to engage the entire population in the information and communications technology revolution. Of special importance is greater democracy in policymaking and the engagement of key players and stakeholders in regional agenda building. The strategy must involve long-term goals and social perspectives about science and technology and industrialization.

2) The region needs to revamp its education and training institutions. Major gaps exist in the quality of education, in maintaining a proper balance between secondary and tertiary education and between science and technology and other fields. Qualified scientists and technologists are in critically short supply. Every school should be connected to the internet. An Arab multimedia university should be established as soon as possible. Basic computer literacy programs for all Arabs must be implemented with provisions for long distance electronic education.

3) Building an info-structure is the foundation of this social project. This means building broadband network and mobile computing technology. Every house should be linked to the network and new buildings must be electronically conduit-ready.

4) The region needs to develop supporting laws and regulations, networks and clusters of firms to create affordable applications with local content.

5) The Arabs have to be careful to balance the new knowledge and techniques with traditional values. A comprehensive education system, on-line information services, networked electronic communities and IT appreciation sponsored by the media can strengthen traditional values.

6) Strong, visible and credible incentives that encourage innovation should be implemented. An interface between users and producers should be quickly developed. Sub-contracting networks should be formed at the enterprise level or for specific clusters of companies. An emphasis should be placed on forging strong links between production, research and development and reverse engineering, on developing and using consultancy systems, on improving and strengthening the technology import capability, and on discouraging harmful and wasteful turn-key projects.

7) A plan is needed to transform key Arab states into centers of excellence in multimedia and content building. These areas can leverage the transformation to the entire region.

8) Much of what is recommended will not bring about a transition if a minimum threshold of Arab technological development is not achieved. Governments need to lead the movement from the top down while society and stakeholders lead it from the bottom up. This full societal program is along the lines of what has been achieved in Malaysia.

9) A favorable macroeconomic environment is crucial. Recent literature suggests a fixed exchange rate regime and a stable and credible monetary policy are important for acquiring technology in a world still heavily dependent on importing technology.

Source: Kuborsi, 2001.

Economic Research Forum - **73**

vation during the period 1989-1993. It measured innovation as a function of firm size, market structure, profits and skill level of the labor force.

The survey found that innovation increases with company size up to a point, then decreases. That is contrary to the finding of studies in developed nations where innovation generally continues to increase with size. The study also found that higher profits are associated with increased innovation and that the skill level of the workforce, measured by average wage and salary levels, has a positive effect on the probability the firm will innovate. This demonstrates the importance of new technology and the role played by technical employees for innovation in Turkey's economy.

Firms using intensively imported capital goods are also more likely to innovate. This indicates that Turkey's trade liberalization has helped innovation. However, other channels of technology transfer, such as technology agreements or foreign direct investment in Turkish manufacturing, do not appear to have significantly affected innovation.

FDI often helps innovation, particularly when joint ventures and multinationals transfer technology and management skills to their local partners. But if the local partner is technologically weak or if the main motivation of the foreign firm is to gain access to the domestic market, such investment may not result in innovation. This is probably what occurred in Turkey between 1989 and 1993, when foreign partnerships appear to have had no positive effect on innovation.

In theory, joint ventures can also help other firms innovate through technology spillover. Competitors may adopt a new technology to hold onto market share, and joint ventures may introduce technology to other firms by subcontracting work. However we conclude that the impact of FDI in Turkey was limited to creating jobs and bringing in foreign exchange and didn't diffuse technology among local firms.

In conclusion, findings indicate that benefits of trade liberalization on the innovation activities of firms are only part of the equation. The lack of impact of FDI on innovation is particularly significant since the role of this channel of technology transfer will increase in the future.

Intellectual Property Rights: the Case of Pharmaceuticals

Intellectual property rights have become highly controversial in the pharmaceutical industry. In spite of traditional arguments about ownership rights and the impact on innovation and development, developing countries have not altogether accepted the imposition of a global intellectual property rights regime. The pharmaceutical industry in the Middle East faces a tremendous challenge as countries increase compliance with the Trade Related Aspects of Intellectual Property Rights (TRIPS) agreement of the World Trade Organization and the intellectual property rights conditions in the European Union's trade agreements with Mediterranean countries. The challenge is especially big in countries like Egypt, Jordan, Iran and Saudi Arabia, whose pharmaceutical industries grew up outside the TRIPS regime. The industry will have to reorient and reposition itself to adjust to the new rules.

The Arab Pharmaceutical Industry

The total pharmaceutical market in Arab countries grew by 10 percent in 1999 to $5.98 billion. Saudi Arabia has 21 percent of the Arab market, which consists of 234 companies, including 15 under establishment. Syria has 22 percent of the region's pharmaceutical companies, the largest number in the Arab world, followed by Egypt, with 18 percent. (See Table 4.8 below.)

Investment in Arab pharmaceutical industries reached $4 billion in 1998. The industry employs more than 50,000 people. Multinational corporations are investing in joint venture factories in large markets such as Egypt to gain access to the large and growing local market. Firms in smaller markets find it more difficult to establish joint ventures with global leaders, particularly as the whole region moves into compliance with TRIPS and Arab-Arab trade expands with greater economic integration.

Despite a surge in pharmaceuticals production in the last 25 years, the Arab world remains a net importer. Between 1975 and 1999, consumption per capita and the per capita share of domestically produced medicine both grew almost four fold, while the population doubled. Consumption grew to

Table 4.8: Pharmaceutical Market Size In the Arab World 1999

Country	Market Size ($m)	Domestic Product ($m)	Domestic Product (%)	Number of Factories
Saudi Arabia	1230	246	20%	13
Egypt	1000	890	89%	41
Iraq (1989)	475	166	35%	6
Algeria	550	137	25%	12
Morocco	490	416	85%	23
Syria	360	270	75%	52
Libya	230	–	–	1
Tunisia	260	65	25%	18
UAE	220	44	20%	2
Jordan	180	66	37%	25
Yemen	220	33	15%	3
Lebanon	180	21	12%	6
Sudan	135	67	50%	16
Kuwait	120	–	–	1
Palestine	130	45	35%	6
Qatar	60	–	–	–
Oman	65	–	–	2
Bahrain	40	–	–	1
Mauritania	25	–	–	–
Somalia	6	–	–	–
Eritrea	5	–	–	–
Total	5981	2751	46%	234

Source: Jordanian Association of Pharmaceutical Manufacturers, 2001.

$5.98 billion from $785 million, while domestic production grew to $2.75 billion from $345 million. The ratio of domestic production to consumption grew to 46 percent in 1999 from 44 percent in 1975, an almost negligible improvement over a quarter of a century.

The Future of Arab Pharmaceuticals

The pharmaceutical industry must reposition itself in a way that improves quality and competitiveness while adhering to intellectual property rights. Several factors should be addressed in the short term in order to set the stage for a viable long-term strategy.

- Smaller firms must merge to achieve the critical mass needed for competent research and development and to gain expertise in state-of-the-art marketing techniques such as packaging. The local industry lacks both. Not all firms have to merge. But if proper partnerships are established, big firms can harness the spirit and creativity of the start-ups.
- Medium-sized and small firms must join in joint ventures to expand markets. For example, the small market in Jordan is a deterrent to foreign investors. Unless assurances are in place that a significant percentage of output will be sold in the domestic market many multinational companies would be reluctant to enter into joint ventures. Successful in-country joint ventures are few and occur usually with older and larger firms. Small firms may find their only option is to exit.
- Alternatively, local pharmaceutical companies may enter into strategic partnerships whereby they become resellers of patented products in regional markets, thereby realizing their market access advantages and their knowledge and expertise in their markets.

Adjustment will prove costly for the Arab pharmaceutical industry in the short term, especially in the absence of a public-sector policy aimed at compensating or alleviating some of the burden. Many small firms will not be able to operate in a new structure that requires research and development. Some will risk losing their regional markets as various countries become compliant with the TRIPS agreement. To deal with the imminent trauma, the public sector needs to put a clear policy of assistance in place, possibly with significant contributions from donor countries and agencies whose countries and constituencies will reap immediate benefits from the implementation of TRIPS. Public sector assistance to the industry should use a cluster approach of analysis and design, provide assistance from special funds and be in complete partnership with the private sector.

Tunisian Competitiveness: an Approach Based on Patents

Tunisia's economy is becoming increasingly open since it signed a partnership agreement with the European Union, joined the General Agreement on

Table 4.9: Development of Domestic Pharmaceutical Production and Consumption in the Arab World during 1975-1999

Year	Population (millions)	Domestic Output ($ m)	Consumption ($ m)	Output/ Consumption	Per Capita Share of Output ($)	Per Capita Share of Medicine ($)
1975	140	345	785	44%	2.6	5.6
1980	163	700	1800	39%	4.2	11
1993	240	1590	3425	46%	6.6	14
1994	247	1760	3890	45%	7.1	15.7
1995	254	1900	4300	44%	7.4	16.9
1996	262	2150	4567	47%	8.2	17.2
1997	270	2340	4960	47%	8.6	18.4
1998	278	2539	5478	46%	9.1	19.7
1999	284	2751	5981	46%	9.6	21

Source: Compiled from files of Jordanian Association of Pharmaceutical Manufacturers, 2001.

Box 4.2.
The Jordanian Pharmaceutical Industry

The first Jordanian pharmaceutical company was established in 1962. By 1999, the number of registered pharmaceutical companies reached 61. With overall sales growing to $207 million in 1999 from $68 million in 1991, Jordan's pharmaceutical industry has become an important source of export revenue and a major employer, as well as the best performing pharmaceutical industry in the Arab world. Pharmaceutical exports were $141 million in 1999, third after potash and phosphates.

Whether this trend will continue remains to be seen, given that most exports are to traditional markets that are fast becoming adherents to the TRIPS agreement. Jordan's accession to the WTO in 2000 and its signing of the EU-Jordan Association Agreement in 1997 both impose significant covenants on Jordanian industry in the field of intellectual property rights, particularly in pharmaceuticals.

The Structure of the Industry

Jordan now has more than 61 factories for human medicines as well as seven for veterinary drugs. The local market is $163 million, of which $97 million, or 60 percent, is imported. Some 68 percent of production is exported. Generic medicines comprise 85 percent of output.

In 1999, 85 percent of exports were to Arab countries—Saudi Arabia, Iraq, Algeria, Sudan, UAE, Yemen and Libya. To ensure greater access to markets and to benefit from more strategic locations, Jordanian businessmen have established joint ventures in manufacturing in Portugal, the United States, Saudi Arabia, Tunisia and Algeria. They are considering further joint ventures in Yemen, Sudan and Ethiopia.

A number of complementary industries have emerged. These include businesses that provide raw materials for medicines, capsules and packaging. Cooperation is being developed between industry and Jordan's eight pharmacy colleges, from which about 900 pharmacists graduate annually. Jordanian pharmaceutical industry spend only a tiny 2 percent of their gross revenue on research and development.

Research and development has focused on two areas, formulation and stability studies and bioequivalence studies. Multinational companies do research in three additional areas—critical and complex synthesis compound studies, clinical studies and toxicology studies—and it is in these areas where most new drug development occurs. So while the Jordanian pharmaceutical industry has concentrated research only on developing new formulas for existing patented drugs, the multinational companies are continuously developing new patented pharmaceutical products.

Jordan's IPR Commitments

Jordan's main intellectual property rights commitments arise from the EU-Jordan Association Agreement, which requires that it grant effective protection to intellectual, industrial and commercial property rights in accordance with the highest international standards.

The three principle elements of the TRIPS agreement are:
• Minimum adequate standards and procedures for the protection of intellectual property rights (IPR)
• Effective enforcement of these standards
• The availability of a dispute settlement mechanism

In the past, Jordan's own intellectual property rights laws protected the formulation of medicine, but to comply with TRIPS Jordan will have to protect also the final product. In other words, Jordanian manufacturers will no longer be able to use different methods to produce a patented pharmaceutical product and thus obtain a Jordanian patent. In the future, new products will have to be demonstrated as different from patented products.

Source: Bashir Al-Zu'bi and Yusuf Mansur, 2001.

Tariffs and Trade and prepares for the elimination of the Multi Fiber Agreement (MFA) in 2005. Tunisian enterprises will soon face a tidal wave of competition that will threaten their market share and limit their chances of expansion unless they obtain the technology needed to adopt quickly.

Tunisian companies must put into place more efficient procedures, improve production quality and create new products and services. Patents and labor structure data give an indication of how well they might fare based on inventive activity.

Tunisia had 1,720 deposited patents in the decade from 1984 to 1994. The patents were concentrated in three areas: mechanical and electrical industries, chemical industries and various manufacturing industries (Table 4.10).

Among mechanical and electrical industries patents, 17 percent were in the category of forging metals and 45.5 percent were in manufacturing machinery and agricultural and industrial equipment. Among chemical industries, 53 percent were in the category of other basic chemical industries and 40 percent were in pharmaceutical industries. Various manufacturing industries included 37 percent in the category of paper, printing and publishing industries and 36 percent were in various industries.

An examination of the patents by nationality found that Tunisians represented 16.6 percent of the total number, or 285, with the majority in the three dom-

inant sectors. This prevalence of patents in the three areas conforms to the global trend. Competition is strong in these sectors and inventions need to be protected. In recent years the trend has changed to favor general application technologies, a category which comprises computerization and communications applications.

The patents were awarded to three groups: firms, individuals and research centers. Some 77.4 percent were awarded to firms, 21 percent to individuals and 1.6 percent to research centers. Among the foreign applicants, almost 90 percent were awarded to firms, while among Tunisians, 82 percent were awarded to individuals, 14.7 percent to firms and 3.2 percent to research centers affiliated to three engineering schools, Tunis, Sfax and Gabés.

This high ratio of patents awarded to individuals in Tunisia makes it hard to evaluate inventiveness in the economy. The effort deployed and the value of the patent itself are hard to quantify in applications by individuals. Most patents have little chance of being used unless someone commits to an investment. On the other hand, national enterprises registered only 390 inventions per year in manufacturing from 1973 to 1994, with a total of 8,581 enterprises at the end of 1994. This low patent production can be explained in different ways.

First, the small size of enterprises, both in capital and labor force, limits their ability to generate new inventions. In manufacturing, 98.6 percent of the

Economic Research Forum - **77**

Table 4.10: Distribution of Patents into Sectors and Evolution over Time

Sector	1984	1985	1986	1987	1988	1989	1990	1991	1992	1993	1994	Total
Agriculture and fisheries	0	0	1	0	1	0	0	0	0	0	0	2
Agriculture and food production	4	2	6	4	7	2	2	7	6	8	3	51
Materials for construction & ceramics & glass	14	5	2	2	3	3	3	4	3	2	2	43
Mechanical and electrical industries	65	73	65	52	51	59	58	46	25	51	58	603
Chemical industries	115	111	66	62	61	60	73	51	63	45	38	745
Textiles, clothing and leather industries	1	1	5	2	0	1	4	4	1	4	5	28
Various manufacturing industries	8	8	18	11	10	14	10	12	18	26	28	163
Mining industries	0	0	0	0	0	0	0	1	0	0	0	1
Oil extraction and refining industries	1	3	1	1	1	4	2	2	2	2	3	22
Water production and distribution	1	1	1	1	0	0	0	0	0	0	2	6
Building and civil engineering	4	12	2	11	3	1	8	3	2	4	5	55
Various trade services	0	0	0	0	0	0	0	0	0	1	0	1
Total	213	216	167	146	137	144	160	130	120	143	144	1720

Source: National Institute for Patents, Tunisia, 1994.

enterprises employ at least 300 people but only 8 percent are considered big in terms of capital. Second, the Tunisian economy was highly protected at the time. Quotas on imports of raw materials slowed expansion. Investment regulations designed to protect non-competitive sectors raised the entry barriers for new firms. A structural adjustment program to liberalize prices, investments and imports was begun only in 1986 and completed in 1991. Third, the percentage of managers was very low, with higher management or engineering averaging only 7.7 percent of all workers. Finally, the cost of purchasing a patent, 0.3 million dinars in 1994, was very low.

Among the 83 percent of the patents filed by non-Tunisians, most were in the same dominant sectors —chemical industries, mechanical and electric and various manufacturing industries—and most were filed by EU countries, particularly France, Germany and Italy. Some were co-filed with Tunisians. During the period, Tunisia's dominant foreign trade partner was Europe. This convergence of the proportion of patents with trade patterns shows that the driving force in foreign patent applications in Tunisia was to protect products destined for exports.

Another correlation emerged in the area of foreign direct investment. In 1991, 69 percent of the FDI in Tunisia came from the European Union and 16 percent from the United States. The EU countries best represented were France, Germany, Belgium and Italy.

In conclusion, there is a high correlation between patents, trade and foreign direct investment. The classification of patents according to products is related to trade relations rather than investment. At the end of 1991, 90 percent of the direct investment was made in the energy sector. By the end of 1993, 84 percent of investment was made in textiles, clothing and leather industries.

Manufacturing: How Far is Egypt from the Technological Frontier?

Since the early 1970s, and more intensively since the early 1990s, Egyptian industrial policy has focused on selling state enterprises, cutting government subsidies, liberalizing business and investment laws and lowering trade barriers. As a result, Egypt manufacturers have to compete abroad and at home. Productivity and competitiveness in manufacturing is of key importance.

78 - *Economic Research Forum*

How far Egypt is from the technological frontier and to what extent it can benefit by catching up on a sector-by-sector basis can be seen by comparing it to France, a country with one of the highest productivity levels worldwide. The European Union is Egypt's main trading partner. EU countries such as France will probably soon liberalize their foreign trade even further. This bilateral comparison, based on national production data and prices, therefore provides an indication of the possible consequences of trade liberalization for both sides.

Comparing Productivity and Unit Labor Costs

Some 239 products in 72 industries were matched in France and Egypt. The products represent 39 percent of manufacturing production in Egypt and 16 percent of manufacturing production in France. Food products, textiles and clothing, chemicals and rubber and plastics were explored.

Production prices between the two countries were equalized for each product by a pertinent UVR, or currency conversion factor. The nominal exchange rate in the table shows the actual conversion rate in use. A ratio between the two shows the actual price level of Egypt as a percent of the French level (Table 4.11, Column 7). If the exchange rate is above the UVR, Egypt producer's prices are below those of France. Overall, Egyptian manufacturing prices are 46 percent of those in France. Low price levels were found in apparel and leather products while non-metallic mineral products and electrical machinery and apparatus were higher.

When Egyptian value-added was converted by UVR instead of by exchange rate, the level of output compared to France doubled to 6 percent from 3. The relative number of hours worked in manufacturing (48.4 percent) is considerably larger than that of value added. The difference between the amount of value added and employment is smaller when employment is measured in terms of persons engaged. This is because the number of annual hours worked in manufacturing is 2,500 in Egypt compared to 1,600 in France. Nevertheless, in the context of an economically active population of roughly the same size in both countries, employment in manufacturing in Egypt is surprisingly small.

The first three columns of Table 4.11 compare Egyptian labor productivity per person and per hour to that of France. Using nominal exchange rates, Egyptian labor productivity per person in manufacturing as a whole is 10 percent of that of France. When UVRs are used instead, relative labor productivity doubles to 21 percent. Finally, Egyptian labor productivity per hour relative to France is only 13 percent. Per-hour productivity is lower in Egypt because Egyptian workers work longer hours than do French workers. On the sector level, relative labor productivity is highest in wearing apparel and fabricated metal products and lowest in motor vehicles and textiles.

Egyptian competitiveness depends not only on efficiency but also on production costs. Egypt's relatively low labor costs tend to counterbalance the low productivity of its workers. Relative labor costs depend on three factors: hourly labor costs valued at the exchange rate, labor productivity valued at the exchange rate and the relative price level of manufactures.

Columns 4 to 6 of Table 4.11 show the relative labor costs and their components. Egyptian labor costs only 33 percent of what it costs in France. This is due largely to low labor cost per hour and low Egyptian price levels. Large differences exist among sectors: the lowest unit labor costs are in wearing apparel, tobacco products, and pulp and paper products. The highest unit labor costs were in textiles, furniture and other manufacturing and motor vehicles.

Even though productivity in 1996 was only 13 percent of that of France, Egypt's manufacturing is internationally competitive because hourly labor costs are only 4 percent of those of France and the price level of its products is only 46 percent.

Egypt began losing its price advantage in the second half of the 1990s after prices increased to 60 percent of the French level, mainly because the Egyptian pound appreciated in value. Recent devaluations have somewhat reversed the fall in price competitiveness. But improvements in productivity and related cost savings would probably help much more.

Table 4.11: Labor Productivity and Unit Labor Costs, Egypt/France, 1996

NACE		Labor Productivity:			Relative	Relative	Relative	Relative
		Per Person (Exc. Rate Conversion)	Per Person (UVR Conversion)	Per Hour (UVR Conversion)	Unit Labor Cost	Labor Costs Per Hour	Labor Productivity Per Hour	Price Level
		(1)	(2)	(3)	(4)	(5)	(6)	(7)
15+16	**Food, beverages and tobacco**	**9.6**	**21.6**	**13.1**	**26.7**	**3.5**	**5.8**	**44**
15	Food products and beverages	9.3	21.0	12.8	26.4	3.4	5.7	44
16	Tobacco products	16.3	37.6	21.6	10.6	2.3	9.4	43
17-19	**Textiles, clothing and leather products**	**6.6**	**17.3**	**10.6**	**34.2**	**3.6**	**4.0**	**38**
17	Textiles	5.1	12.5	7.6	47.3	3.6	3.1	41
18	Wearing apparel; dressing and dyeing of fur	14.8	45.7	29.3	9.6	2.8	9.5	32
19	Leather products and footwear	5.9	17.2	11.2	28.6	3.2	3.8	34
20-22	**Wood, paper, publishing**	**14.2**	**30.6**	**20.1**	**20.0**	**4.0**	**9.4**	**46**
20	Wood and wood products, except furniture	7.5	16.2	10.9	35.5	3.9	5.1	46
21	Pulp, paper and paper products	19.2	41.2	26.1	13.6	3.6	12.1	46
22	Publishing, printing and reproduction	10.0	21.4	15.5	36.5	5.6	7.2	46
24-26	**Chemicals, rubber and plastics**	**11.2**	**24.4**	**16.4**	**28.3**	**4.6**	**7.6**	**46**
24	Chemicals and chemical products	8.9	19.5	13.0	34.6	4.5	6.0	46
25	Rubber and plastic products	15.7	38.6	25.2	15.9	4.0	10.2	40
26	Other non-metallic mineral products	13.2	25.1	17.3	27.4	4.8	9.1	52
27-29	**Basic metals, metal products, machinery**	**14.0**	**30.2**	**20.4**	**41.2**	**8.4**	**9.5**	**46**
27	Basic metals	12.2	27.3	18.1	31.8	5.8	8.1	45
28	Fabricated metal products, except machinery	19.7	42.4	29.1	34.3	10.0	13.6	46
29	Machinery and equipment n.e.c.	9.6	20.5	14.1	27.9	3.9	6.5	46
30-33,36	**Electrical, electronic equipment, other**	**10.9**	**19.4**	**12.8**	**36.6**	**4.7**	**7.2**	**56**
30	Office machinery and computers	16.2	34.8	20.1	4.1	0.8	9.4	46
31	Electrical machinery and apparatus n.e.c.	15.8	22.5	15.9	37.6	6.0	11.1	70
32	Radio, television and communication equipment	11.7	25.2	17.0	37.9	6.5	7.9	46
33	Medical, precision and optical instruments	9.6	20.6	13.2	34.2	4.5	6.1	46
36	Furniture and other manufacturing	6.3	13.6	8.1	42.4	3.4	3.8	46
34+35	**Transport equipment**	**7.7**	**16.5**	**8.5**	**36.7**	**3.1**	**4.0**	**47**
34	Motor vehicles, trailers and semi-trailers	6.5	14.0	7.0	40.8	2.9	3.3	46
35	Other transport equipment	9.8	20.9	11.5	30.2	3.5	5.4	47
15-36	**Manufacturing**	**9.7**	**20.9**	**13.3**	**32.5**	**4.3**	**6.1**	**46**

Sources: Cottenet and Mulder, 2001.

Making Small and Medium-Sized Enterprises More Competitive

Governments to some extent have promoted small- and medium-sized enterprises (SMEs) in the belief that they provide the bulk of employment and help alleviate poverty. But in general, macroeconomic policies nonetheless remain biased toward large enterprises, which in most Arab countries have bet- ter access to credit, government services, technology and other facilities. Service providers often prefer to deal with a few but big customers than lots of widely dispersed small companies.

A study of government policies aimed at supporting SMEs in Bahrain, Jordan, Lebanon and Syria looked at whether the programs in place contribute mean- ingfully to their success and competitiveness. The conclusion is that they often do not.

Box 4.3.
Iran: The Potential for Non-Oil Manufactured Exports

The Islamic Republic of Iran continues to depend heavily on exports of crude oil, petroleum products and natural gas for the bulk of its foreign exchange earnings. Though the share of hydrocarbons in export revenue has declined gradually since the early 1980s, when it approached 95 percent, it remains extremely high. In the year ending March 1997 it accounted for $19.3 billion or 86 percent of the total.

Its dependence on oil and gas exports leaves Iran vulnerable to fluctuations in international energy prices. Iran's second socioeconomic and cultural development plan calls for diversifying trade by developing export-oriented industries. This would protect against external shocks, create jobs, increase technological innovation and add domestic value to its rich natural resource base.

However, the quality and price of many Iranian goods are not competitive abroad. Iranian industries, grown flaccid in a highly protected domestic market, will have to adopt more efficient technology, adhere to internationally-recognized specifications, tighten quality control and improve packaging if they are to shift toward more demanding export markets.

Apart from the export of carpets and dried fruits, Iranian trade has long been geared more towards imports than exports. Tariffs, quotas, taxes, valuations, permits and authorizations were designed mainly with the import trade in mind, while infrastructure such as ports, roads and railways were conceived mainly to transport in-incoming goods. Entrepreneurs have tended to be importers.

Because of Iran's natural comparative advantage and low production costs, foodstuffs and processed agricultural products have been favored by exporters. All of the units under study had paid considerable attention to quality, packaging, and catering to customers' tastes.

Constraints on Exports

Foreign exchange controls impose three restrictions on Iranian exporters and have often been cited as the main factor hindering exports. Under Iranian regulations, exporters must sell their foreign exchange earnings to Iranian banks at the official rate, fixed by means of an exchange regime introduced in April 1994. This has prevented businessmen from hedging against inflation, which caused the wholesale price index for exports to rise to 383 in 1995 from 100 in 1990. Forced to buy at ever-increasing prices in Iran while the exchange rate remains fixed, exporters often could not cover the costs of production, packaging, marketing and overheads, and have been unable to compete in international markets.

In addition, domestic producers of manufactured goods destined for export often rely on imported inputs such as raw materials, spare parts and packaging materials to meet the quality and tastes demanded by foreign consumers. The import of these inputs is subject to extensive and complex licensing and approval procedures that pose a formidable burden on manufacturers.

A Plan for Action

In order to encourage manufacturers to diversify away from oil-related exports, the government must:

1. Reduce export procedures to the bare minimum consolidated under a single agency. Realistic targets for non-oil exports should be established in official five-year plans.
2. Streamline procedures for importing the machinery and raw materials needed by industry as well as the issuing of letters of credit.
3. Allow exporters more time to turn over foreign exchange earnings in order to give them a chance to use them to meet their import needs and sustain their production cycles.
4. Allow exporters to sell their foreign exchange earnings at market rates. This would increase the incentive to export and help reduce smuggling and the under-valuation of Iranian exports.
5. Stop setting official minimum export prices for Iranian goods.
6. Encourage barter trade with some poor countries, especially the least developed countries that are unable to pay the full export value in foreign exchange. This would help Iranian exporters penetrate these markets.

Source: United Nations Industrial Development Organization, 1999.

SMEs don't get the same access to training that large companies do. Most suppliers of training courses have difficulty reaching small entrepreneurs and training programs often are not geared to the specific problems that small firms face. Entrepreneurs interviewed for the study were generally reluctant to take training and indicated they obtained information for their businesses by visiting factories, reading or from previous jobs, saying that they did not trust development agencies or training institutions.

The region's support institutions have strived to provide business information. But entrepreneurs in the four countries generally complained that their efforts have been unsuccessful. Most entrepreneurs did not know where to get information or were not aware that it was available. Very few of the small entrepreneurs had computers or were aware of the existence of electronic commerce.

Institutions provide very little marketing assistance to small firms. Most support for SMEs is limited to help in displaying products at fairs and exhibitions and in offering management training rather than marketing training. This is partly explained by the fact that most small firms have no exportable products, and thus are ignored by governments.

Lack of Programs to Enhance Competitiveness

Most support institutions and agencies dealing with SMEs are developing programs to provide credit and advice, to upgrade technical and managerial skills and to inform them about macroeconomic and environmental policies. Few programs emphasize inter-firm cooperation, the importance of forming networks, clusters and self-help groups to improve their competitiveness.

Several factors impede the creation of networks and cooperation between firms in the four countries. Most industries are scattered geographically. Very little inter-firm cooperation exists. Trust between entrepreneurs is absent. There are few business associations for small industries. Industries are generally isolated and their market is limited to the area where they are located. They are also isolated with respect to information they can obtain on competitors, new technology and export markets.

Assessing Business Development Organizations

Although there are a number of business development organizations working in the four countries, some lack qualified staff and others are overly bureaucratic. Often their activities lack focus. They are scattered and unintegrated and have little follow-up. The most effective programs are ones that avoid credit activities and provide services in a specific sector such as trade, agriculture or industry. But the programs need to reach larger numbers of clients in order to be effective. Information technology can provide new opportunities for business organizations to operate on a larger scale. With few exceptions, most of the service delivery organizations are government organizations. Most use a social rather than a business-like approach, even though the best organizations are those that operate commercially and not as charities.

Governments Need to Do More

Governments must help business development organizations reach many more entrepreneurs—in the thousands rather than in the hundreds. One way to do this is by means of information technology. The management and structure of the organizations need to be changed in a major way. They must become larger, more sector-specific and business-like, and be driven by demand. They must learn to become facilitators, developing databases for entrepreneurs, assisting companies to export through e-commerce, creating links with universities and helping them subcontract work out to other businesses when needed.

Business development organizations could encourage the use of the internet and introduce tools such as e-mail, networking, e-commerce and on-line marketing, training, banking and information retrieval. They could also help enterprises within an industry create networks and cooperate to deal with the impact of globalization and increase their competitiveness. Networks of 10 to 20 firms can be formed and encouraged to cooperate in the development, design and marketing of new products. At the same time, SMEs should be organized into mutual support groups or associations to help provide services and share experience.

Box 4.4.
The Role of Private Manufacturing In Egypt

Egyptian industry faces serious structural challenges brought about by increasing external competition and the gradual removal of foreign trade barriers, the absence of an institutional infrastructure to provide support and incentives for competition and a lack of good management.

Unless all the parties involved make changes, industry will face problems that could hurt the Egyptian economy. Government and industry need to cooperate to develop an industrial policy that identifies competitive advantages enjoyed by Egyptian manufacturers and suggests sectors where they can potentially compete.

The government must:

1) Give priority to education and training and create links between education and the labor market.
2) Reduce transaction costs, protect property rights and enact legislation that prohibits monopolies. This can be accomplished through the judicial and other state institutions.
3) Reduce bureaucracy and create transparency in decision making and communication.
4) Create flexible labor laws, harmonious industrial relations and reduce taxes to support economic growth.
5) Direct foreign direct investment into areas that can open new export markets. There is no doubt that current FDI inflows are creating jobs but most manufacturing projects have failed to boost exports. One reason may be limited foreign investment in manufacturing with export potential, such as the food industries, textiles, electronics and garments.

Private manufacturers can also play a role. The most difficult steps are the ones that should come first: entering the market and building credibility. They can expect little help from Egyptian support institutions, which lack hands-on experience and knowledge of world markets and of the standards that govern international trade. Private industry needs to define its competitive advantages in terms of cost and quality.

Among the information they need is which product varieties the market will accept, what are the most efficient distribution channels and who are the buyers. Egyptian companies must rethink their operation methods and management practices to determine whether a better way can be found to produce higher quality goods at lower cost.

Source: Lutft Mazhar (2001).

More cooperation needs to be established between these organizations at the national and regional level. This is increasingly necessary in a world dominated more and more by large economic groupings.

Arab Chambers of Commerce Must Help Develop Industry

The most important organizations representing the private sector in the Arab region are chambers of commerce and industry and their related federations. Membership in these chambers has been growing and the quality of their services has improved. In general, the chambers have three major responsibilities. They organize and represent the interests of the private sector, they provide consulting, and they offer a variety of business services such as training, seminars and conferences.

The special needs of Arab industry, combined with the rapid spread of technology and information, impose new responsibilities on Arab chambers. These must now help private industry more effectively via new initiatives, appropriate training to raise standards, improve competitiveness and quality, and to encourage investment in new technology.

In parallel, they should provide legislative and structural information to help modernize industries and update tax regulations. This could encourage capital investment and provide an incentive for research and development. Chambers could also encourage regional industrial integration by working towards eliminating trade barriers, setting up coordination programs and providing guidance to investors toward high-value-added industries and manufacturing. Finally, chambers could promote sub-contracting and mergers among Arab companies.

GAFTA Falls Short of Expectations

Under the Great Arab Free Trade Area (GAFTA) agreement, which came into effect in 1998, Arab countries must eliminate all tariff and non-tariff barriers on products of Arab origin within ten years of the date they sign the treaty. As of January 2001, 14 Arab countries had joined and had lowered duties by 40 percent.

The agreement is a major step towards achieving more regional integration. However, several loopholes and violations of the agreement are undermining its effectiveness. These include an extensive list of exceptions from immediate trade liberalization, the failure to address existing taxes and charges similar in effect to tariffs, the imposition of additional non-tariff barriers and the lack of a dispute settlement mechanism.

To overcome these obstacles, members must set tight deadlines. Otherwise it will be hard for many member countries to comply even within ten years. Some GAFTA members continue to be concerned that the agreement will have costly negative social and economic effects and may lead to increased unemployment, at least in the short term. Some countries that have not moved as far ahead in reforms are concerned they will not be able to compete as well as others.

GAFTA can be improved by linking it to programs to increase productivity and by encouraging the role of the private sector in countries where industry is still dominated by the state. It can also be improved by linking it to plans for advancing technology, encouraging environment-friendly industry, developing local skills, untangling bureaucracy and providing credit facilities.

GAFTA needs authority to remove non-tariff barriers and to deal with dumping and discrimination. Non-tariff barriers in particular undermine the effectiveness of GAFTA by constraining trade. They encourage countries to make exceptions even for products that compete with those from non-Arab countries. It is important that GAFTA adopt detailed and well-defined rules of origin.

Regional trade in manufactured products needs to be developed. More investment must be made in industry, especially in the manufacture of export products. Arab exports have been dominated by extractive industries, with mineral fuels making up about two-thirds of the total. Manufacturing contributes only 16 percent, of which a quarter was textiles and garments.

Other steps might include expediting border procedures for food products, whose shelf lives are limited, unified standards and specifications for pharmaceuticals and protection against the dumping of textiles. Long-term trade agreements should be considered for fertilizers to assure market access.

GAFTA has so far fallen short of expectations. Arab countries still send only 8 percent to 10 percent of their exports to other Arab countries. New investment is modest and appears to be stagnating. Unless Arab governments put some muscle into the agreement, GAFTA will continue to stagnate. Two major steps must be taken made. They must create an Arab supervising body to solve problems and they need to establish a fund to help ease the transition to freer trade.

References

Al-Zu'bi, Bashir and Yusuf Mansur. 2001. "The Pharmaceutical Industry in Jordan and Intellectual Property Rights." Background paper to *Economic Trends in the MENA Region*. Cairo: Economic Research Forum.

CAPMAS. *Annual Industrial Output Statistics.* Various issues.

CAPMAS. *Annual Statistics on Production in Manufacturing.* Various issues.

CAPMAS. *Statistics on Employment, Wages, and Work Time.* Various issues.

Chevallier, A. and D. Unal-Kesenci, 2000. "La productivité des industries méditerranéennes." Paper presented at FEMISE conference. Marseille, 17-18 February.

Cottenet, Héléne and Nanno Mulder. 2001. "The Competitiveness of Egyptian Manufacturing: An International Perspective." Background paper to *Economic Trends in the MENA Region*. Cairo: Economic Research Forum.

ESCWA. 1999. *Small and Medium Enterprises: Strategies, Policies and Support Institutions.* December.

Ghali, Sofiane. 2001. "An Analysis of the Tunisian Firms Competitiveness: A Patent Approach Export Competitiveness: Where Does The Middle East & North Africa Region Stand?" Background paper to *Economic Trends in the MENA Region*. Cairo: Economic Research Forum.

Ghantous, Elias. 2001. "The Role of Private Sector Institutions in Industrial Development in Arab Countries." Background paper to *Economic Trends in the*

MENA Region. Cairo: Economic Research Forum.

Hanel, P. 1994, "Interindustry Flows of Technology: An Analysis of the Canadian Patent Matrix and Input-Output Matrix for 1978-I989." *Technovation,* 14 (8), pp. 529-548.

INSEE. 1997. *Rapport sur les Comptes de la Nation.*

Kubursi, Atif. 2001. "New Economy and Industry in the Arab Region." Background paper to *Economic Trends in the MENA Region.* Cairo: Economic Research Forum.

Lanjouw, J.O. and Cockburn, 1, 2000. "Do Patents Matter? Empirical Evidence after the GATT." NBER., Working Paper 7497, January.

Mansour, Antoine. 2001. "Competitiveness of SMEs and Enterprise Support Policies And Programmes." Background paper to *Economic Trends in the MENA Region.* Cairo: Economic Research Forum.

Mansur, Y. et al. 2000. *User's Manual of the Jordan-EU Association Agreement.* Freidrich Naumann Foundation, 2000.

Mazhar, Lotfi. 2001. "The Role of the Private Manufacturing Sector in the Economic Development in Egypt." Background paper to *Economic Trends in the MENA Region.* Cairo: Economic Research Forum.

MMIS Management Consultants. 2000. "The Pharmaceutical Industry in Jordan, Current Situation and Future Prospects." Amman, Jordan.

OECD. 1997. "Patents and Innovation in the International Context." OCDE/GD (97) 210, Paris.

Pamukçu, Mehmet Teoman. 2001. "Trade Liberalization and Innovation Decisions of Firms: A Case Study for Turkish Manufacturing Industries." Background paper to *Economic Trends in the MENA Region.* Cairo: Economic Research Forum.

Qasem, S. 1998. *R&D Systems in the Arab States, Development of S&T Indicators.* UNESCO.

SCEES. 1996, *Enquête de Branche; Enquête Annuelle d'Entreprises.*

Scherer, F.M. 1983. "The Propensity to Patent." *International Journal of Industrial Organization,* 1, pp. 107-128.

Serhal, Mai. 2001. "The Private Industrial Sector in Arab Countries and the GAFTA, An Analysis of Implementation." Background paper to *Economic Trends in the MENA Region.* Cairo: Economic Research Forum

SESSI. 1996. *Enquête de Branche; Enquête Annuelle d'Entreprises.*

U.S. Patent and Trademark Office Web Site.

UNESCO. 1998. *World Science Report.*

UNIDO. 1999. "Islamic Republic Of Iran Industrial Sector Survey On The Potential For Non-Oil Manufactured Exports." Nc/Ira/94/01d/08/37, UNIDO.

World Bank. 2000. *World Development Indicators,* Washington, DC.

CHAPTER FIVE

LABOR MARKETS AND HUMAN RESOURCE DEVELOPMENT

The Challenge to Provide Jobs

The world economy must create 500 million new jobs over the next decade to absorb the new entrants to the labor market. MENA countries alone will have to create five to six million jobs every year—or even more if current unemployment is to be reduced. How will MENA countries respond to the challenge?

Bucking the Trend

The answer depends on many factors, but the broad trends have changed little: recent falls in birth rates have not yet had a significant impact on the labor force, which continues to grow by 3 percent a year; unemployment has increased up to 20 percent, and in a few countries such as Algeria and Yemen has reached almost 30 percent; the public sector and the informal economy continue to account for most jobs. As much as half the urban population in countries like Egypt, Morocco, Algeria and Iran now work in the informal sector; employers tend to discriminate against women, and youth, offering them fewer jobs at less pay.

With few exceptions, MENA economies have grown slowly in the last few years. MENA's GDP only grew by an average 3.4 percent a year from 1965 to 1998, while low income countries as a whole grew by an average 5.9 percent. MENA per capita GDP grew by 0.2 percent compared to 3.7 percent in low income countries.

Productivity in the region was low in the 1990s despite a rapid increase in the number of people of working age. Human capital was misallocated or simply left idle. To improve economic performance, MENA governments must shift away from employing people in their public sectors, which are among the largest in the world, and whose low productivity knocked an estimated 8.4 percentage points off GDP growth from 1985 to 1995.[1] The small enterprise sector should be promoted and incentives introduced for enterprises to become formal. Education and training would yield better results if driven more by demand.

Alleviating Youth Unemployment

In MENA countries as a whole, at least 20 percent of the total population is between 15 and 24 years old. Only in Bahrain, Qatar and the United Arab Emirates is the number less than 15 percent (Annex Table A5.3). Moreover, with the notable exception of Egypt and Iran, their percentage of the total increased in the last two decades. In absolute numbers, MENA youth have been growing by at least the global average of 3 percent a year, and in many countries have exceeded it. In Yemen the number of youth grew by 4.9 percent, in Oman 4.3 percent, in Qatar and Jordan 3.8 percent, in Libya 3.7 percent and in Sudan and Syria 3.4 percent. The result has been a marked growth of the youth labor force at a time when it has been decreasing in developed countries.

Unemployment has affected youth more than others. In Egypt, unemployment in 1995 was 10.8 percent overall, but 25.5 percent for women and men aged 15 to 20 and 39.4 percent those aged 20 to 25. Moreover, of the 1.9 million who were unemployed in that year, 95.5 percent were first-time job seekers, mainly young women and men.[2] Recent estimates indicate that in 2000, the labor market was still heavily biased against youth.

Economic Research Forum - **87**

Table 5.1: Selected MENA Countries: Employment, 1973-2015
(Annual growth rates in percent)

| | Employment Growth | | | | | Unemployment Rate (in percent) | |
| | | Of Which | | | | | |
	Estimated 1973–1994 [1]	Required 2000–15	Working Age Population	Participation Rate [2]	Unemployment Reduction [3]	Latest Available Estimate	Targeted 2000–15
Algeria	3.2	5.0	2.7	1.0	1.3	28.0	14.0
Egypt	1.4	3.6	2.2	1.0	0.4	12.0	6.0
Iran	2.6	4.1	2.5	1.0	0.6	14.0	7.0
Jordan	n.a.	4.4	2.8	1.0	0.6	15.0	7.0
Morocco	3.6	3.6	2.1	1.0	0.5	13.0	6.0
Tunisia	2.3	3.6	3.1	1.0	0.6	15.0	7.0

Sources: Employment, 1975–2000: ILO Yearbook, various years, except Iran: national estimates; working age population projections: World Development Report Database, World Bank, 1999.
1: Or closest available.
2: Level in percent of labor force.
3: Contribution in points to the desired increase in employment.

MENA governments have tried to alleviate youth unemployment in three major ways. They have guaranteed to employ graduates, but this has been expensive and has sapped the government service of its efficiency. They have provided credit to small- and medium-sized enterprises through institutions such as Egypt's Social Fund for Development, but results have been disappointing, since such enterprises need to develop skills such as product design, marketing and business management. The consequence has been a relatively high mortality rate of "youth schemes." Finally, they have provided training. This has been important, although training programs need to be carefully targeted at youth, driven by market demand, and developed with more consultation with private enterprises [3].

Certainly, active labor market policies have a role to play. But the most effective way to reduce youth unemployment is to increase demand in the economy as a whole.[4]

The New Demography and Labor Markets

After decades of expansion second only to Sub-Saharan Africa, population growth in the 1990s decelerated sharply across much of MENA. Household surveys confirm that a decrease in fertility rates occurred in the Maghreb, much of the Mashreq and to a lesser extent the Gulf countries. In the first part of the 21st century, the defining feature will be a rapid change in the age structure marked by a rise in the share of the working-age group aged 15 to 64 and a shrinking of the dependent group under 15 years of age.

Employment in the MENA region will have to grow by more than 4 percent a year to absorb the working-age population's expansion. Examples from six MENA countries with high unemployment highlight the challenge (Table 5.1). In Algeria, whose 28 percent unemployment is the highest in the region, the working-age population is expected to rise by 2.7 percent a year from 2000 to 2015 and the labor force by 3.7 percent, as increasing numbers of people seek jobs. Just halving the unemployment rate by the end of 2015 would require employment to grow by 5.0 percent and real GDP by 6.5 percent in each of the next 15 years. This compares to the 3.2 percent average annual increase in employment from 1973 to 1994 and 2.9 percent real in GDP. Prospects in Tunisia and Egypt are somewhat better, given their mature age structures and lower unemployment rates. Yet both will also face tremendous pressure to generate growth and create jobs.

88 - *Economic Research Forum*

In all the non-oil countries in the region, the need to create jobs and speed up GDP growth will be greater than before, even when compared to the impressive record achieved during the oil boom era. Employment growth requirements will be higher than those registered in the fastest job-creating region of Latin America, where employment grew by 2.9 percent a year from 1990 to 1997 on average, and East Asia and the Caribbean, where it grew by 2.3 percent.

Demand for Housing Could Create Jobs

As has happened elsewhere, notably during the baby boom in the US,[5] the rising number of young adults in the labor force goes hand in hand with an increase in demand for housing construction, a labor-intensive activity. Moreover, preliminary data show that a substantial shortage of housing units has been building up in MENA since the late 1970s, with a disproportionate effect on young adults and the poor.

Six MENA countries, Algeria, Egypt, Iran, Jordan, Morocco, and Tunisia, with a total working age population of 125 million in 2000, will need 3.5 million new homes a year, at a time when deliveries are currently running at less than 0.7 million (Table 5.2). Since housing construction typically accounts for 3 percent of GDP and 5 percent of employment in these countries, the acute need for housing could result in a large number of new jobs.

The demand for low- to medium-income housing has not been met partly because policymakers in many countries of the region have invested elsewhere, notably in industry. In some countries, there is a glut of luxury housing, but weaker application of property rights prevents land and homes to be used as collateral for loans. In Egypt, acquiring a title to and a construction permit for desert land requires 77 bureaucratic steps in 31 different offices, which would need 6 to 14 years to complete.[6]

Further, countries such as Algeria and Egypt have virtually no mortgage market at all, while Morocco's is minimal. Jordan stands out in MENA in that its stock of mortgages is equivalent to 10 percent of GDP. By contrast, the mortgage stock in Europe is equivalent to 30 percent of GDP, and in the United States it is over 60 percent.

Unemployment in Select MENA Countries

The Case of Egypt

Addressing parliament in January 2001, the prime minister declared that the government's most important task is to "create the largest number of job opportunities possible for youth and to reduce the size of accumulated unemployment." The debate that followed was intense, and the government announced a plan to create some 900,000 jobs in the fiscal year starting July 2001-2002.

Unemployment in Egypt, already on the increase, has been accelerated by a marked slowdown in the economy and a decline in demand for Egyptian labor in oil-rich countries and elsewhere. Because many people work in informal jobs, unemployment is often difficult to measure. Government statistics estimate the average jobless rate at 8 percent, or 1.5 million, during the last three years, down from 10 percent in the early 1990s. Others estimate the rate at 11.7 percent, or even as high as 14 or 15 percent,[7] which would mean as many as 2.5 million workers without jobs.

The size of the labor force has been skyrocketing by an annual 2.7 percent, with some 733,000 graduates entering the labor market each year. To absorb the new entrants and reduce unemployment by 100,000 a year, the economy would need to create 833,000 new jobs a year. It now creates only 380,000.

Some 95 percent of the unemployed in 1996 were first-time job seekers, up from 77 percent in 1986, according to the 1988 and 1998 Labor Force Sample Survey. Unemployment was higher among women than among men. Underemployment in the informal economy accounted for 54 percent of total employment in the private sector in 1998. So far, the informal sector has provided the greater part of demand for employment (accounting for 34.7 percent of growth in total employment, 1988 to 1998).

For the unemployment problem to be alleviated, GDP growth must speed up to 6 to 7 percent a year from the current 4.5 percent, incentives must be provided to employment-intensive industries and greater priority must be given to both the large and small-scale private sector and less to the government, public and agriculture sectors.

Economic Research Forum - **89**

Table 5.2: Selected Countries: Key Housing Data, 2000
(In million housing units)

	Existing	Stock	Working Age Population [1] Growth Rate (million)	(percent)	Desired Housing Stock [2]	Replacement [3]	Desired Flow Shortfall Reduction [4]	Population Growth [5]	Total	Average Actual Flow	
Algeria	4.0	(1997)	18.2	(2.7)	10.9	0.1	0.1	0.3	0.5	0.1	(1995–97)
Egypt	12.6	(1995)	38.7	(2.2)	23.2	0.3	0.3	0.5	1.1	0.2	(1986–92)
Iran	11.2	(1998)	40.2	(2.5)	24.1	0.3	0.3	0.8	1.4	0.3	(1995–97)
Jordan	0.6	(1996)	2.8	(2.5)	1.7	...	...	...	0.1	...	
Morocco	4.1	(1994)	18.0	(2.1)	10.8	0.1	0.1	0.2	0.4	0.1	(1995–97)
Pakistan	20.0	(1997)	81.8		49.0	0.5	0.6	1.5	2.6	0.3	(1997)
Tunisia	1.5	(1990)	6.2	(2.0)	3.7	...	...	0.1	0.1	0.1	(1995–96)
Total seven MED countries	62.0	(...)	205.9	(...)	123.4	1.3	1.4	3.4	6.1	1.1	(...)
France	28.2	(1996)	38.9	(0.2)	23.3	0.3	0.0	0.1	0.4	0.4	(1995–96)
Italy	19.7	(1991)	39.2	(-0.6)	23.5	0.2	0.1	-0.1	0.2	0.2	(1993–94)
United Kingdom	23.6	(1991)	38.2	(...)	22.9	0.2	0.0	0.0	0.2	0.2	(1995–96)
United States	102.3	(1990)	181.0	(0.7)	109.0	1.0	0.0	0.8	1.8	1.4	(1995–96)
Total four industrial countries	173.8	(...)	297.3	(0.4)	178.4	1.7	0.1	0.8	2.7	2.2	

Sources: United Nations: ECE, Trends in Europe and North America, 1988/99; Compendium of Human Settlements Statistics, 1995; Housing and Building Statistics for Europe and North America, 1998/99; and staff estimates.

1: Estimated working age population in year 2000 and average annual growth rate, 2000–15. Source: World Development Report database.

2: Sixty percent of estimated working age population in year 2000.

3: One-fortieth (1/40) of existing stock for MED countries, 1 percent for industrial countries.

4: Elimination of the gap between actual and desired stock over a 30-year period at a steady geometric rate; no correction is made for the discrepancies.

The International Labor Organization's National Employment Program has recommended implementing a "quick fix" of the existing system, then instituting long-term reforms to generate growth by encouraging investment in employment-intensive industries. Egypt's government should also invest more in education and training.

The Case of Syria

Syria's new government has put employment at the top of its agenda for economic reform, and a Ministry of Planning program aims to create some 440,000 jobs over the next five years at a cost of $1 billion.

The population has grown by 3.3 percent over the last three decades, one of the highest rates in the world. At this pace, the population will increase to 20 million in 2005 from 16.5 million in 1999. As in other developing countries, the population is young, with 44.8 percent under 14 years. As a result, the labor force, which numbered 4.7 million according to the Multipurpose 1999 Survey, will grow by an estimated annual 3.5 percent to 4.0 percent. Some 60 percent of the labor force lives in urban areas.

The economy has been sluggish. GDP contracted by 1.5 percent in 1999, but is expected to grow by 3.5 percent in 2001, thus catching up with population growth. Unemployment has risen in recent years. Recent estimates put the number anywhere from 8 percent to 20 percent. The 1999 Multipurpose Survey puts unemployment at 9.5 percent, or 432,000 persons, with an additional 150,000 new workers entering the labor market every year.

In Syria, unemployment falls disproportionately on youth. Unemployment among people aged 14 to 24 was estimated at 42.4 percent in 1999. It has reached 10 percent in rural areas compared to 8.9 percent in urban areas. It also falls disproportionately on the illiterate and those with only a primary or secondary education. These categories account for 82.4 percent of the total unemployed. It is often hidden. As many as 34 percent of workers are employed in the informal sector. Some 99,000 people, or 25 percent of the labor force, worked less than three hours a day in 1999.

To alleviate unemployment, Syria will have to create 400,000 to 500,000 jobs a year, boost GDP growth above the current 3.4 percent, perhaps by double, reform its laws to favor private entrepreneurship, and encourage exports. The textiles sector may be a particularly promising export area.

The Case of the Palestinian Territories

The Palestinian workforce soared to 770,000 workers in 2000 from 283,000 in 1995.[8] The working-age population has been increasing at 4.5 percent a year.[9] The number of working-age people participating in the labor market rose to 42.5 percent of the total in the second quarter of 2000 from 39 percent in 1995.[10] The work force is disproportionately young, with 60 percent of the working-age population 15 to 34 years old and 20.9 percent 35 to 44 years old.[11] Palestinian workers are more educated than before. Some 23.7 percent have completed 13 or more years of education and 29.7 percent 10 to 12 years. Only 3.6 percent are illiterate, according to the Labor Force Survey of the Palestinian Central Bureau of Statistics.[12]

Some 22.3 percent of the labor force worked in Israel as of June 2000, of which 56 percent worked in construction. In the West Bank and Gaza Strip, another 22.3 percent worked in construction, which has been gaining at the expense of agriculture, which absorbs only 13.4 percent of the labor force. Some 14.4 percent worked in manufacturing and the rest in trade, transport and services.

After the Intifada began at the end of September 2000, Israel imposed an economic blockade on the Palestinian territories and restricted the movement of people, often sealing off towns completely. Israel stopped raw materials and other inputs from reaching factories, destroyed agricultural land and prevented farmers from reaching their fields. The number of unemployed thus jumped to 316,000 in the fourth quarter of 2000 from 170,000 in June 2000, and unemployment to 39.7 percent from 8.8 percent. In Israel, 130,000 Palestinians lost their jobs and tens of thousands of others lost their jobs in the Palestinian territories.

The situation in the Palestinian labor market is the worst it has been since Israel first occupied the territories in 1967, and is likely to deteriorate further.

The Case of Tunisia

Unemployment in Tunisia has increased over the last decade and is now above 15 percent. Urban unemployment is rising and includes an increasing proportion of the young and educated. The labor force is growing at a faster rate than the total population, where fertility has been falling.

Women are participating in the labor force at a much higher rate. While the number of working men has grown by less than 2 percent, the number for women has surged by more than 3.4 percent (Figure 5.1).

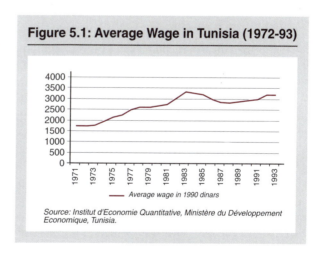

Figure 5.1: Average Wage in Tunisia (1972-93)

Source: Institut d'Economie Quantitative, Ministère du Développement Economique, Tunisia.

The labor force is increasingly educated, though about 60 percent of workers have never attended secondary school, received vocational training or have any well-defined skills. However, the number of first time job seekers who are young and had a secondary or higher education rose to 58.5 percent in 1997 from 46 percent in 1994. The percentage of educated girls seeking jobs is nearing that of men. Most educated Tunisians, 139,000 out of 160,000, work in services, in government or in state-owned enterprises. However, public employment has been dropping. People are moving out of agricultural jobs and into manufacturing and services.

Tunisia's labor market is organized on the pattern of France's. It has minimum wages, collective wage negotiations, compulsory social and health insurance and restrictive hiring and firing rules. Layoffs often end up in court or involve complicated procedures. When firing is authorized, firms must make severance payments, often expensive. While this high degree of regulation tends to help those who are already employed, it limits their mobility and raises the cost of hiring new workers, which in turn may harm employment rates overall.

However, the labor market is far more flexible than it appears. Regulations are enforced only in the formal sector. Because of its greater flexibility, the informal sector has absorbed a substantial part of the labor force, and its share of the total labor force has been increasing. Despite the onerous wage-setting procedures, average real wages have tended to fluctuate over time and in some periods have fallen. Rigidities might have aggravated unemployment, but their effect seems small.

In the long run, wage increases do not seem to increase unemployment permanently. Nor do increases in productivity. This is confirmed by data that show that firms using more modern technologies are hiring more labor and paying higher salaries.[13]

The GCC Labor Market: Private vs Public

Labor markets of the Gulf Cooperation Council (GCC) countries have two exceptional elements: a rapid expansion of government jobs to employ local citizens and the extensive use by private business of foreign workers. The GCC's own citizens filled 26 percent all jobs in 1995, down from 33 percent in 1985 and 61 percent in 1975, according to data published by the GCC Secretariat, statistical offices and research institutions. Only 5.9 percent of the Kuwaiti labor force worked in private business in 1995.

Table 5.3: Kuwaiti and Expatriate Labor
(in thousands)

Occupation	Kuwaiti	Non-Kuwaiti	Total	(%) Kuwaiti
Doctors & scientists	1.29	4.95	6.25	20.70
Engineers	2.95	13.78	16.73	17.70
Economists & lawyers	5.54	17.95	23.49	23.60
Teachers	24.74	22.75	47.49	52.10
Artists & sociologists	6.46	5.78	12.24	52.80
Mngt. & supervisors	30.46	31.94	62.41	48.80
Business & salesmen	3.51	27.74	31.25	11.20
Clericals & policemen	74.77	57.55	132.32	56.50
Medicine tech.	4.06	12.72	16.79	24.20
Tech. in engineering	6.83	14.04	20.87	32.70
Skilled labor	8.86	91.07	99.93	8.90
Semi-skilled labor	0.92	50.53	51.45	
Services & agriculture	1.48	72.50	73.98	2.00
Other unskilled labor	12.74	526.70	539.44	2.40
Total	**184.63**	**950.00**	**1134.60**	

Source: Ministry of Planning, Kuwait and author's estimates for 1995.

Table 5.4: UAE National and Expatriate Labor
(in thousands)

Occupation	UAE	Non-UAE	Total	(%) UAE
High level mgr. & off.	9.43	38.73	48.16	19.6
High level profession	9.48	77.30	86.78	10.9
Technicians	5.69	44.71	50.40	11.3
Clerks & related	9.01	47.78	56.79	15.9
Services & sales	14.60	213.66	228.25	6.4
Farmers & hunters	1.74	78.71	80.46	2.2
Craftsmen	2.09	280.70	282.79	0.7
Semi-skilled	3.36	127.26	130.62	2.6
Unskilled	4.19	50.70	54.90	7.6
Military	31.23	24.03	55.26	56.5
Total	**90.82**	**983.59**	**1074.40**	

Source: Economic Establishment Survey, Ministry of Planning and author's estimates for 1995.

In the UAE, only 8.7 percent did so. The rest, more than 90 percent in both countries, held public sector jobs. Any remaining public sector jobs were filled mainly by other Arabs and Asians. The result has been to swell government institutions, decrease efficiency and drive up government spending. GCC countries finance these jobs through their considerable oil revenue and sometimes by the returns on their public investments abroad.

In the public sector, Kuwaitis and Emiratis tend to be biased toward office jobs, particularly in the military, teaching, non-science professions and in senior management. Among working Kuwaitis, 41 percent are clerics and policemen, 17 percent are managers and supervisors and 13 percent are teachers. Fewer than 7 percent work in the remaining professions, with less than 4 percent working as medical technicians and engineers. Emiratis are under-represented in most occupations, apart from the military, where they fill 56 percent of total positions. In Kuwait, however, nationals have relatively higher participation rates as teachers, social scientists, managers and supervisors and clerics. They generally fill more than 50 percent of the jobs in these areas.

Most private sector jobs are occupied by foreigners. The number of private sector jobs filled by local citizens does not exceed 2 percent of the total in either Kuwait or the UAE. Private business owners in the GCC employ foreigners because they tend to be far less expensive than their own citizens.

The situation in Kuwait and the UAE illustrates the problem faced by other GCC countriesl. In 1995, the private sector accounted for 70 percent of all workers in Kuwait and 83 percent the UAE. Despite this, less than 5 percent of private workers in either of the two countries were local citizens. The number of Kuwaitis working in non-oil manufacturing was 2.5 percent, construction 1.9 percent and private community and personal services 1.2 percent. At the same time, Kuwaitis filled more than 63 percent of all government jobs and Emiratis 34 percent in their respective countries.

However, the local population is growing by over 3 percent a year, and more women are also working. The result has been increasing numbers of people wanting jobs. From 1985 to 1995, the number of working-age Kuwaitis grew by 6.2 a year, Qataris by 5.2 percent and Emiratis by 5.5 percent.[14]

Table 5.5: Number of Workers in Kuwait & UAE by Activity, Sector and Nationality, 1995
(in thousands)

Activities	Private			Public			Private			Public		
	Kuwaiti	Non-Kwt	Total	Kuwaiti	Non-Kwt	Total	UAE	Non-UAE	Total	UAE	Non-UAE	Total
Agriculture	0.04	12.31	12.35				2.25	78.35	80.60			
Crude oil				3.71	2.63	6.34				3.16	6.25	9.40
Manufacturing	1.41	55.04	56.45	4.37	3.79	8.16.	3.46	116.16	119.62	0.07	2.32	2.39
Electricity	2.04	1.87	3.91	2.61	2.39	4.99				3.32	20.08	23.41
Construction	1.24	64.41	65.65				1.70	152.60	154.30			
Trade & transport	7.09	103.47	110.57	8.96	14.12	23.08	21.46	303.74	325.20	0.14	2.57	2.71
Finance	1.93	6.03	7.96	0.76	0.36	1.12	2.44	14.19	16.63	0.02	0.74	0.77
Real estate	0.89	7.84	8.73				2.25	26.96	29.21			
Social services*	3.86	318.04	312.91				5.06	169.59	174.65			
Gov. services				141.59	79.82	221.57				45.49	90.03	135.52
Total	**18.51**	**569.01**	**578.52**	**161.99**	**103.11**	**265.25**	**38.61**	**861.60**	**900.21**	**52.20**	**121.99**	**174.19**

Source: Annual Establishment Survey and unpublished data provided by Department of Accounting, the Ministry of Planning, Kuwait. For UAE data: Economic Establishment Survey, national accounting publications of the Ministry of Planning
Excluding domestic help.

If current plans to encourage the private sector and sell off state-owned enterprises go through, GCC governments will no longer be able to create the same number of jobs for their citizens. Graduates leaving schools and universities will have to find jobs in private business or remain unemployed.

The first signs of an employment crunch have appeared, aggravated by both regional and international factors. Two Gulf wars had already set back development and cost Kuwait's economy and labor markets dearly. After the 1990 war with Iraq, less skilled foreign workers replaced skilled workers, reducing productivity. The 1983 Manakh stock market crash left an $80-billion mountain of debt that is still being serviced. Kuwait, like other countries of the Gulf region, is particularly vulnerable to falls in oil prices (1986, 1998), which worsen the region's investment climate, decreasing demand for labor.

One employment strategy has been to limit foreign workers by restricting work permits, and the Kuwaiti government has now begun to replace 10 percent of foreigners working in the public sector with Kuwaitis each year. However, the number of Kuwaiti citizens seeking jobs rose considerably in the 1990s and is set to rise further, and there is now less scope for them in the public sector. GCC policymakers will have to apply new macroeconomic policies, encourage private businesses to hire more national workers, offer training programs to direct and re-orient job seekers toward the private sector and create funds to finance new jobs for graduating citizens.

In the future, GCC countries may also have to top up the wages of their citizens or subsidize businesses that hire Gulf nationals or introduce taxes to increase the cost of employing foreigners, either by applying a per capita labor tax or by charging more for health and other social welfare programs provided to foreign workers. They could also adopt a national program to train and re-orient new graduates towards the private sector.

In Kuwait, the National Assembly recently approved a law adopting many of these policies. The UAE has taken a somewhat different approach. It has set up specialized units in private businesses to train nationals and create links between the Ministry of Labor and Social Affairs and private businesses to create jobs for nationals.

Relaxing Restrictive Labor Regulations

Do Labor Laws Hurt Company Profits?

The region's labor laws are rigid. But in many cases enforcement is feeble and prone to corruption, and most businesses have found ways to get around the law. For example, Egyptian labor law restricts the right of an employer to fire a worker after a probation period. But many firms ask new workers to sign an undated resignation before issuing an employment contract.

Nevertheless, if structural factors are a reason for unemployment, they also provide some protection in times of economic stagnation, when job creation slows and unemployment can mean ruin in the absence of a social safety net. Further, too flexible a labor market in many MENA countries might push down already low and declining wages and increase poverty. Minimum wage regulations are rare in the region.

A 1994 World Bank survey provides evidence against labor regulations as a major impediment to enterprise profitability in Egypt (Box 5.1). It shows that Egypt's present labor law is much less important to profitability than other factors such as tax rates, tax collection, the high cost of finance, price instability and stagnant demand.

A test of how rigid labor markets are is the behaviour of real wages. Since the mid-1980s real wages have declined in the region, especially in the private sector and among women. In Egypt, real wages in public enterprises plummeted by the mid-1990s to about 70 percent of their 1985 level. In the private sector, the collapse of wages was even greater, down to about half, and poverty has increased.

Do Flexible Labor Laws Hurt Workers?

Encouraged by international financial institutions, some Arab countries are considering relaxing their rigid labor laws. Although this may have a sound economic basis, some argue that it could be politically dangerous. The emergence of powerful new business interests in the wake of structural adjustment programs may result in laws that leave workers vulnerable.

94 - *Economic Research Forum*

Box 5.1.
Labor Laws and Profitability in Egypt

A survey of 208 enterprises undertaken by a World Bank team for its 1994 Private Sector Development Study looked at 22 factors that impede profitability. Enterprises were divided into four categories based mainly on number of employees. The study appears to indicate that, overall, small enterprises suffer more impediments to profitability than do large ones. Both micro and medium enterprises suffer a similar, intermediate level of impediment, though due to different factors.

Among 22 factors, labor regulations and requirements was the fourth least important in impeding profitability in micro enterprises and the seventh least important in both small and medium enterprises. Only in large enterprises, which account for less than one tenth of private non-agricultural employment, did it rank high—the fifth most burdensome.

By comparison, the high level of taxes was considered the heaviest impediment to profitability for all size categories except micro enterprises, where it was superceded only by lack of demand and customers and by inflation and price instability.

Source: Fergany, 2001.

Reform of labor laws is an important component of structural adjustment. Under a law being proposed in Egypt, employers would be allowed to terminate workers without compensation. The law would ease hiring constraints and introduce private employment agencies and training firms to increase labor market flexibility.

However, this flexibility must be balanced, if it is not to weaken the bargaining power of workers, who are becoming increasingly dissatisfied with their union leaders and other representatives who are often coopted by the government or by interest groups. In Egypt, modifications to the Labor Unions Law in 1995 exacerbated a rift between union leadership and the rank and file. In addition, workers are still fighting a draft labor law completed several years ago, even after the government-dominated labor union approved it. In consquence, the government has not yet submitted it to parliament, fearing unorganized and disruptive labor action in the current climate of slow growth, high unemployment and poverty.

Any changes to labor laws must come as a complete reform package that spurs growth and generates jobs. The package must include an effective social safety net that provides a minimum level of benefits, particularly in the event of unemployment. The judicial system must be made able to resolve labor disputes swiftly. Legal procedures in many MENA countries are cumbersome and courts increasingly

overloaded. Because governments of the region are frequently the largest employer, their low wage structure is often a model for private business. Bad reward structures and poor administration encourage corruption and induce employees to take on second jobs or to moonlight.

Women In The Labor Force

The negative consequences of privatization, such as cuts in government jobs and expenditure, and growing unemployment fall disproportionately on women.[15] This is because women workers in the region concentrate in a small number of economic activities, are less mobile and face barriers in many professions. On the other hand, market reforms have created jobs for women in labor-intensive trade-related services and in export industries such as textiles, garments, fruits, flowers and, increasingly, in electronics assembly. Morocco and Tunisia are examples in the MENA region where this has happened.

Comparing Egypt and Turkey

A comparison of women's wage and salary work in Egypt and Turkey's urban areas (1998-1994)indicates that females engaged in wage employment as a share of the total female population increased to 13 percent in Turkey, from an earlier 10 percent. This compares to an increase of one percentage point in Egypt over the same period, from 16 to 17 percent.

Some 34 percent of women worked in the public sector in Turkey in 1994, compared to nearly 80 percent in Egypt in 1998. Despite cuts in public expenditures in Egypt between 1988 and 1998, government employment continued to grow by 4.8 percent per year, or nearly double the rate of overall employment growth. Women's share in this sector increased to 39.7 percent from 37.4 percent.

However, the reduction in state-owned enterprise employment in Egypt hit women hard. By 1998, only 15.5 percent of all state-owned enterprise employees were women, compared to 16.6 percent ten years earlier. The private sector did not take up the slack. By 1998, only 12.8 percent of all working women had jobs in the private sector, compared to 15.7 percent ten years earlier (Table 5.6).

Table 5.6: Distribution of Wage and Salary Employment in Urban Areas by Sector and Gender, Ages 15-64 Turkey and Egypt, (%)

		Government	SOE	Private	Other	Total
Turkey 1994						
	Male	17.3	12.4	69.8	0.5	100
		71.5	88.3	80	53.1	79.1
	Female	26.0	6.3	66.1	1.7	100
		28.5	11.7	20	46.7	20.9
	Total	19.1	11.1	69.0	0.7	100
		100	100	100	100	100
Egypt 1988						
	Male	32.2	24.4	43.0	0.4	100.0
		62.6	83.4	84.3	50.0	75.5
	Female	59.3	15.0	24.6	1.1	100.0
		37.4	16.6	15.7	50.0	24.5
	Total	38.9	22.1	38.5	0.5	100.0
		100	100	100	100	100
Egypt 1998						
	Male	37.7	14.5	47.5	0.3	100.0
		60.3	84.6	87.2	73.7	74.3
	Female	71.8	7.7	20.2	0.3	100.0
		39.7	15.5	12.8	26.3	25.7
	Total	46.5	12.7	40.5	0.3	100.0
		100	100	100	100	100

Sources: Egypt - LFSS 1988 and ELMS 1998. Turkey - IDS 1994.

There is little sign that women's share in the Turkish public sector has changed since 1994. At the same time, both Egypt and Turkey say they want to reduce public hiring. As a result, women will have to rely increasingly on the private sector for employment.

Despite their lower overall participation in paid employment, the proportion of urban Turkish working women with private sector jobs in 1994 was more than double that of their Egyptian counterparts in 1998. Turkish female wage and salary workers work in the private sector at only slightly lower rates than their male counterparts. In Egypt, only one fifth of Egyptian female wage and salary workers worked in the private sector in 1998, compared to nearly half of male workers. If government employment indeed contracts, Turkish women will more likely find jobs than Egyptian women.

Women: The Workforce is Changing

Turkish women tend to get jobs earlier than Egyptian women (Figure 5.2, Panel B). However, among 20 to 25 year-old Egyptian women, the percentage of women with jobs soars above that of their Turkish counterparts. This is the age at which government jobs open up to them. Turkish women tend to quit their jobs at younger ages than Egyptians. However, in both countries there was a trend toward extending their employment in the period under consideration. In Egypt, it was only public-sector jobs from which women delayed retirement.They continued to work in private sector jobs. In Turkey, however, the tendency to retire early remained until early retirement benefits were eliminated in 1999.

In Egypt, female wage and salary work in the private sector drops off significantly by age 35, when most women have married and have children. In Turkey, there is an initial drop off when women reach their early twenties, but a significant proportion continue to work in the private sector well into their forties. A comparison of age profiles from 1988 and 1998 in Egypt also indicates that the public sector curtailed the hiring of young people.

Overall the results indicate older women in Egypt seem to be holding on to their government jobs out of concern that state employment will decline in the future. The brunt of cutbacks in the state enterpris-

96 - *Economic Research Forum*

es seems to be falling on younger women who are unable to get alternative jobs in the private sector. This suggests that there are cultural factors at play, and that the private sector in Turkey is more hospitable to married women than in Egypt.

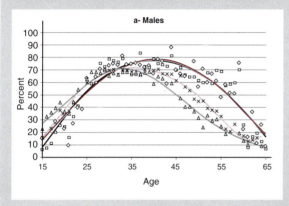

Figure 5.2: Wage and Salary Employment Ratios in Urban Areas by Age and Gender Egypt 1988, 1998 and Turkey, 1988, 1994

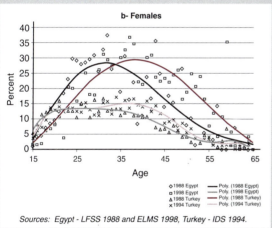

Sources: Egypt - LFSS 1988 and ELMS 1998, Turkey - IDS 1994.

Women: Education Matters

Total and wage employment of urban women with less than higher secondary education in both Egypt and Turkey is relatively low. Most lesser-educated women are self-employed or do family labor. The wage and salary labor market in both Egypt and Turkey is still essentially closed to women who have not attained a higher secondary certificate.

The share of females with higher secondary education or above increased to 30 percent in 1998 in Egypt from 18 percent in 1988, and to 22 percent in 1994 in Turkey from 14 percent in 1988 (Annex Table A5.6). Women with higher secondary diplomas and above have much better access to wage and salary work. Such certification appears to be a necessary threshold in both countries, but more so in Egypt. Wage and salary employment for educated women nearly triples in Turkey and goes up six-fold in Egypt (Annex Table A5.6). A few years ago, this level of education would have translated into a wage and salary job, primarily in the public sector, but as governments pare down jobs, the incidence of unemployment will rise. This will impact seriously on women-headed households, or households that depend on a second income to meet rising costs.

The Gender Gap in Egypt and Turkey is Widening

Women are restricted from working in certain fields, the areas where they can find jobs are over-supplied, and, as a result, wages are low. In Egypt, the wage gap remained stable at 11 percent from 1988 to 1998 (Table 5.7). In Turkey, the gap widened significantly in favor of men from 1988 to 1994. When all wage workers are taken into account, women's wages were 6 percent lower than men's wages in 1988 and 18 percent lower in 1994.[16]

It appears that the gap in wages in favor of men for both Egypt and Turkey remained constant or increased in the period under consideration. In Egypt, because female employment shifted toward the government sector, the gap is relatively small; in state-owned enterprises or the private sector, the gap is higher and increasing over time. In Turkey, the widening differential is consistent with an increasing share of private and casual employment, where the gender gap is significantly higher than the government or state-owned enterprise sectors.

Lessons on the Gender Gap in MENA

Falling real wages of female workers and the growing gender gap in favor of males indicate that the falling rates of female employment are not due to constraints on labor supply, but the outcome of a variety of economic, social and cultural factors.

Box 5.2.
Employment Profiles of Women, Egypt and Turkey,1988-1998

Egypt:

Women comprised 39 percent of the labor force in 1998, up from 35 percent in 1988. The total number of working women grew by an average 3.4 percent a year. About 28 percent of working women were in cities. In urban areas, women comprised 30 percent of the total labor force, up from 25 percent in 1988. The total number of working women in the cities grew by an average 3.8 percent a year. The share of women working in agriculture increased to 70 percent of the total female work force from 65 percent ten years earlier.

In 1998, about 46 percent of women working in urban areas worked in community and personal services, including jobs in government, the primary employer of women. Some 32.3 percent worked in urban agriculture, mainly home-based animal husbandry and the processing of dairy products for home consumption, up from 20.7 percent ten years earlier. The share of woman working in trade fell from the 14.5 percent recorded in 1988, while those in manufacturing also fell from the 11.2 percent recorded in 1988. The total number of women working in trade increased somewhat, while the number in manufacturing remained stable. Within manufacturing, fewer women worked in state-owned enterprises while the number working in the private sector doubled, albeit from a low base.

Women comprised 30 percent of the total urban labor force in 1998, up from 25 percent ten years earlier. Most of the increase is accounted for by a rise in the number of women working in urban agriculture. In 1998, women comprised 73 percent of all people working in urban agriculture compared to 52 percent in 1988. These were almost entirely unpaid family workers. When urban agriculture is excluded, the share of wage-earning women among all working women in the cities increased. In 1998, 89.0 percent of urban working women received wages, 5.8 percent were self-employed and 3.2 percent were unpaid family workers. In 1988, 83.7 percent received wages, 6.7 percent were self-employed and 6.8 percent were unpaid family workers.

The share of women working in finance, insurance and real estate in 1998 jumped to 29 percent of the work force from 24 percent in 1988. Their share in community and personal services work remained constant at about 39 to 40 percent and in manufacturing at about 13 to 14 percent, but in trade declined to 16 percent from 19 percent.

The total number of wage-earning workers increased by about 30 percent, from about 1.1 million to 1.4 million. The number of casual female workers decreased to about 17,000, or 1.2 percent of all women workers, from about 27,000, or 2.5 percent. The number of self-employed women rose to 94,000 in 1998 from 88,000 in 1988, while the number of unpaid family workers declined to 51,000 in 1998 from 89,000 in 1988.

Women worked longer hours than they did ten years earlier. Self-employed women worked 49.4 hours per week in 1998 compared to 37.7 hours in 1988. Unpaid family workers worked 35.5 hour per week, up from 27.1 hour in 1988, and regular casual workers worked 41.2 hours per week, up from 39.3 hours.

Turkey:

In Turkey, total employment grew to about 22 million in 1998 from about 19 million in 1988, an average annual increase of 1.5 percent. The portion of the urban population who were employed increased to 45 percent from 38 percent, or an annual 3.2 percent, while the portion of the country's population living in cities decreased to about 66 percent from 58 percent.

Women comprised 29 percent of the labor force in 1998, down from 31 percent in 1988. The total number of working women grew by an average 0.76 percent a year. About 27 percent of working women were in cities, up from 19 percent ten years earlier. In urban areas, women comprised 18 percent of the total labor force, up from 15 percent in 1988. The total number of working women in cities grew by an average 4.8 percent a year.

Turks working in agriculture decreased to about 43 percent of the total work force from about 50 percent, although the absolute number increased slightly. The share of women working in agriculture fell to 70 percent of the total female work force from 79.5 percent ten years earlier.

In 1998, about 45.9 percent of women working in urban areas worked in services, up from 39.4 percent in 1988, about 26.9 percent in manufacturing, down from 31.4 percent, and about 8.8 percent worked in agriculture, down from 15.4 percent. Of the total that worked in commercial services in 1998, about 32 percent were women, up from 26 percent in 1988, of those in community and personal services about 28 percent, up from 20 percent, and those in manufacturing about 17 to 18 percent, little changed from 10 years earlier.

Among women working in urban areas, 82.3 percent, or 1.4 million, earned regular or casual wages, up from 75.1 percent, or 792,000, in 1988. Those performing unpaid family work decreased to 9.2 percent, or 158,000, from 13.9 percent, or 147,000 in 1988, and those who were self employed fell to 6.2 percent, or 106,000, from 10.1 percent in 1988. The number of casual female workers increased to 107,000 from 73,000, but their share in the urban female labor work force decreased to 7.5 percent from 9 percent.

Self-employed women worked an average 40.4 hours in 1998, up from 33.3 hours in 1988, unpaid family workers worked 38.3 hours per week, down from 41.3 hours in 1988 and regular wage and salary workers worked an average 44.6 hours in 1998, up from 42.8 hours in 1988.

Source: Assaad and Tunali, 2001.

Table 5.7: Gender Wage Differential Corrected Estimates, Wage and Salary Workers only
(percent)

	Corrected Wage Differentials		
	Egypt 1988	Egypt 1998	Turkey 1994*
Government	-3.0	-3.0	-11.3
SOE	-13.9	-25.9	-10.4
Private	-22.1	-29.5	-22.9
Private – regular	-34.3	-36.2	-20.5
Private – irregular	-7.7	-21.3	-26.7
All wage workers	-11.3	-11.3	-16.5
	Turkey 1988		Turkey 1994
Regular wage workers	-5.8		-16.4
All wage workers	-5.8		-18.2

Source: Assaad and Arntz, 2001 and Dayioglu, 2001.
Notes: Gender wage Differential is calculated as (fem. hr. wage - male hr. wage)/(male hr. wage).

The contrast between Egypt and Turkey suggests that the relatively greater openness of the Turkish labor market to women with lower levels of education, and to female wage workers in general, is probably due to Turkey's greater success in developing labor-intensive export-oriented industries, such as textiles, garments, and leather products, areas that typically welcome women employees. Similar trends can be observed in Morocco and Tunisia.[17]

Policies that discourage the growth of labor-intensive export-oriented industries, such as overvalued exchange rates, have the unintended consequence of reducing female employment. There is also evidence from Egypt that women are more likely than men to prefer jobs that are close to their homes.

This suggests that policies that concentrate private sector employment in industrial parks and new towns outside existing population centers are likely to constrain women's participation. For entry to the private sector, policies or regulations that increase the cost to employers of hiring women such as long paid and unpaid maternity leave need to be revisited, and child care provisions provided, especially in urban locations, where the extended family network is starting to break down.

Labor Markets and Poverty Reduction

Poverty has been rising in the Arab world since its economies slowed down in the mid-1980s.[18] Real wages have fallen, income inequality widened and unemployment, especially among the young, has risen.[19] Households in MENA are now poorer, unemployment has increased and worker remittances from abroad have declined (Table 5.8). In addition, adults have more debt than did their parents and are likely to pass even greater debt on to their children, while the old and those unable to work receive little government support.

The Role of Social Protection in MENA

The need for effective safety nets is recognized by all countries in MENA, but, with the exception of the oil-rich countries, demand for welfare services far exceeds supply. Current social programs in MENA were largely drawn up in the early 1980s, when oil revenues pushed up growth to about 7 percent a year.

Box 5.3.
Objective and Subjective Poverty in Egypt

A survey of households in Egypt in early 1996 measured poverty in two ways. To estimate "subjective" poverty, the surveyors asked informed respondents in each household if they were "having any difficulties in affording food or clothing." To estimate "objective" poverty, expenditure was compared. A household was considered to be living in poverty if its expenditure was less than two-thirds the average per capita expenditure for the entire country. Some 35.5 percent of households were below the subjective poverty line and 37.3 percent below the objective poverty line. The study explored labor issues involved in determining levels of poverty. It looked at the following:

Access to Gainful Activity:

Both subjective and objective poverty decrease as more people engage in gainful activities, here defined as self-employment or employment by others. (Table 1). The fewer people working in a household, the more trouble the household tends to have obtaining basic needs.

Level of Earnings:

To measure the effect different types of employment have on poverty, workers were divided into six categories: agricultural self-employment, non-agricultural self-employment, government employment, public enterprise employment, private non-agricultural employment by others and agricultural employment by others. Their earnings were compared also to the poverty of the households they lived in (Table 2).

More than half of all households where a member worked for hire in agriculture were below the objective poverty line, though somewhat fewer were below the subjective poverty line. Poverty tended to be far less among self-employed agricultural workers than among those working for others, probably because the self-employed generally own their houses and grow some of their food on their own land.

Table 1: Household Engagement in Gainful Activities and Poverty
Poverty Rates, Proportion of Working Adults to the Total

	Lowest 20%	2ND 20%	3RD 20%	4TH 20%	Highest 20%
Objective poverty	36.2	44.0	45.6	30.8	29.5
Subjective poverty	39.3	38.2	38.2	31.4	31.4

Source: Nagi, Saad Z., 2000, "Poverty in Egypt: Human Needs and Institutional Capacities."

Table 2: Employment Categories (18 Years of Age and Over), Earnings, and Poverty Rates

	Employment Status						
	Self/Non-Agr. (%)	Self/Agr. (%)	Govt. (%)	Pub. Sec	Priv/Non-Agr. (%)	Priv/Agr. (%)	Total unemployed (%)
Earnings							
None		1.0				25.2	4.7
Up to 1500	17.1	15.6	34.5	16.9	30.0	28.3	27.0
> 1500 - 3000	29.7	36.1	49.5	57.3	50.1	39.0	44.8
> 3000 - 5000	29.7	25.3	12.7	19.6	16.5	6.3	16.1
> 5000 - 10000	12.8	15.3	3.2	5.9	2.5	1.3	5.2
> 10000	10.8	6.7	0.1	0.3	1.0		2.1
Poverty Rates							
Objective	30.4	35.7	30.0	35.7	43.5	52.9	47.5
Subjective	26.5	24.0	29.0	38.9	40.3	37.4	37.6

Source: Nagi, Saad Z., 2000, "Poverty in Egypt: Human Needs and Institutional Capacities."

Workers employed by the government or in public enterprises tended to have earnings at the bottom of the overall scale. Despite this, fewer households of government employees were below either the subjective or objective poverty lines than in other categories, although this was not the case with the households of public enterprise employers. The poverty rates of households with members working in the informal sector were among the highest of all categories. An enterprise was considered here to be informal if it was not registered with the government and its workers were not covered by social insurance. An average 62 percent of all workers in non-agricultural private business, both self-employed or with jobs, worked in the informal sector. Their mean earnings were LE 2,852, roughly half the LE 5,731 pounds earned by workers in formal enterprises.

Among the unemployed, many more people were objectively poor than subjectively poor. This is because many unemployed are young, well-educated and living with their parents or other relatives.

Market's Distributive Equity:

As an example of unequal distribution that contributed to poverty, the study showed that women tended to make far less money than men and were more often unemployed. A sample of university-educated men and women aged 26 to 30 showed that the mean earnings of women was LE 1,432, only 56.9 percent that of the mean LE 2,516 earned by men.

Work Related Benefits:

Insurance, compensation and other benefits for workers who retire, become ill or disabled or die help ease their poverty or that of their families. A high rate of objective poverty among retired Egyptians indicates that benefits have been inadequate. This is backed up by a 1991 World Bank report, which warned that the lack of adequate benefits meant the most vulnerable members of the society would not be protected as economic adjustment policies were put in place. A rise in objective poverty rates to 37.3 percent in 1995 from 30.8 percent in 1990-91 seems to bear this out.

Source: Nagi, 2001.

Table 5.8: Worker's Remittances in Selected MENA Countries 1970-1995
($ million)[1]

Country	1970	1980	1985	1990	1995
Algeria	211	241	313	321	n.a.
Egypt	29	2,696	3,212	3,744	3,417
Jordan	16	n.a.	1,022	500	n.a.
Morocco	63	989	967	1,995	1,890
Tunisia	89	207	351	539	590
Yemen	60	n.a.	1,391	1,366	n.a.
Total	415	5,004	7,469	8,892	6,351
TOTAL[2]	188	4,666	4,823	6,653	6,282

Note: n.a. = Not available.
[1] *Official international remittances include both monetary transfers to banks and exchange imports.*
[2] *Sum of remittances for countries for which data are available for all five years 1970-1995.*
Source: World Development Report, various years.

This is one of the highest growth rates among all developing regions. Remittances from oil-rich countries helped the region as a whole, and governments created a wide range of formal social protection mechanisms (Table 5.9). They spent more on health and education, thereby improving labor mobility and productivity. Public works, such as expanded and improved infrastructure. employment programs and guaranteed employment schemes provided jobs for the working population. Governments increased food subsidies, gave cash assistance to the neediest and expanded pension schemes.

With few exceptions, governments set aside very little increased revenues as a provision for the day when oil prices fell. Economies had for the most part not diversified away from oil, the private enterprise sector remained underdeveloped, guaranteed employment in government services contiued. Regional economies contracted and the value of local currencies fell, making imports, including food, more expensive. Lacking money, governments cut back their social programs and food subsidies.

Most of the poor in the MENA region live in rural areas and work in agriculture. Formal methods of social protection have rarely reached them. Unemployment is higher than in cities. Agricultural

Table 5.9: Social Sector Expenditure in 1995 (Percentage of GDP)

Country	Food Subsidies (1)	Cash & In-Kind Transfers (2)	Public Works (3)	Public Pension (4)	Total (1+2+3+4) (5)	Housing (6)	Health (7)	Education (8)	Total (6+7+8) (9)	GRAND TOTAL (5+9)
Algeria	0.0	1.5	0.3	2.6	4.4	5.5	3.3	6.1	14.9	19.3
Egypt	1.7	0.3	0.3	2.5	4.8	2.0	1.6	5.4	9.0	13.8
Iran	2.9	1.2	-	1.5	5.6	1.5	2.4	4.0	7.9	13.5
Jordan	0.0	1.5	-	4.2	5.7	0.7	3.7	6.0	10.4	16.1
Lebanon	-	0.9	-	-	0.9	-	1.5	3.7	5.2	6.1
Morocco	1.7	0.1	0.7	1.8	4.3	0.1	1.3	5.5	6.9	11.2
Tunisia	1.7	1.0	0.4	2.6	5.7	1.7	3.0	6.5	11.2	16.9
Yemen	3.6	0.2	0.2	0.1	4.1	0.7	1.7	6.2	8.6	12.7

Notes: Social assistance includes cash and transfers but excludes public works.
Source: Various World Bank reports and recent Social Safety Net Updates, 1995-2000.

Table 5.10: Population Below the Poverty Line (%)

	Survey Year	Rural	Urban	National	Survey Year	Rural	Urban	National
Algeria	1988	16.6	7.3	12.2	1995	30.3	14.7	22.6
Egypt	1981	24.2	22.5	26.0	1997	29.1	23.1	26.5
Jordan	1987	23.7	16.6	18.7	1992	29.0	22.0	24.0
Morocco	1990-91	18.0	7.6	13.1	1998-99	27.2	12.0	19
Tunisia	1990	13.1	3.5	7.4	1995	13.9	3.6	7.6
Yemen	1992	19.2	18.6	19.1	1998	26.9	21.8	25.4

Sources: Algeria: Poverty Assessment, 1997; Jordan: Ministry of Social Development 1987 and 1992; Yemen: HBS 1992 and HBS 1998; Morocco: Poverty Update, 2000; Tunisia: Social Conditions Update, 2000; Egypt: Alleviating Poverty during Structural Adjustment, 1991; IFPRI, A Profile of Poverty in Egypt, 1997.

work is seasonal and subject to natural calamities such as drought. Public services, education and health provisions, potable water, sanitation and power have not spread as widely in rural areas, and the services and infrastructure that exist are of poorer quality (Table 5.10).

A number of policies common to most MENA countries have compounded poverty. These include high tariffs and imports barriers and an emphasis on government employment and spending as the main means of providing social protection.

Formal Labor Insurance and Pensions

Social insurance is a pressing area for MENA. It is expected that by 2025, the number of elderly will have risen by 4 percent a year, while the rest of the population grows by 1.4 percent. This will add new pressure to labor insurance and pension systems already under strain. The old-age dependency ratio is deteriorating steadily. Despite favorable demographics, pension fund reserves are already underfunded, and some are in deficit.

Governments have often invested social insurance proceeds for political reasons, and returns have been low. This has weakened pension funds, and, because of their vast size, has also harmed the broader economy. Increasing urbanization, slow economic growth and growing unemployment mean social insurance schemes need to expand. before it becomes too costly to reform. Further, international experience suggests that social insurance reform requires time, serious analysis and great political will to build a consensus before changes can be made.

Pension schemes in the region are mandatory.[20] They are similarly based on partially-funded systems and operate on the "pay-as-you-go" principle with defined benefit plans. The payment of contributions is frequently evaded, and schemes are inflexible, offering little choice. On paper, benefits appear to be generous, in some countries promising up to 70 or 80 percent of a worker's salary at retirement. However, none of the schemes is indexed to inflation, and ultimate benefits depend on discretionary adjustments by the government. This creates uncertainty and makes workers view their contributions as a tax.

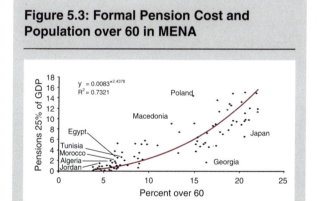

Figure 5.3: Formal Pension Cost and Population over 60 in MENA

Source: "Pension Systems in MENA", World Bank, 1999.

Payroll taxes for pensions are high by international standards. They account for 8 percent to 14 percent of total labor costs in the main schemes of Algeria, Libya, Morocco and Tunisia and more than 23 percent in Iran and Egypt.[21] If health, family allowances and other social insurance contributions are included, they can account for between 13 and 40 percent of labor costs. Important differences emerge, however, when considering details such as whether there is a ceiling on taxable earnings.

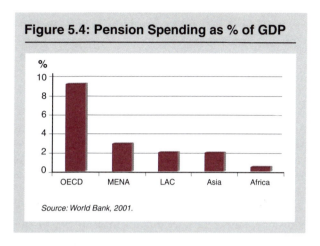

Figure 5.4: Pension Spending as % of GDP

Source: World Bank, 2001.

Although coverage rates are low, they are comparable to those in countries with similar levels of per capita income. Some 20 percent of Morocco's labor force is covered and about half of Egypt's. Across the region, between 18 and 34 percent of the working-age population is covered.[22] Some people are not required by law to contribute. However, most of the population is uncovered because they are in the informal sector, or have evaded payroll and other taxes. These will end up with no pension.

Pension finances are deteriorating. At present there are more than 10 people in the general population between the age of 20 and 60 for every person over the age of 60. But it is estimated that only three to five workers pay into government social insurance funds for every person who collects benefits. These ratios are likely to worsen unless the problem is addressed.

Pension funds are not managed efficiently. Even though their substantial reserves tend to dominate local capital markets, their return on investment is usually lower than that of private investments with comparable risk. In some systems, pension fund investments are actually making a loss. Tunisian, Egyptian and Yemeni funds have made significant losses over the past few years, mainly because governments use the funds to subsidize other state programs.[23] Algeria uses its pensions to finance social assistance. Tunisia until 1992 used them to finance public housing and to this day continues to use them to finance small unemployment assistance programs.

Most MENA countries need to assess the efficiency of current social insurance systems and bring workers who are not paying contributions into the system. Tradeoffs may have to be considered when deciding pension budgets, safety nets and intervention in the labor market.

Child Labor

A smaller percentage of children work in the MENA region than do in other developing regions. Nonetheless, child labor is a concern, especially in Yemen, Morocco and Egypt, where rates are still relatively high. Throughout the region, children are among those with the highest poverty rates. In Morocco, some 24 percent of children below the age of 15 are poor, compared to 16 percent of adults. The figures for Jordan are similar (Figure 5.5). In Egypt, a new initiative offers community services to disabled children and provides help to reintegrate street children into society. Jordan, Morocco, Yemen and other countries in the region are experimenting with similar programs. This is an area where governments could expect to draw on support from NGOs.

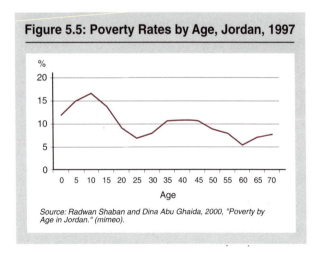

Figure 5.5: Poverty Rates by Age, Jordan, 1997

Source: Radwan Shaban and Dina Abu Ghaida, 2000, "Poverty by Age in Jordan." (mimeo).

Training

Too many training programs in the region produce poor results. Often funded from payroll contributions, they are costly, dominated by governments and supply driven. They often act as programs of last resort for dropouts from the formal education system. They are not sufficiently geared to the needs of the market, and lack facilities and equipment.

The Broader Safety Net

Social protection measures can be made more effective and cost efficient if they are tied to development and if local communities are given a greater say in decision making. The usefulness of social funds (in terms of sustainability and their share of the poor's total spending) is limited.

Table 5.11: Food Subsidy Expenditure (% of GDP)

	1990	1999
Algeria	4.3	0.0
Egypt	4.4	n.a.
Jordan	3.4	0.3
Morocco	1.3	1.7
Tunisia	2.4	1.2
Yemen	3.7	0.3
Average	3.3	0.7*

Notes: *Excluding Egypt.
Source: World Bank, 1999.

Microfinance at low or or even negative interest rates is more of a transfer than a contribution to sustainable development. Public work projects that pay high wages or have a low share of labor in their total cost are seldom an efficient way to make people less vulnerable to poverty, and they do not reduce unemployment significantly (Table 5.11). Food subsidies create economic distortions and, if universal, are appropriated by people who don't need assistance. Though embryonic in most of the region, child protection schemes such as child labor and disability programs are a promising area, especially if civil society is allowed to participate.

Governance is another important aspect of social protection. The quality of administration can be measured in many different ways, such as how often governments repudiate contracts, the risk of expropriation, law and order, the quality of bureaucracy and lack of transparency. The better the governance, the better the economy performs. A cumbersome

Box 5.4.
How Poor Communities in Yemen Cope

To assess the coping mechanisms of poor communities in Yemen, a 1998 social protection field study targeted communities identified as very poor by their level of household income—in this case less than 5,000 riyals per month. The 1998 food poverty line, as defined by Yemen's statistical office, was about 2,500 riyals per person per month, or 20,000 riyals for a household of three adults and five children.

The study asked the participants to prioritize how they would spend an additional 5,000 riyals per month. More than 85 percent said they would spend the entire amount on food. Four percent would spend some on clothing, four percent on repaying loans, and fewer than 1 percent on medicine or medical treatment.

How do these families survive? Informal lines of credit helped in the short term. Some 47 percent of those questioned owed money to relatives or neighbors and 42 percent owed money to local retailers or traders. Some 60 of the participants owed up to 20,000 riyals, 15 percent up to 40,000 riyals and 9 percent up to 100,000 riyals. In such poor communities, the capacity to repay is extremely low: around 65 percent of those who had borrowed had not paid back their debts, 15 percent had partially repaid them and only 20 percent had fully repaid them.

The study revealed that the unpaid or partly paid debt, especially to retailers or traders, was essentially a running line of credit, with the debtors paying off what they could when they were able. Debts to family and neighbors were usually much smaller and tended to be repaid quickly. The participants did not mention public assistance programs as a possible source of income in times of crisis. Indeed, very few public assistance programs had reached into these communities, and none of the participants was aware of assistance available from the Social Development Fund.

Source: World Bank, 2001.

---

bureaucracy in particular can directly hinder the assessment of the needs of the poor and the payment of benefits. In most cases, governance has improved in MENA over time, though there is still significant scope for improvement (see Institutional Country Risk Guide indicators-ICRG in Chapter Two).

Informal mechanisms of social protection complement and support government efforts. The MENA region is characterized by strong kinship networks (Box 5.4). Households rely on relatives to mitigate crises and to conserve or acquire resources. These networks spread the risks of local catastrophes and strengthen a group's economic and social capital. Studies conducted in the West Bank and Gaza show that the closer the kinship and community ties, the higher the informal support. Conversely, informal support is lowest in Palestinian refugee camps, where dispersal and dispossession have weakened kinship relations.

Notes

[1] C. Pissarides, 2001.
[2] Radwan, 1998.
[3] For detailed appraisal see ILO, 2000.
[4] *Ibid.*, pp. 37-54.
[5] Mankiw and Weil, 1989.
[6] De Soto, 1997.
[7] Assaad, 1999.
[8] Palestinian Central Bureau of Statistics, 1997, and Palestinian Central Bureau of Statistics, 2001.
[9] World Bank Group, 2000.
[10] The Palestinian Central Bureau of Statistics, 2000.
[11] Abu Shokor. 1999. pp. 27.
[12] Palestinian Central Bureau of Statistics, 2000.
[13] Boughzala, 2001.
[14] Girgis, 2000.
[15] The material presented in this section is drawn from a study funded by an ERF research grant (ERF99-US-103).
[16] It appears that the low gender differential in 1988 in Turkey is due to the apparent overstatement of the hourly wages of female part-time wage workers, many of whom were teachers. Since the wage is calculated as the monthly earnings divided by the relevant number of hours worked, the overstatement is most probably due to an understatement in the number of hours, possibly out of confusion of hours in the class room for total hours of work for teachers. Since we are not sure whether such an overstatement of wages for female part-timers also occurred in 1994, it is hard to be totally confident about the trend in the gender differential in Turkey from 1988 to 1994.
[17] Moghadam, 1998.
[18] Handoussa and Tzannatos, 2001.
[19] A. Ali and I. El-Badawi, 2001.
[20] This section draws from Borsch-Supan, Palacios and Tumbarello, 2000.

[21] These figures refer to total payroll tax rates as a share of gross wage plus employer payroll contributions.

[22] In Yemen, coverage is even lower than in Morocco. A recent study has found that fewer than one third of eligible private sector employees participate in the pension scheme, and that the informal sector is likely to be very large.

[23] While data on returns are not available for the rest of the countries, reserves have been channeled to socially desirable purposes in Iran and Algeria, with negative rate of returns.

References

Ali, A. and I. El-Badawi. 2000. "The Labor Market and Poverty in the Arab World: Some Preliminary Results". Paper presented at ERF's Seventh Annual Conference, Amman, Jordan, October.

Abu Shokor, A. 1999. "Mid-term Employment Strategy in Palestine 2000–2004, Palestinian Employment Program." International Labor Office, Palestinian Labor Department, Ramallah.

Abu-Shokor, A. 2001. "Labor Market and Human Resource Development in the Palestinian Territories." Background paper for *Economic Trends in the MENA Region*. Cairo: Economic Research Forum.

Al-Qudsi, S. 2001. "Gender In the GCC." Background paper for *Economic Trends in the MENA Region*. Cairo: Economic Research Forum.

Assaad, R. and I. Tunali. 2001a. "How Market-based Reforms Affect Labor Market Outcomes by Gender: A comparison of Egypt and Turkey." Background paper for *Economic Trends in the MENA Region*. Cairo: Economic Research Forum.

Assaad, R. and I. Tunali. 2001b. "Changes in the Employment Profiles of Women: Egypt and Turkey, 1988-1998." Background paper for *Economic Trends in the MENA Region*. Cairo: Economic Research Forum.

Assaad, R. 1999. "Matching Severance Payments with Worker Losses in the Egyptian Public Sector." *World Bank Economic Reviews*, 13, 1: 117-53.

Börsch-Supan, A., Palacios, R. and P. Tumbarello. 2000. "Pension Systems in the Middle East and North Africa: A Window of Opportunity." World Bank, Middle East and North Africa Region (mimeo).

Boughzala, M. 2001. "Search for Employment in Tunisia: An Empirical Assessment." ERF research project.

Boughzala, M. 2001a. "Why is the Rate of Unemployment Persistently High in the MENA Countries." Background paper for *Economic Trends in the MENA Region*. Cairo: Economic Research Forum.

Boughazala, M. 2001b. "Unemployment in Tunisia." Background paper for *Economic Trends in the MENA Region*. Cairo: Economic Research Forum.

De Soto, H. 1997. *Dead Capital and the Poor in Egypt*. Cairo: Egyptian Center for Economic Studies.

Dhonte, P., Bhattacharya, R. and T. Yousef. 2000. "Demographic Transition in the Middle East: Implications for Growth, Employment and Housing." IMF Working Paper 00/41.

Economic Research Forum. 2000. *Economic Trends in the MENA Region*. Cairo, Egypt.

Fergany, N. 2001. "Labor Market Regulation, Employment Generation and Poverty in Arab countries, Evidence from the Egyptian Case." Background paper for *Economic Trends in the MENA Region*. Cairo: Economic Research Forum.

Girgis, M. 2000. "National Versus Migrant Workers in the GCC: Coping with Change". Paper presented at the Third Mediterranean Development Forum, Cairo, March.

Handoussa, H. and Z. Tzannatos (eds.). 2002. *Employment Creation and Social Protection in the Middle East and North Africa*. Joint WBI/ERF publication, American University in Cairo Press.

International Labor Organization. 2000. *Employing Youth: Promoting Employment-Intensive Growth*. Geneva.

Khorshid, M. 2001. "Labor Market Structural Imbalances in the GCC Countries." Background paper for *Economic Trends in the MENA Region*. Cairo: Economic Research Forum.

Mankiw, G. and D. Weil. 1989. "The Baby Boom, the Baby Bust, and the Housing Market." *Regional Science and Urban Economics*, 19, pp. 235-58.

Moghadam, V. 1998. *Women, Work and Economic Reform in the Middle East and North Africa*. Boulder: Lynne Rienner.

Nagi, S. 2001. "Labor Market Participation and Poverty Reduction." Background paper for *Economic Trends in the MENA Region*. Cairo: Economic Research Forum.

O'Higgins, N. 2001. "Youth Unemployment and Employment Policy: A Global Perspective." ILO, Geneva.

Palestinian Central Bureau of Statistics. 1997, 2000a, 2000b and 2001. Labor Force Survey, Ramallah, Palestine.

Pissarides, C. 2001. "Labor Markets and Economic Growth in MENA." Economic Research Forum (mimeo).

Radwan, S. 2001a. "The Problem of Youth Unemployment in the MENA Region." Background paper for *Economic Trends in the MENA Region*. Cairo: Economic Research Forum.

Radwan, Samir. 2001b. "Unemployment in Egypt and Syria." Background paper for *Economic Trends in the MENA Region*. Cairo: Economic Research Forum.

Radwan, Samir. 1998. "Towards Full Employment: Egypt into the 21st Century." Cairo: Egyptian Center for Economic Studies.

Tzannatos, Z. 2001. "Reducing Vulnerability: the Role of Social Protection in the Middle East and North Africa." Background paper for *Economic Trends in the MENA Region*. Cairo: Economic Research Forum.

United Nations. 1998. *World Population Prospects*. Geneva

World Bank. 2000. *Develpment News*. West Bank and Gaza Strip. October, Washington, D.C.

World Bank. 2001. *World Development Indicators.* Washington, D.C.

Yousef, T. 2001. "The New Demography of MENA." Background paper for *Economic Trends in the MENA Region.* Cairo: Economic Research Forum.

Annex

Table A5.1: Demographic Trends

Country	Total Population (millions) 1998	Average Annual Population Growth Rate (%) 1980-98	Average Annual Population Growth Rate (%) 1998-2015	Age Dependency Ratio [a] 1980	Age Dependency Ratio [a] 1998	Total Fertility Rate Births Per Woman 1980	Total Fertility Rate Births Per Woman 1998
Algeria	29.9	2.6	1.7	1.0	0.7	6.7	3.5
Bahrain	0.6	3.6	1.5	0.6	0.5	5.2	3.4
Comoros	0.5	2.6	2.5	1.0	0.9	7.2	4.5
Djibouti	0.6	4.5	2.0	0.9	0.8	6.6	5.2
Egypt, Arab Rep.	61.4	2.3	1.5	0.8	0.7	5.1	3.2
Iran, Islamic Rep.	61.9	2.6	1.7	0.9	0.7	6.7	2.7
Iraq	22.3	3.0	2.0	0.9	0.8	6.4	4.6
Jordan	4.6	4.1	2.3	1.1	0.8	6.8	4.1
Kuwait	1.9	1.7	2.5	0.7	0.6	5.3	2.8
Lebanon	4.2	1.9	1.2	0.8	0.6	4.0	2.4
Libya	5.3	3.1	2.0	1.0	0.7	7.3	3.7
Mauritania	2.5	2.7	2.3	0.9	0.9	6.3	5.4
Morocco	27.8	2.0	1.4	0.9	0.6	5.4	3.0
Oman	2.3	4.1	2.2	0.9	0.9	9.0	4.6
Qatar	0.7	6.5	1.4	0.5	..	5.6	2.7
Saudi Arabia	20.7	4.4	2.9	0.9	0.8	7.3	5.7
Sudan	28.3	2.3	2.1	0.9	0.7	6.5	4.6
Syrian Arab Republic	15.3	3.1	2.1	1.1	0.8	7.4	3.9
Tunisia	9.3	2.1	1.2	0.8	0.6	5.2	2.2
Turkey	63.5	2.0	1.2	0.8	0.5	4.3	2.4
United Arab Emirates	2.7	5.3	1.9	0.4	0.4	5.4	3.4
West Bank and Gaza	2.7	..	3.5	..	1.0	..	5.9
Yemen, Rep.	16.6	3.7	2.8	1.1	1.1	7.9	6.3
East Asia & Pacific	1817.1	1.5	0.8	0.7	0.5	3.0	2.1
Europe & Central Asia	474.6	0.6	0.1	0.6	0.5	2.5	1.6
Latin America & Carib.	501.7	1.8	1.3	0.8	0.6	4.1	2.7
Middle East & North Africa	285.7	2.8	1.8	0.9	0.7	6.2	3.5
South Asia	1304.6	2	1.5	0.8	0.7	5.3	3.4
Sub-Saharan Africa	627.1	2.8	2.2	0.9	0.9	6.6	5.4

[a] *Dependents as a proportion of working age population.*
Sources: World Development Indicators, 2000.

Table A5.2: The Structure of the Labor Force

Country	Population Aged 15-64[a] (millions)		Total (millions)		Labor Force[b] Female % of Labor Force		Average Annual Growth Rate (%)		Activity Rates			
									Men		Women	
	1980	1998	1980	1998	1980-98	1998-2010	1980	1998	1980	2000	1980	2000
Algeria	9.3	17.6	4.9	9.9	3.9	3.4	21.4	26.36	41.1	48.2	11.1	18.8
Bahrain	0.2	0.4	0.1	0.3	4.4	..	10.9	20.08	60.3	62.8	10.3	21.9
Comoros	0.2	0.3	0.2	0.2	2.6	..	43.1	42.34	51.1	51.9	39.6	39.4
Egypt, Arab Rep.	23.1	36.6	14.3	22.7	2.6	2.8	26.5	29.72	50.7	52.3	18.9	23.5
Iran, Islamic Rep.	20.2	36.3	11.7	18.6	2.6	3.4	20.4	25.94	47.0	44.3	12.4	17.0
Iraq	6.7	12.5	3.5	6.0	3.0	2.9	17.3	19.02	44.1	43.9	9.6	11.1
Jordan	1.0	2.6	0.5	1.3	5.2	3.6	14.7	23.28	39.2	43.9	7.2	15.0
Kuwait	0.8	1.2	0.5	0.7	2.1	4.4	13.1	31.22	55.0	52.9	11.1	26.7
Lebanon	1.6	2.6	0.8	1.4	3.0	2.6	22.6	29.04	47.7	42.4	12.6	20.3
Libya	1.6	3.1	0.9	1.5	2.7	2.4	18.6	22.14	47.7	42.4	12.2	13.7
Mauritania	0.8	1.3	0.7	1.2	2.5	2.6	45.0	43.76	53.5	52.5	42.8	40.0
Morocco	10.2	17.3	7.0	10.8	2.4	2.5	33.5	34.66	47.7	52.1	24.1	27.8
Oman	0.6	1.2	0.3	0.6	3.5	2.6	6.2	15.74	51.9	41.6	4.1	9.6
Qatar	0.2	0.5	0.1	0.4	7.5	..	6.7	14.12	67.1	71.0	8.1	23.3
Saudi Arabia	5.0	11.6	2.8	6.8	4.9	3.2	7.6	14.82	50.5	49.9	4.9	11.9
Sudan	9.8	16.2	6.9	11.1	2.6	2.8	26.9	29.02	53.4	56.0	19.7	23.7
Syrian Arab Republic	4.2	8.3	2.4	4.7	3.7	3.7	23.5	26.48	42.7	46.1	13.6	17.4
Tunisia	3.5	5.8	2.2	3.6	2.9	2.2	28.9	31.18	48.0	53.4	20.1	25.4
Turkey	24.9	41.2	18.7	29.8	2.6	1.8	35.5	37	53.6	59.2	30.4	36.4
United Arab Emirates	0.7	1.9	0.6	1.4	4.9	1.8	5.1	14.12	73.9	66.6	8.8	19.9
West Bank and Gaza	..	1.3	..	..	..	..	..	..	31.7	33.6	3.4	4.3
Yemen, Rep.	4.0	8.1	2.5	5.3	4.2	3.1	32.5	27.98	41.2	45.0	18.1	17.9
East Asia & Pacific	820.0	1,206.0	719.0	1,026.0	2.0	1.1	42.6	44.5				
Europe & Central Asia	274.0	315.0	214.0	236.0	0.5	0.5	46.7	46.1				
Latin America & Carib.	201.0	313.0	130.0	212.0	2.7	2.0	27.8	34.4				
Middle East & North Africa	91.0	166.0	54.0	94.0	3.1	3.0	23.8	26.9				
South Asia	508.0	777.0	392.0	573.0	2.1	2.1	33.8	33.1				
Sub-Saharan Africa	195.0	330.0	170.0	275.0	2.7	2.5	42.3	42.2				

[a] Population aged 15-64 is the number of people who could potentially be economically active.
[b] Total labor force comprises people who meet the ILO definition of economically active population: all people who supply labor for the production of goods and services during a specified period. It includes both the employed and the unemployed.

Sources: World Development Indicators 2000
World Development Report 2000
Yearbook of labor Statstics, ILO 2000

Table A5.3: Youth[1] Employment Trends

| Country | Youth Population (000's) | | | | | | Indicators of Youth Economic Activity | | | |
| | 1980 | | | 1995 | | | Economically Active Youth, % of Total | | Change per Year,1990-95% | |
	Male	Female	% of Total Population	Male	Female	% of Total Population	Male	Female	Male	Female
Algeria	1869	1796	19.6	3020	2893	21	26	30	2.4	5.9
Bahrain	42	33	21.6	42	40	14.6	11	19	-4.3	2.4
Egypt	4608	4291	20.3	5982	5595	18.6	22	26	1.6	3.3
Iran	3938	3831	19.8	6681	6409	19.1	26	34	2.2	5.5
Iraq	1288	1230	19.4	2083	1986	20.3	25	26	2.2	4.2
Jordan	299	268	19.4	592	551	21.3	27	35	3.5	7.4
Kuwait	139	109	18	156	155	18.4	17	20	-6.2	-3.3
Lebanon	263	281	20.4	303	298	20	24	36	0.8	2.7
Libya	276	259	17.6	531	514	19.3	24	37	3.3	5.9
Mauritania	143	146	18.6	226	225	19.8	29	29	2.9	2.9
Morocco	1951	1990	20.3	2889	2778	21.4	27	33	1.7	2.5
Oman	104	95	17.6	192	189	17.2	19	27	2.4	9
Qatar	27	17	19	34	30	11.6	6	13	-1.1	10.2
Saudi Arabia	998	783	18.5	1671	1633	18.1	17	31	-0.2	6.5
Sudan	1784	1750	18.9	2788	2731	20.7	26	27	3	4.2
Syria	875	836	19.7	1493	1448	20.7	28	35	2.7	4.8
Tunisia	702	669	21.3	927	886	20.2	25	36	1.1	1.9
Turkey	4623	4351	20.2	6645	6317	21.3	28	31	2.7	3.3
UAE	120	59	17.6	165	132	13.4	9	19	3.7	7
Gaza Strip	54	45	22	78	67	18.4	26	36	5.2	10.2
Yemen	700	813	18.4	1608	1435	20.3	31	29	5.3	4.6

1: The standard UN defenition classifies "youth" as those age 15-24.
Source: UN Statistical Charts and Indicators on the Situation of Youth, 1980-95, New York, 1998.

Table A5.4: Employment by Economic Activity

Country	Agriculture				Industry				Services			
	Male % of Male Labor Force		Female % of Female Labor Force		Male % of Male Labor Force		Female % of Female Labor Force		Male % of Male Labor Force		Female % of Female Labor Force	
	1980	1992-97[a]	1980	1992-97[a]	1980	1992-97[a]	1980	1992-97[a]	1980	1992-97[a]	1980	1992-97[a]
Algeria	27	18	69	57	33	38	6	7	40	45	25	36
Bahrain	4.1	1	0	0	36.4	57	6.7	32.4	59.5	41	93	67
Comoros	70.4	..	93.4	..	12.2	..	2.6	..	17.3	..	4	..
Egypt, Arab Rep.	46	32	10	43	21	25	14	9	34	43	76	48
Iran, Islamic Rep.	36	30	50	..	28	26	17	..	35	44	33	..
Iraq	21	12	62	39	24	19	11	9	55	69	28	52
Jordan	..	6	..	4	24	27	7	10	76	66	93	87
Kuwait	2	2	0	0	36	32	3	2	62	67	97	98
Lebanon	13	6	20	10	29	34	21	22	58	60	59	68
Libya	16	7	63	28	29	27	3	5	55	66	34	68
Mauritania	65	..	79	..	11	..	2	..	24	..	19	..
Morocco	48	4	72	3	23	33	14	46	29	63	14	51
Oman	52	48	24	20	21	22	33	35	27	30	43	45
Qatar	3.1	..	0	..	30	..	0	..	67.3	..	100	..
Saudi Arabia	45	20	25	12	17	21	5	6	39	59	70	82
Sudan	66	64	88	84	9	10	4	5	24	26	8	11
Syrian Arab Republic	..	23	..	54	..	28	..	8	..	49	..	38
Tunisia	33	22	53	20	30	32	32	40	37	44	16	38
Turkey	45	30	88	65	22	29	5	13	33	41	8	21
United Arab Emirates	5	9	0	0	40	30	7	3	55	61	93	98
West Bank and Gaza	..	..	..	..	..	..	..	..	..	..	..	..
Yemen, Rep.	60	50	98	88	19	22	1	6	21	29	1	7
Europe & Central Asia	26	..	26	..	43	..	31	..	31	..	43	..
Latin America & Carib.	..	22	..	13	..	28	..	13	..	50	..	74
Middle East & N. Africa	39	..	47	..	25	..	14	..	37	..	40	..
South Asia	64	..	83	..	14	..	10	..	23	..	8	..
Sub-Saharan Africa	62	..	74	..	14	..	5	..	24	..	22	..

a. Data for the most recent year available.

Sources: World Development Indicators, 1999 & 2000;

World Development Indicators 2000;

World Development Report 2000;

Yearbook of Labor Statstics, ILO, 2000.

Table A5.5: Education

| | Illiteracy Rate | | | | Net Enrollment Ratio | | | | Expected Years of Schooling | | | |
| | Male % of Males Aged 15 and Above | | Female % of Females Aged 15 and Above | | Primary | | Secondary | | Males | | Females | |
	1980	1998	1980	1998	1980	1997	1980	1997	1980	1997	1980	1997
Algeria	45.7	23.5	76.1	45.7	81.6	96	43.4	68.5	10	12	7	10
Bahrain	21.4	9.8	40.7	18.8	80.6	98.2	80.8	87.2	..	..	..	..
Comoros	43.8	34.5	60.5	48.4	66.4	50.1	36	35.7	..	..	..	..
Djibouti	43.609	25.982	74.44	48.616	29.2	31.9	19.4	19.6	..	..	..	..
Egypt, Arab Rep.	46.5	34.5	75.2	58.2	72	95.2	43.3	75.1	..	12	..	10
Iran, Islamic Rep.	38.3	18.3	60.7	32.6	72.1	90	49.5	81.2	..	12	..	11
Iraq	52.5	36.1	78.3	56.8	96.9	74.6	65.6	42.9	12	..	9	..
Jordan	17.9	5.8	46.1	17.4	73	..	52.8	..	12	..	12	..
Kuwait	25.7	16.8	39.3	21.5	84.5	65.2	81.4	63.2	12	9	12	9
Lebanon	17.3	8.5	37.1	20.9	..	..	..	..	..	..	..	..
Libya	28.6	10.4	69.5	34.6	99.9	99.9	82.9	99.9	13	..	11	..
Mauritania	59.2	48.3	79	69	..	..	..	..	..	...	..	..
Morocco	58	39.7	84.6	66	62.1	76.6	36.4	37.7	8	..	5	..
Oman	48.5	22	83.9	42.5	42.8	67.7	20	66.6	5	9	2	9
Qatar	28.2	20.2	34.6	18.3	86.1	83.3	70.6	73.3	..	..	.	..
Saudi Arabia	32.9	17.2	67.1	35.6	49	60.1	36.8	58.7	7	10	5	9
Sudan	49	32	81	56.6	..	..	..	..	..	..	..	..
Syrian Arab Republic	27.8	12.8	66.2	41.9	90.1	94.7	47.9	42.3	11	10	8	9
Tunisia	41.7	20.6	68.8	42.1	82.6	99.9	40.4	74.3	10	..	7	..
Turkey	17	7.1	45.9	25	81.2	99.9	42.2	58.4	..	11	..	9
UAE	33.1	26.6	42.1	22.9	74.9	82	62.6	77.8	8	10	7	11
West Bank and Gaza	..	..	..	..	..	..	..	..	..	..	..	..
Yemen, Rep.	61.8	34.3	94.5	77.3	..	..	..	..	..	..	..	..

Sources: World Development Indicators, 1999 & 2000;
World Development Indicators 2000;
World Development Report 2000.

Table A5.6: Employment Ratios in Urban Areas by Educational Attainment, Sector and Gender, Egypt, 1988, 1998 and Turkey 1988, 1994

Turkey					Egypt				
Educational Attainment	Males		Females		Educational Attainment	Males		Females	
	1988	1994	1988	1994		1988	1998	1988	1988
Total Employment									
Illiterate	68	68	8	14	Illiterate	84	79	17	25
Read and write	70	76	9	17	Read and write	84	81	10	15
Primary	81	83	10	16	Primary and lower sec.	48	50	9	10
Lower secondary	52	56	10	13	Higher secondary	59	58	37	30
Gen. higher secondary	63	69	29	27	Post-secondary	76	81	61	50
Tech. higher secondary	74	84	40	40	University	84	85	60	64
University	86	89	68	74	All	70	66	24	28
All	74	76	13	19					
Wage Employment									
Illiterate	41	38	3	6	Illiterate	51	48	4	3
Read and write	39	45	5	8	Read and write	58	52	4	3
Primary	54	55	7	9	Primary and lower sec.	35	37	6	4
Lower secondary	35	39	8	9	Higher secondary	50	47	36	24
Gen. higher secondary	45	49	27	23	Post-secondary	65	68	61	49
Tech. higher secondary	57	68	36	37	University	68	71	59	61
University	65	66	65	68	All	52	50	16	17
All	49	51	10	13					
Public Sector Employment									
Illiterate		2		*	Illiterate	17	12	1	1
Read and write		5		*	Read and write	31	22	1	1
Primary		9		1	Primary and lower sec.	17	14	3	2
Lower secondary		14		2	Higher secondary	32	25	30	20
Gen. higher secondary		24		11	Post-secondary	45	49	54	41
Tech. higher secondary		29		18	University	52	51	46	51
University		46		51	All	29	26	12	14
All		16		4					
Private Sector Wage Employment									
Illiterate		36		6	Illiterate	34	36	3	2
Read and write		40		7	Read and write	27	30	3	2
Primary		45		8	Primary and lower sec.	18	23	3	2
Lower secondary		25		6	Higher secondary	18	22	6	4
Gen. higher secondary		25		12	Post-secondary	21	19	7	7
Tech. higher secondary		38		19	University	17	21	12	10
University		20		17	All	22	24	4	4
All		36		9					

Sources: Egypt, LFSS 1988 and ELMS 1998. Turkey, LFS 1988 and IDS 1994.
*Notes: * indicates that results for cells with fewer than 20 observations are suppressed.*
Employment ratios are expressed as a percentage of the population of the relevant subgroup.
Blank cells indicate that no information is available in regard to the employment ratios.

In this Series from the Economic Research Forum

Employment Creation and Social Protection in the Middle East and North Africa: The Third Mediterranean Development Forum
Edited by Heba Handoussa and Zafiris Tzannatos

Institutional Reform and Economic Development in Egypt
Edited by Noha El-Mikawy and Heba Handoussa

The Egyptian Labor Market
Edited by Ragui Assaad

Human Capital: Population Economics in the Middle East
Edited by Ismail Sirageldin

The Economic Research Forum for the Arab Countries, Iran and Turkey (ERF) is a regional non-government, non-profit research and networking organization. ERF's mission is to promote independent policy-relevant research in economics and related fields, to disseminate the results of research activity to scholars, policy-makers and the business community, and to function as a resource base for researchers through its data bank and documentation library. ERF does not advocate any one policy line, but provides a platform for the exchange of a wide range of views on regional economic issues. E-mail: erf@idsc.net.eg - Website: www.erf.org.eg